IMAGES
of America

ESPAÑOLA

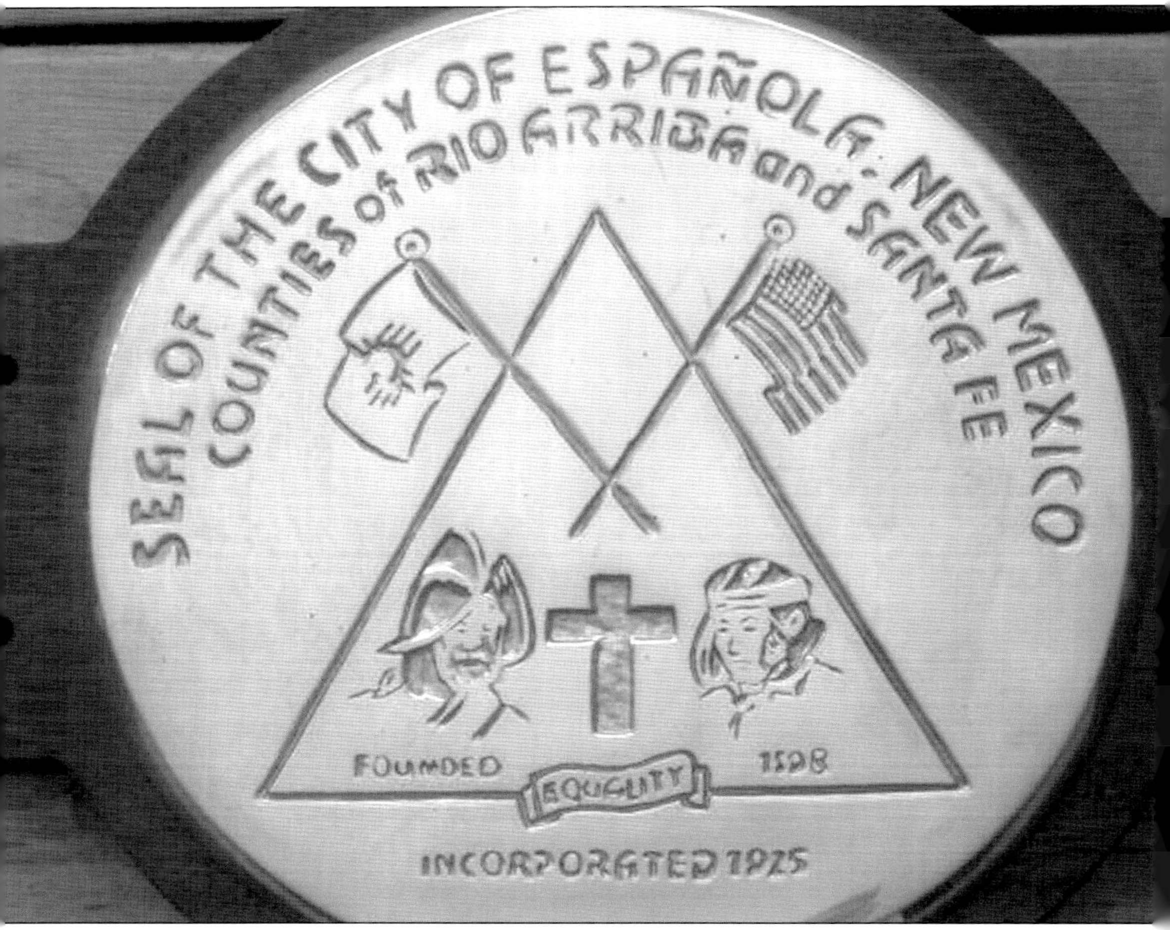

This early example of the seal of Española depicts the three cultural streams that flow together, creating the unique character of the city. (Joe Duran and Richard Lucero.)

On the Cover: The Lions Club float delights the crowd at the Española Fiestas Parade on July 11, 1948. (Ross Olivas.)

IMAGES
of America

ESPAÑOLA

Camilla Trujillo

ARCADIA
PUBLISHING

ISBN 978-0-7385-7967-2

Published by Arcadia Publishing
Charleston, South Carolina

Printed in the United States of America

Library of Congress Control Number: 2011931722

For all general information, please contact Arcadia Publishing:
Telephone 843-853-2070
Fax 843-853-0044
E-mail sales@arcadiapublishing.com
For customer service and orders:
Toll-Free 1-888-313-2665

Visit us on the Internet at www.arcadiapublishing.com

To my father, who taught me to wear the past like a well-loved coat and anticipate the future like Christmas morning; and to Margaret Caperton. Thanks, Will and Bill.

Contents

Acknowledgments

To everyone who helped me on this project, you have my deepest gratitude. Muchisimas gracias. Que Dios les bendiga.

Willie Atencio and Father Javier from Santa Cruz de la Cañada Parish; Irene Vigil and Zenaida Hall from San Gabriel Historical Society; Daniel Comstock, Judy Machen, and Rebecca Collinsworth from Los Alamos National Labs and the Los Alamos Historical Museum; Joe Duran, Dino Martinez and family from Lovin' Oven; and Richard Lucero, former mayor of the City of Española.

Ree Mobley from the Museum of International Folk Art; Tina Whitegeese from the Santa Clara Pueblo Puyé Cliff Dwellings; Juan and Ella Martinez from McCurdy School; Leopoldo Trujillo from Chimayo Trading Post; Catherine Baudoin from University of New Mexico; Daniel Kosharek from the Palace of the Governors Photo Archives; Cheryl Muceus from the Florence Hawley Ellis Museum at Ghost Ranch; Joseph Merhege and Salvador Corona Chavez from Española Valley Farm; Adair Margo Fine Arts; the Tom Lea Institute; and Jared, Kristie, Stacia, Lauren, and Jim from Arcadia Publishing.

Maclovia Quintana, Joan Logghe, Katherine Bennett, Beth Ann Sanchez and family, Linda Pedro, Felix and Sadie DePaula, Albert Wilson, Carlos Valdez and Dr. Gerald Rodriguez, Rosa Weiss, Bill Caperton and Will Caperton de Montoya, Sam and Debbie Montoya, Elvira Martinez, Max and Frances Vigil, Wilfredo Vigil, Aggie Trujillo, JoAnn Garcia Lucero, and Tony and Jessie Borrego. Aurelia Gomez, Ofilia Quintana and family, Ross and Isabel Olivas, Severo Gonzalez and family, Joe and Belle Becker, Martha Archuleta, Clare Cresap Villa, Bob Wilson, Joan Drace Quintana, and my mother, Lydia Trujillo de Roybal.

I owe an especially large debt of gratitude to my friend Jonathan Gordon, whose sharp mind, nurturing meals, late-night coffee, and mutual love for the Española Valley kept me on track. Gracias!

Introduction

Sometimes I like to park at the Dream Catcher Movie Theatre, look a little to the west, and imagine the first European colonists coming up the great Arroyo Seco into the Valley. I feel the earth tremble under the wheels of ox-drawn wooden *carretas*. A big cloud of dust announces the arrival of the 500 voyagers and their 7,000 head of cattle. Like a dark and dusty wave, they drop like over-ripe fruit on this hot August day in 1598, over the sand hills, into the Rio Santa Cruz. If I could make myself invisible, I would walk among them until I found my ancestor, Isabel Robledo, whose father Pedro had died on the journey, north of Las Cruces. The hill at whose foot he is buried was named for him, and to this day it is known as Cerro Robledo. I might know Isabel by her red hair. No doubt she was resourceful, sturdy, and persevering. Her husband was a Romero; their daughter, Ana, died fleeing the Pueblo Revolt in 1680.

It is not difficult, today, to imagine Española as it was in 1880, when it was known as Vega de los Vigiles. The irrigated fields of El Guache, Angostura, and Corral de Piedra still exist, quietly maintained by descendents of the Vigiles, the Salazares, and the Rodrigues. My family, the Roybals and Romeros from the Nambé River valley, were members of Santa Cruz Parish when it reached as far east as Las Truchas, west to Los Alamos, north to San Juan Pueblo and beyond, and south to the pueblos of Santa Clara, San Ildefonso, Pojoaque, and Nambé.

I was baptized in 1956 at the church in Pojoaque, which was at that time within Santa Cruz Parish. Because the Catholic Church of the 16th to 19th centuries kept very good records, many families of the Santa Cruz, Nambé, and north central Rio Grande River valleys can trace their lineage back to the 1705 *reconquista* by Don Diego DeVargas, or even further back to the Oñate Colony. Until the Mexican-Spanish War of 1820, the Spanish church and government were two branches of the same tree. It's easy to see why it was a tradition for large families to dedicate one of their sons to the priesthood, and sometimes a daughter to a convent.

The societies of the Santa Cruz church have roots in old Spain. The oldest one is dedicated to Nuestra Señora de Carmen. Another society is La Cofradia de Padre Jesus Nazareno—also known as Los Penitentes. On Holy Thursday Eve, the brothers sing as they approach the church; their *alabados* pierce my soul, and I am taken back to a time before the English language was spoken here. Their ancient song, born out of a dependence on a fiercely loving God, connects us to the Great Mystery.

The same mystery is honored in the winter by the Turtle Dance at Ohkay Owingeh. The male dancers wear hardly any clothing, but they do not seem cold. Their voices sound as if the air itself were singing.

Driving north into the Valley, just before you come to the Sonic Drive-In, you will come to a road sign—"Rio Arriba County"—which welcomes you to the complex community that comprises Española: at least 20 Colonial and Territorial era villages, three Tewa Indian pueblos, and a small city.

My mother is from the smaller village of Pojoaque to the south, my father is from Taos. They met at Farmers' Supply Feed Store. They fell in love, married, and made a home in San Pedro. Dad worked and Mom stayed home raising her children. Life was centered around our three-acre farm and orchard, our sheep, ducks, horses, and chickens. Irrigating with the acequia was as natural as breathing. *Compuerta, tapanco, bordo, mayordomo* . . . these were everyday words of our *acequia* culture, which is still alive, in which water is life.

I encourage my Valley neighbors to tell the stories of our ancestry. Tell the stories to your children and grandchildren. Write them down; record them. The people of the Española Valley—Tewas, Spanish, and Anglos—have made it this far, through many hardships and transitions. We've brought our stories with us. We are our stories.

—Camilla Trujillo

Española before dawn is as quiet as a lady in black lace;
if you close your eyes to neon, and lean on the cottonwood grandmothers
by the acequia, she lives again in beauty.

Española before daylight reveals Quick Stops and gas stations;
she rests like a woman in a brown cotton dress beside the Big River,
under a Russian olive tree filled with blue birds.

Española at midday is a tired mom outside the Wash-O-Mat,
waiting for a maroon Pontiac that will drive her home
past pigeons taking off from parking lot weeds.

And if you're still up at midnight, Española is a teenage girl in green spandex
cruising Riverside with her boyfriend in his magenta low-rider,
from the south Sonic to the north Sonic.
She buys a hamburger and feeds magpies leftover French fries.

—Joan Logghe
La Puebla, New Mexico
Poet Laureate of Santa Fe

One

El Encuentro

It is August 18, 1598, at the northern edge of the Spanish Empire in the New World. A weary caravan, three miles long, arrives at El Valle de San Juan and stops for a while at the Rio Santa Cruz to let the animals drink. Their journey began 750 miles south in Nueva Vizcaya, the site of present-day Chihuahua, Mexico. It has taken them seven months to get here. Their leader, the fierce soldier-explorer Juan de Oñate, has amazingly brought them all this distance safely and soundly, with almost no loss of human or even animal life. The comforts of Spain—which they left behind and which most will not see again—are very far away. This valley is going to be their home.

The caravan consists of about 500 people, half of them civilian men and women of various occupations. Others have hired on to the journey as herders of the 7,000 head of livestock and drivers of the oxen pulling the 80 *carretas* (lumbering carts with huge, solid wooden wheels that carried food, clothing, kitchenwares, medicine, mining, and blacksmithing tools, armaments, and trade goods). Also in the caravan are servants and slaves—mestizos, mulattos, and Indians. At least 100 are soldiers of the Spanish king, who have provided military escort on the long, dangerous trip. And nine are Franciscan friars.

The colonists have answered a call by the viceroy of New Spain. If they settle this remote portion of the empire and stay for five years, the Crown will grant them the title of Hidalgo, the lowest rung of nobility. They will also be given desirable pastureland.

However, the colony upsets an ancient balance, for others have lived on this land for thousands of years. Unstoppable historical forces have been set into motion. It will take 100 years to bring stability to a complex dynamic of invasion, displacement, and resistance. Unique cultural and political exchanges will work themselves out over the course of many generations, unlike anywhere else in the United States. Three hundred and twenty years into the future, the city of Española will emerge from this cauldron.

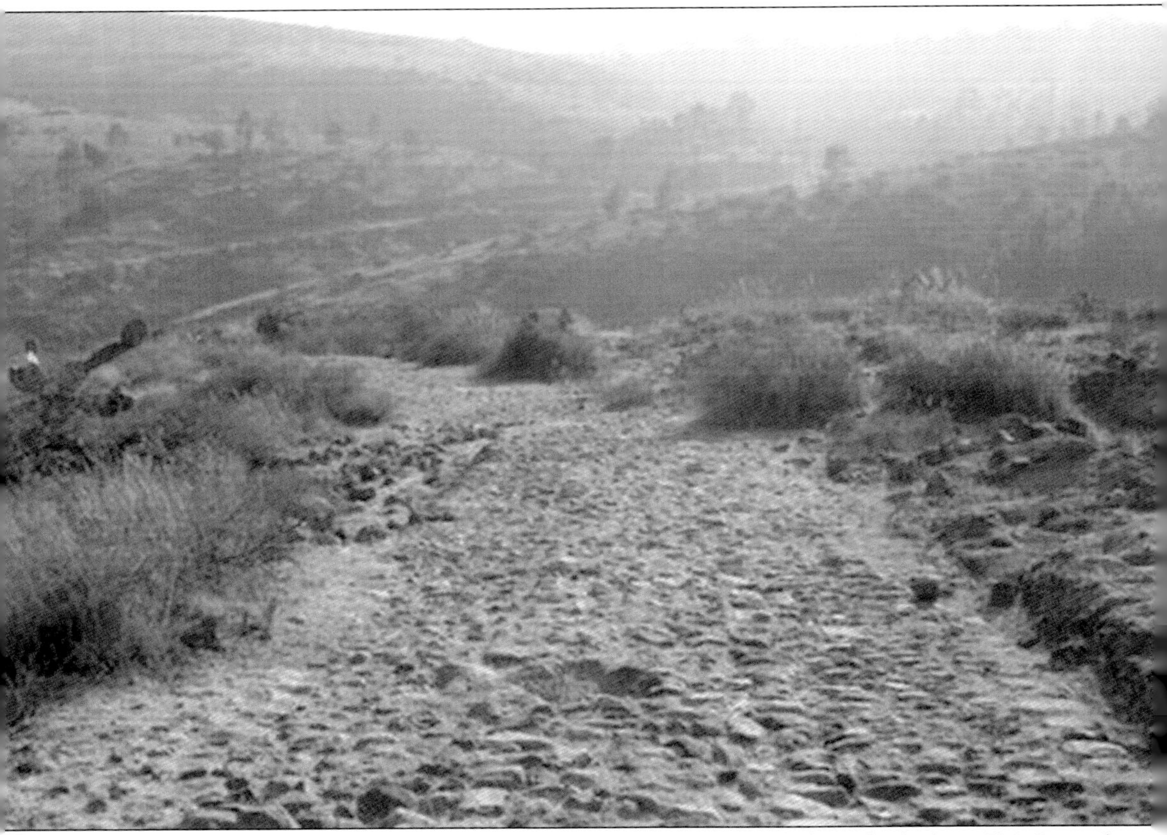

This is a section of the Camino Real, or the Royal Road, as it might have looked in 1598. Spanish engineers constructed the Camino Real, a network of roads built upon ancient native trails thousands of years old. The road that connected Mexico City to New Mexico was known as the Camino Real de Tierra Adentro—the Road of the Inner Lands. It was about 1,600 miles long, and until the 19th century, it was one of the most heavily traveled, continuously used roads in all of the Americas. (National History Museum, Mexico City.)

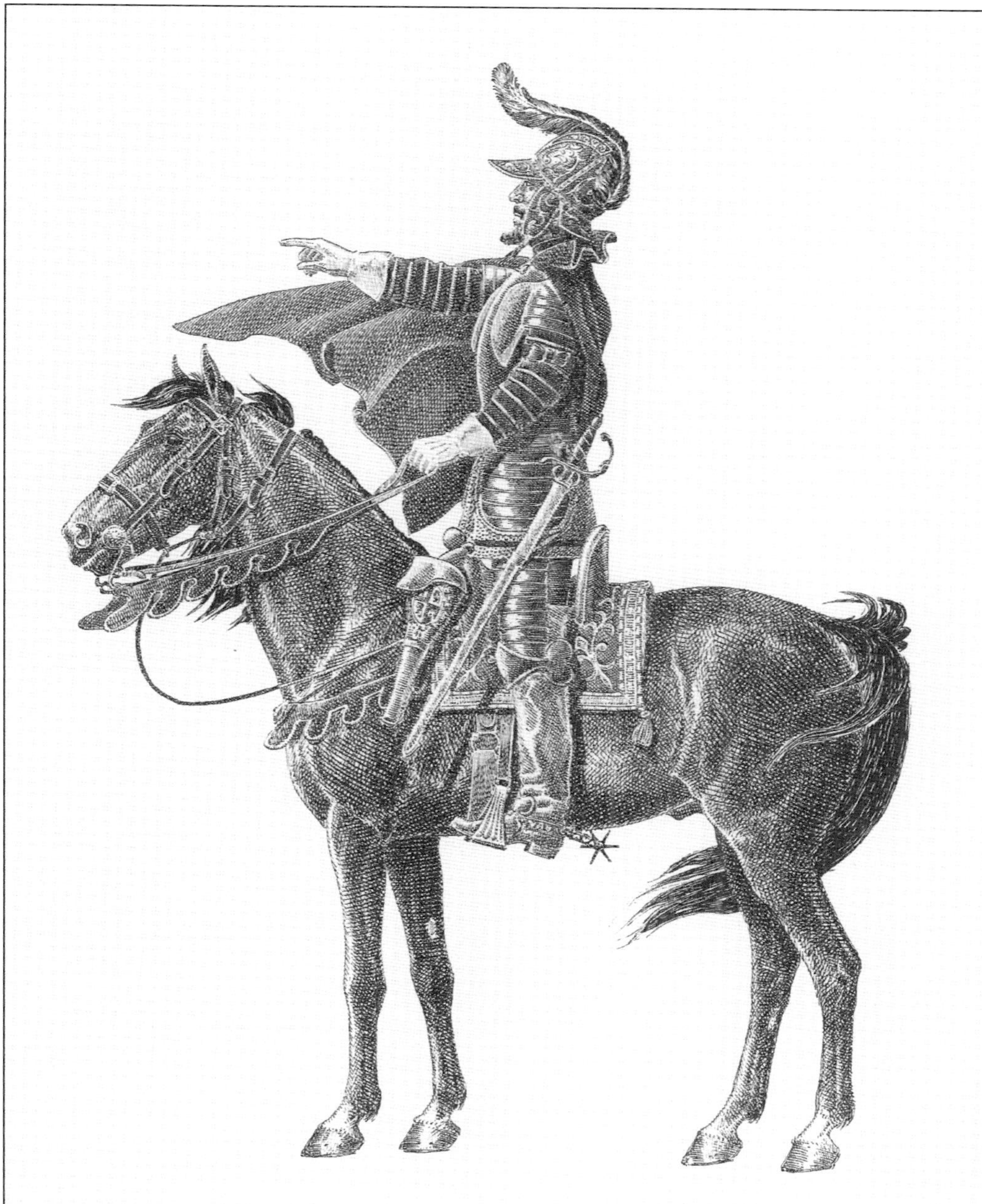

Francisco Vasquez de Coronado (1510–1554) was a provincial governor in Spain when he set off for the New World in 1540. The Spanish had heard rumors of great cities of gold. Coronado explored far into the northern reaches of the kingdom in search of that fabled wealth, but he found only humble communities of farmers and hunters. (Adair Margo Fine Arts, pen and ink drawing by Jose Cisneros.)

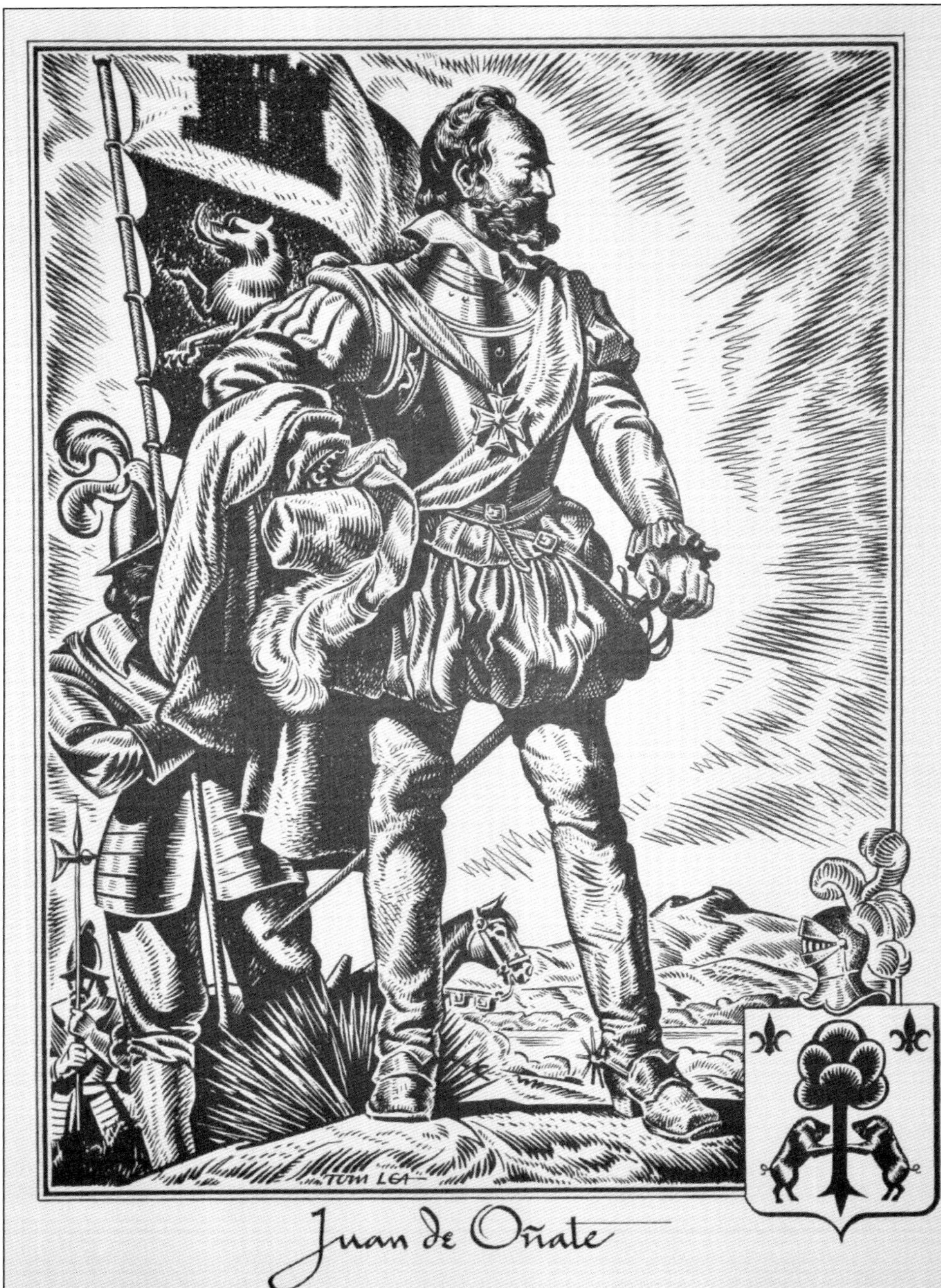

Juan de Oñate (1550–1626) was born in the Americas. His father was a silver baron in Zacatecas, Mexico. Oñate grew up with wealth and privilege. In 1595, King Phillip of Spain contracted him to colonize the northern frontier of the empire. Oñate gathered his colonists in Nueva Vizcaya, present-day Chihuahua, and began his expedition in 1598, following the Camino Real up through Mexico, and crossing the Rio Grande at El Paso del Norte. It was there, on April 30, 1598, that he claimed for Spain all of what is now New Mexico. (Tom Lea Institute.)

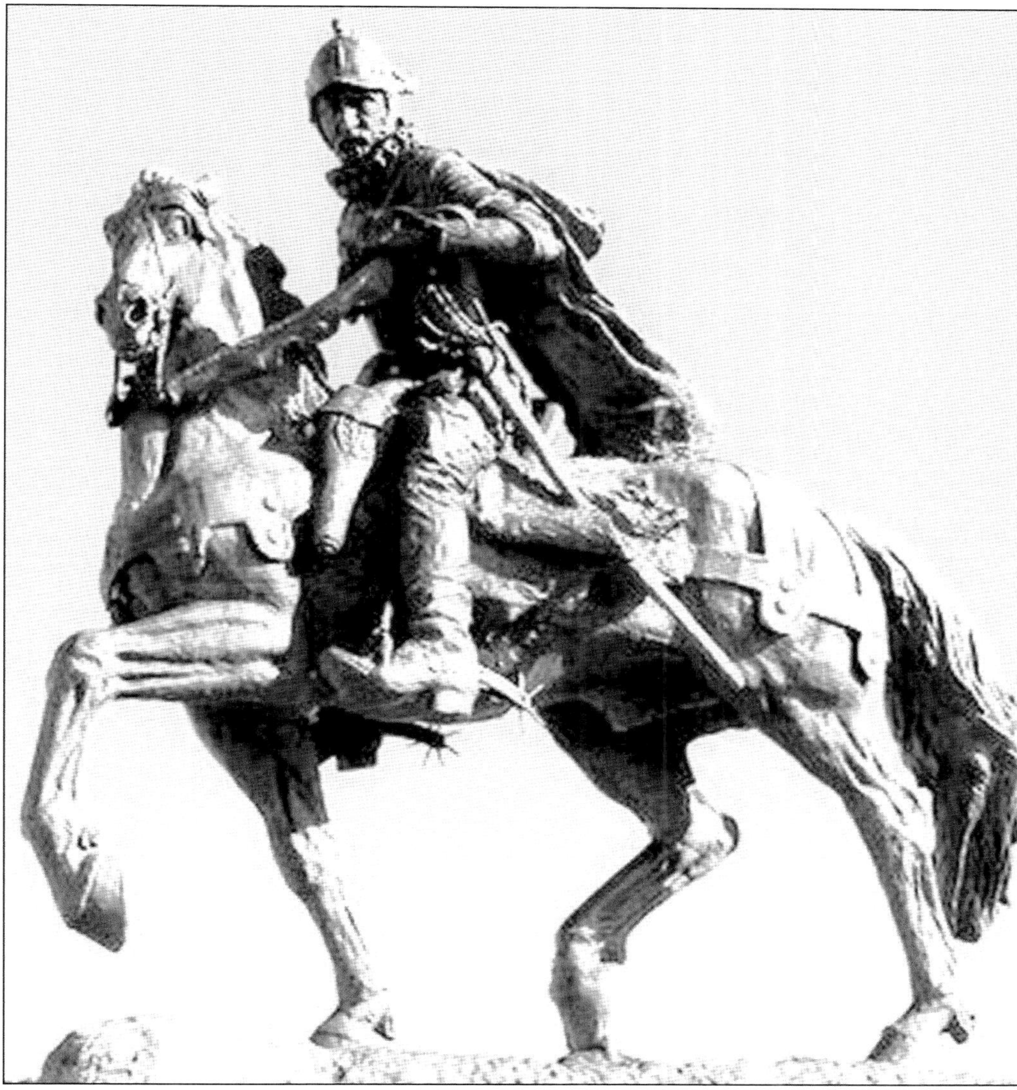

This massive sculpture of Oñate stands at the Oñate Historical Center on the northern end of the Española Valley. In 1998, as New Mexico was celebrating the 400th anniversary of Spanish settlement, some unknown person sawed off the statue's right foot—a symbolic gesture recalling Oñate's brutal conquest of the Pueblo of Acoma, about 65 miles west of present-day Albuquerque. Oñate was so enraged by Acoma's resistance that he decimated the village and ordered his men to cut off a foot of every Acoma man over the age of 25. (Camilla Trujillo.)

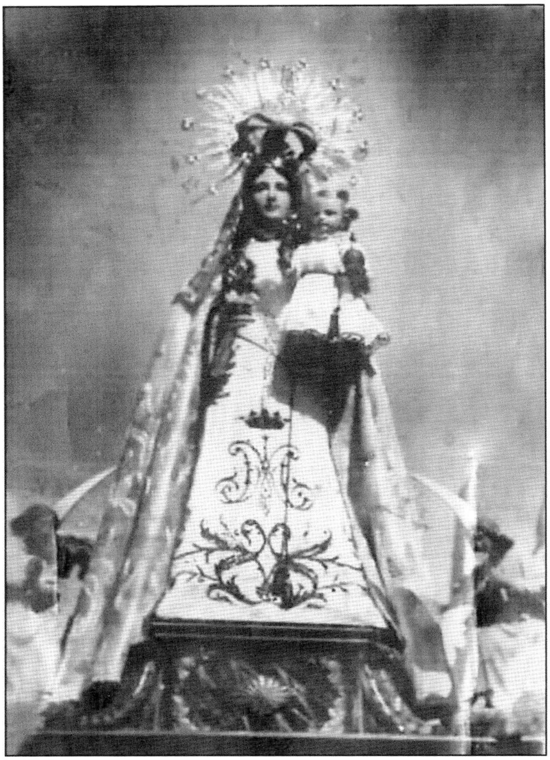

Nuestra Señora de los Remedios accompanied Juan de Oñate and colonists on their journey in 1598. The front of this banner displays an embroidered image of the Virgin Mary, patroness of the Spaniards in the city of Mexico; the reverse side shows the embroidered golden castles of Castile on red and the red lions of León on white. What is believed to be Oñate's original banner is in the possession of the New Mexico Museum and undergoing repair and restoration. (Camilla Trujillo.)

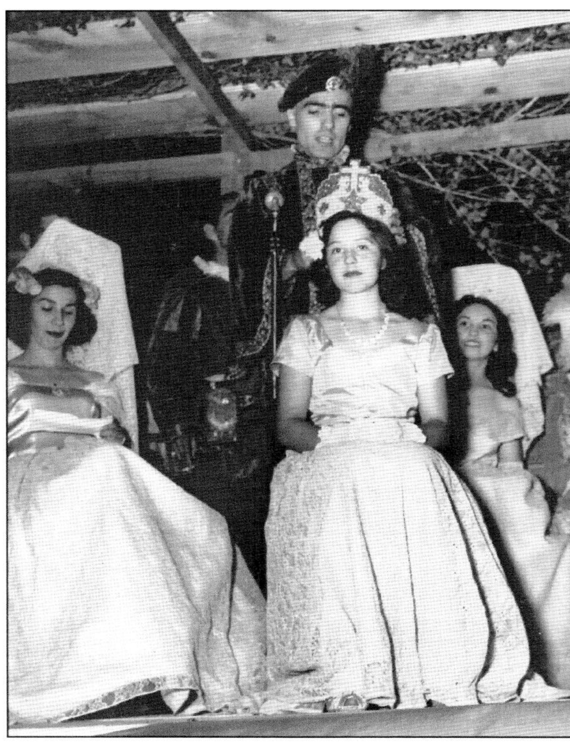

Even 400 years after the arrival of the Spanish colonists, the people of the Española Valley still commemorate their origins through pageantry and ritual. Here, in the Española Fiestas of 1942, La Reina de la Fiesta is being crowned by Oñate. She is played by an unidentified girl whose face communicates the seriousness of this moment. Oñate's eight-year-old son Cristobal is also portrayed in the fiestas by a young boy from the community. (Ross Olivas.)

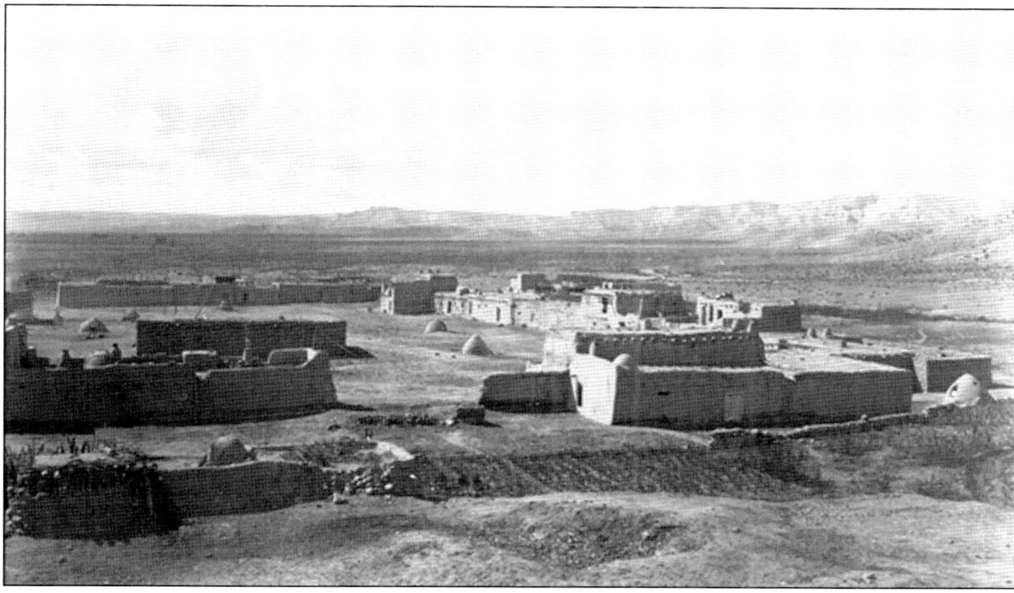

In 1598, the farthest reach of the Camino Real was the Española Valley, home to three Tewa Indian Pueblos: Ohkay Owingeh, San Ildefonso and -- shown above in an early 20th century photograph -- Santa Clara. This timeless view helps readers imagine how the Valley appeared to the first Europeans who came upon it. (Palace of the Governors Photo Archives, photograph by John K. Hillers.)

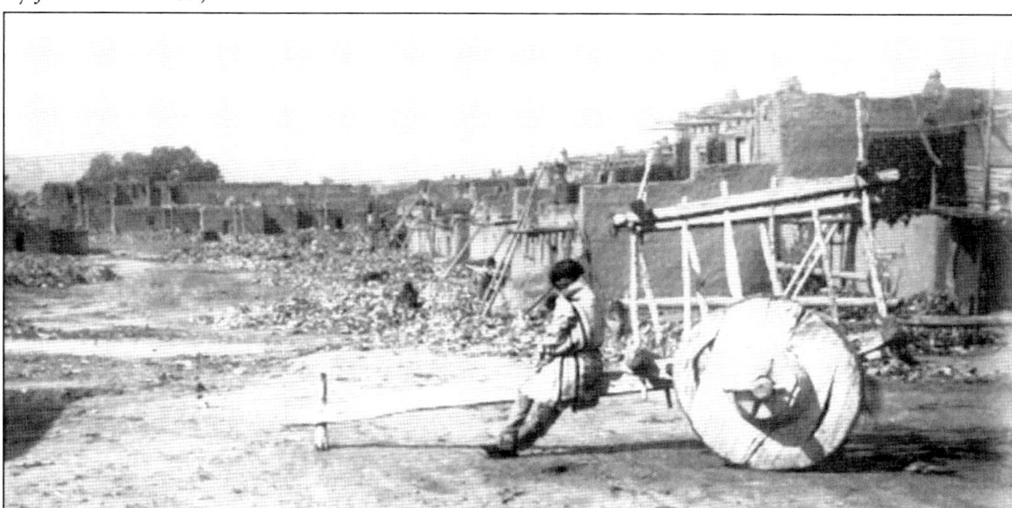

The wooden cart in this photograph—taken at Ohkay Owingeh at the turn of the century—is virtually identical to the *carretas* that colonists used to transport their goods. The *carreta* was very heavy and unwieldy, with huge, spokeless, solid-wood wheels, built to last the journey. The *carretas* were pulled by horses or mules, but when they became stuck in mud or ruts—which happened often—they had to be pulled out with oxen. At one point in the journey, the drivers took some of the wheels off the *carretas* and made them into a floating bridge so that the sheep could cross the raging waters of a river. (Palace of the Governors Photo Archives, photograph by William H. Rau.)

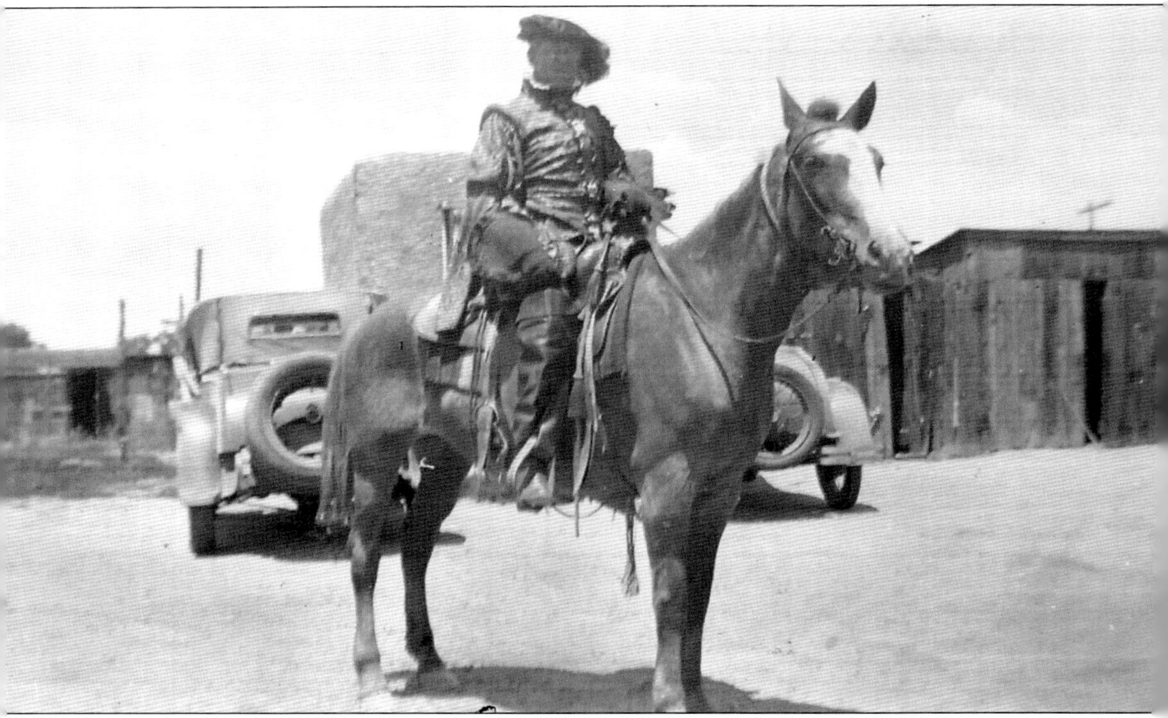

The gallant and beloved Dr. Tobias Espinosa recreates the role of Juan de Oñate for Española Fiestas in 1934. Dr. Espinosa was Española's second mayor, and the first man to portray Oñate in the annual fiestas. (San Gabriel Historical Society.)

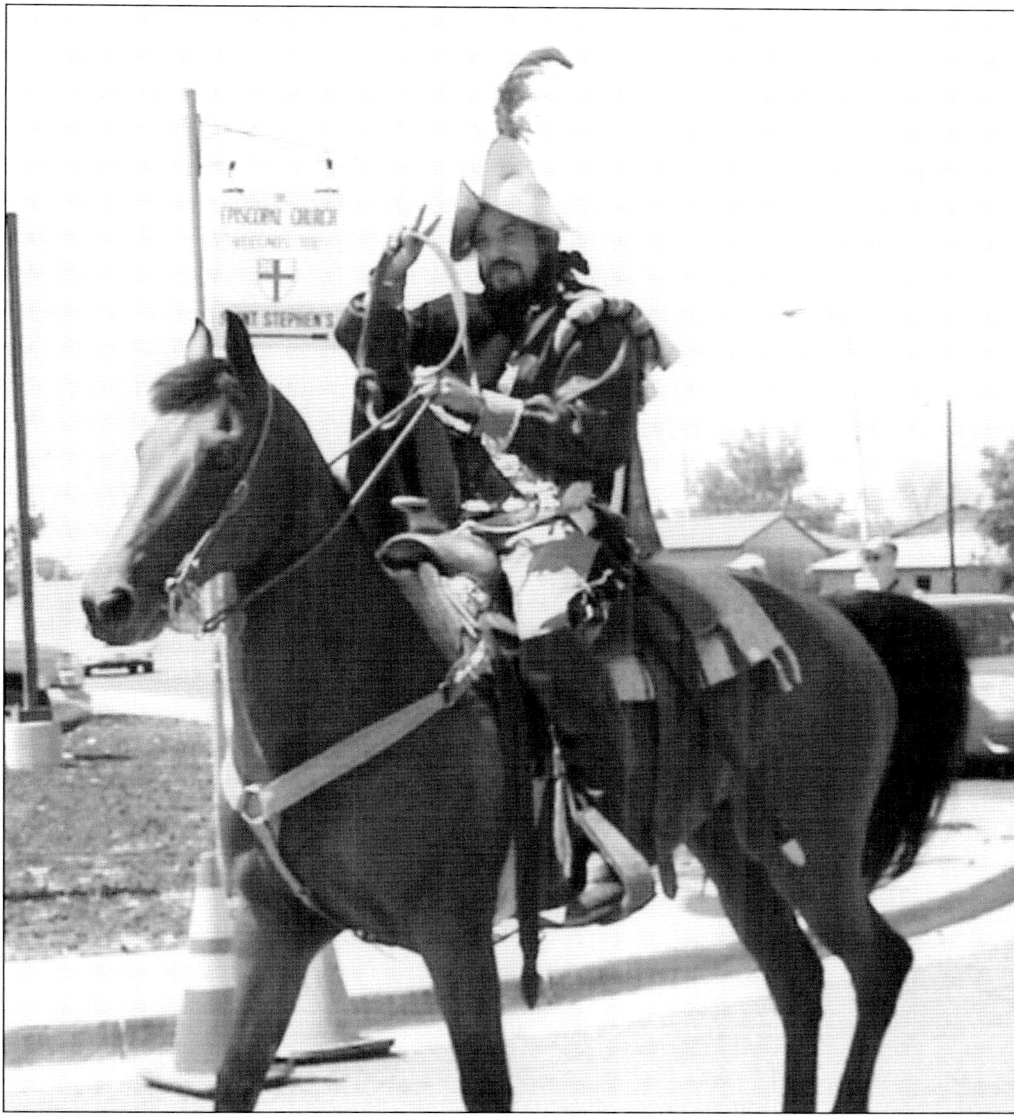

A modern-day Oñate rides up Bond Street in a more recent reenactment of the *encuentro*. (San Gabriel History Society.)

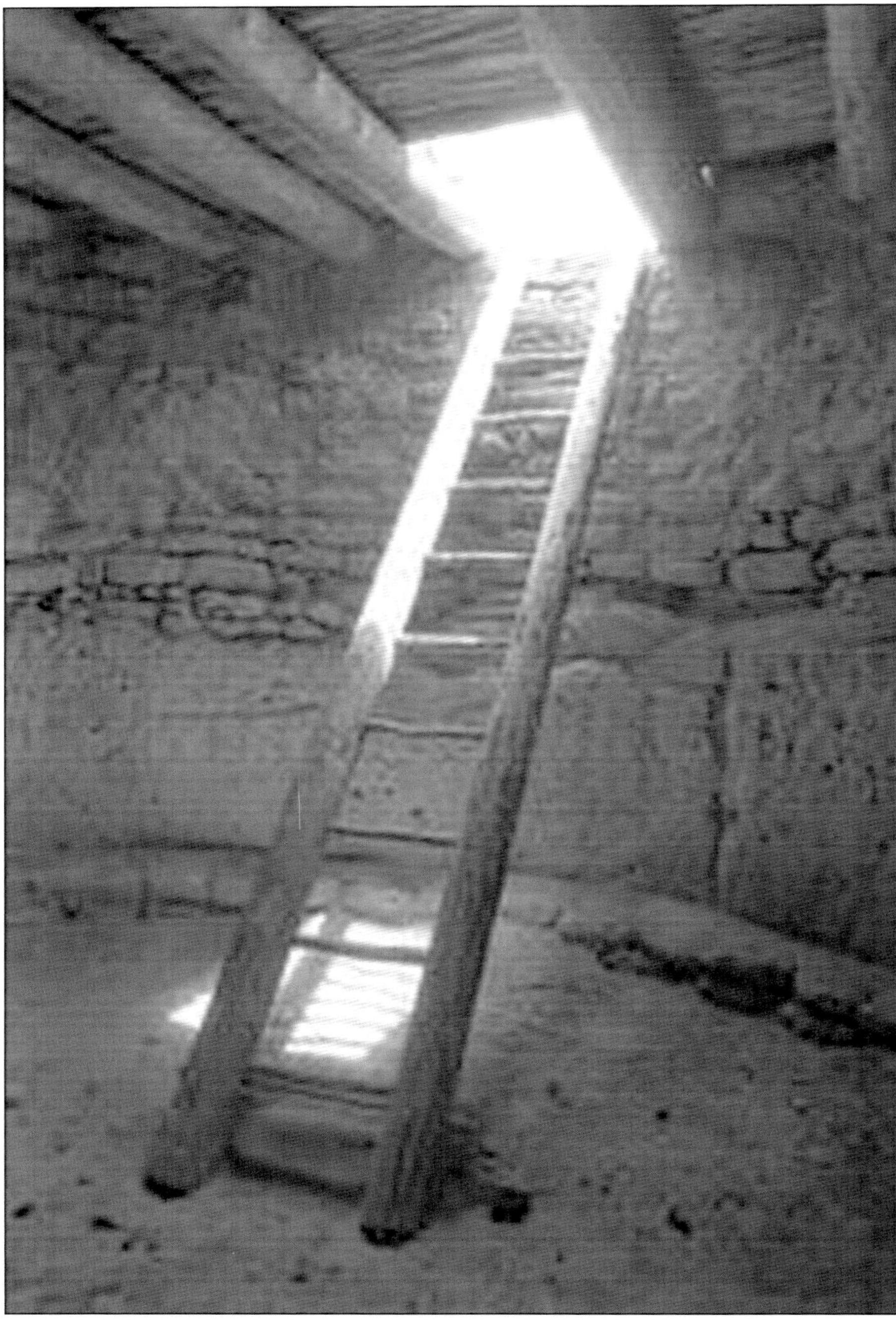

Shown is one of about 740 rooms in the Puye Cliff Dwellings, an astonishing masterpiece of ancient engineering carved into the cliffs of the Pajarito Plateau about 10 miles west of Española. Puye housed more than 1,500 people until 1577, when drought forced residents to abandon it and relocate nearer to the Rio Grande, in an area just south of the Stanley Griego Bridge in present-day Española. The people of Santa Clara Pueblo are the descendants of the inhabitants of Puye. (Puye Cliffs, Santa Clara Pueblo, photograph by Steve Larese.)

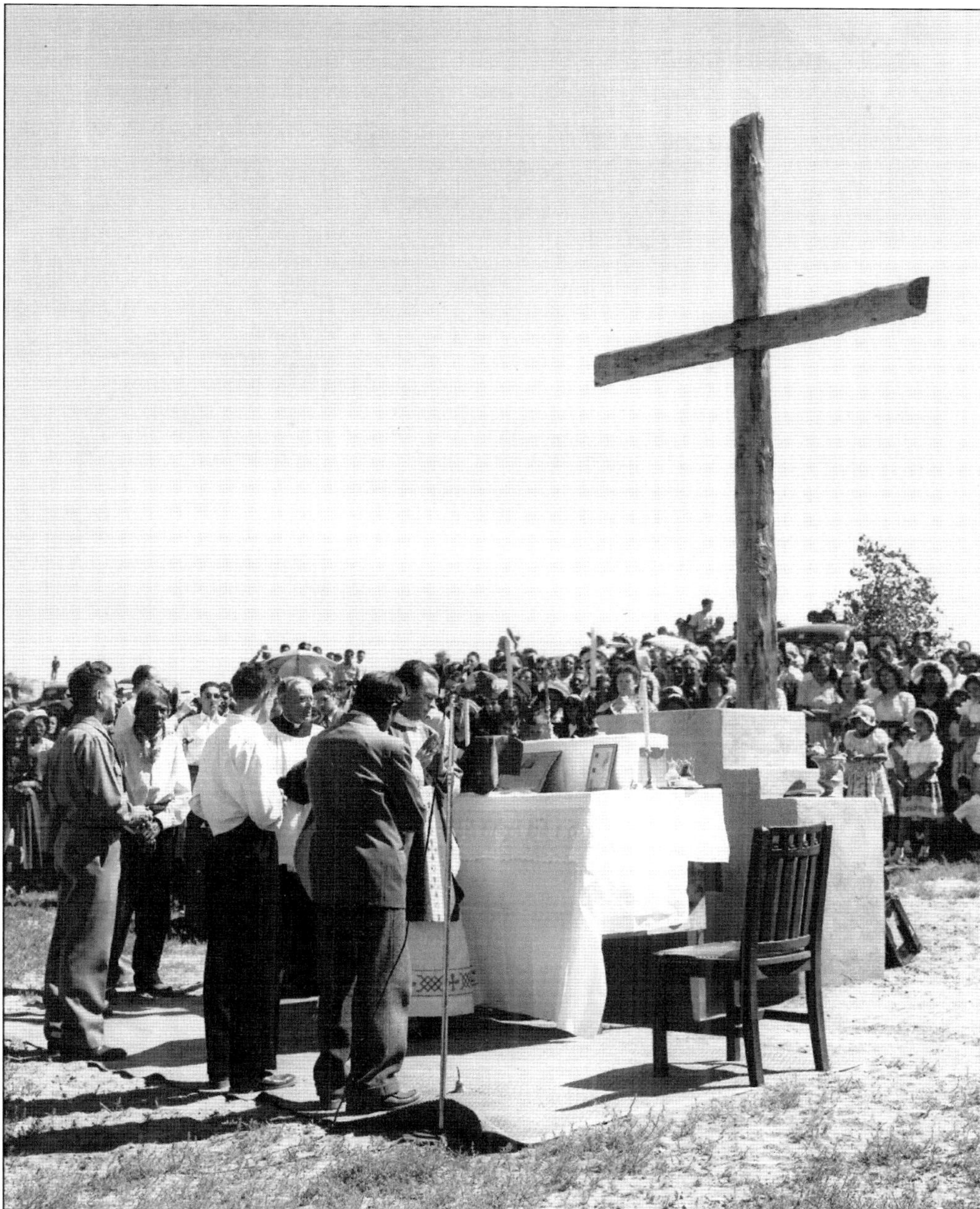

This Catholic Mass, which took place during the 1942 Española Fiestas in San Juan Pueblo, re-creates the Masses offered by the Franciscan friars who accompanied the Oñate expedition. To this day, it is still a part of the annual Española Fiestas. The friars named the pueblo San Juan de los Caballeros, in honor of Oñate's patron saint. The people of the pueblo reclaimed their original name in 2005, and their village is known once again as Ohkay Owingeh. (Ross Olivas.)

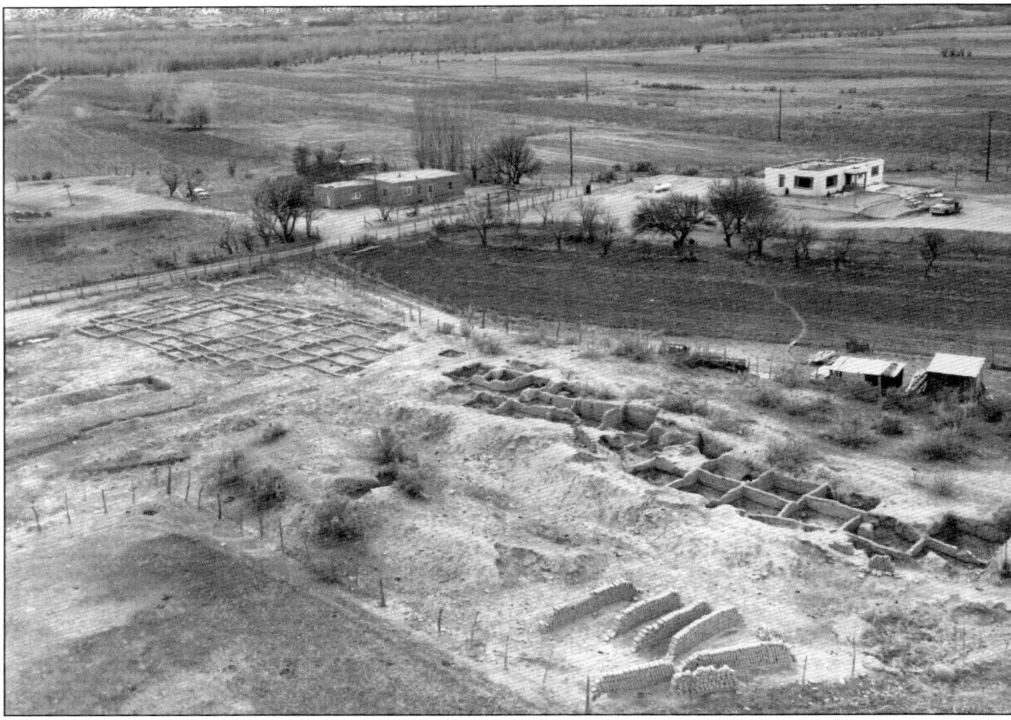

Shortly after establishing the settlement of San Juan de los Caballeros on the east bank of the Rio Grande in the Tewa village of Ohkay Owingeh in August 1598, Oñate relocated his colony across the river to the older Tewa village of Yungue Owingue, or Mockingbird Place. The Spanish called it San Gabriel del Yungue. It appears in these photographs, taken in 1962. San Gabriel was a town of approximately 400 housing units, more adequate for the needs of the Spanish forces. It remained the capital of New Mexico until Gov. Pedro de Peralta, Oñate's successor, founded Santa Fe in 1610. (Maxwell Museum of Anthropology, UNM.)

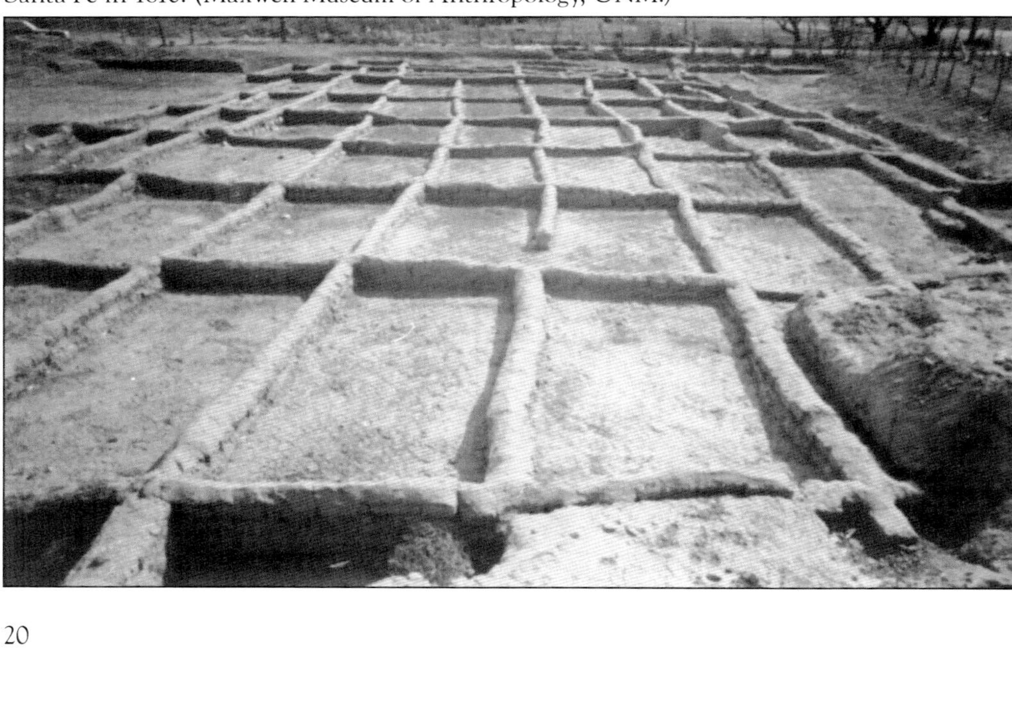

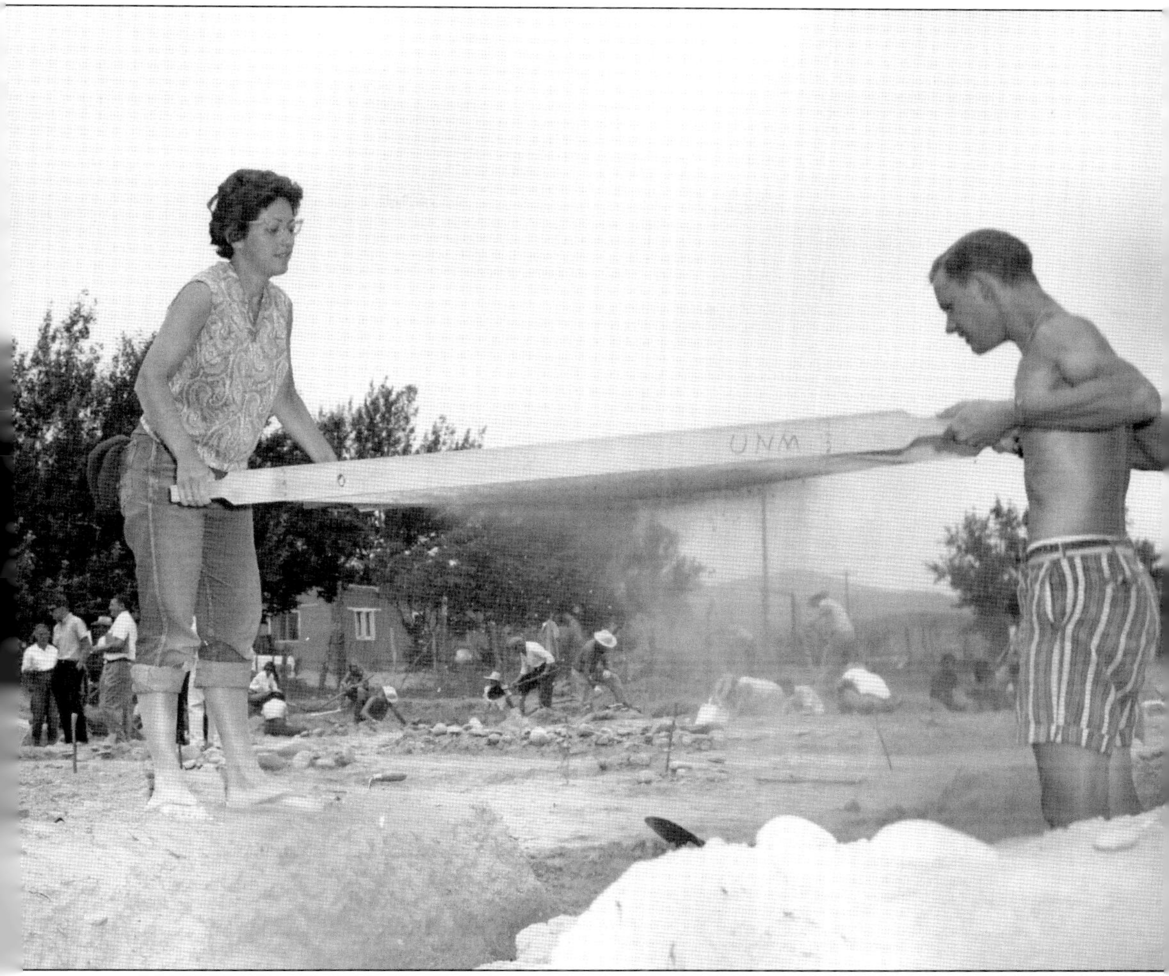

On a hunch, Dr. Edgar Lee Hewett, director of the Museum of New Mexico and the School of American Research in Santa Fe, asked his curator of archaeology, M. Tichy Lambert, to investigate the possible site of the first capital of New Mexico, San Gabriel del Yungue. Despite partial bulldozing of the site by an adobe brick operation, Tichy discovered artifacts that included chain mail and an archer's hat, dating to 1480–1510, the oldest piece of armor ever found in the United States. These important discoveries prompted concern for the preservation of the site. (Maxwell Museum of Anthropology, UNM.)

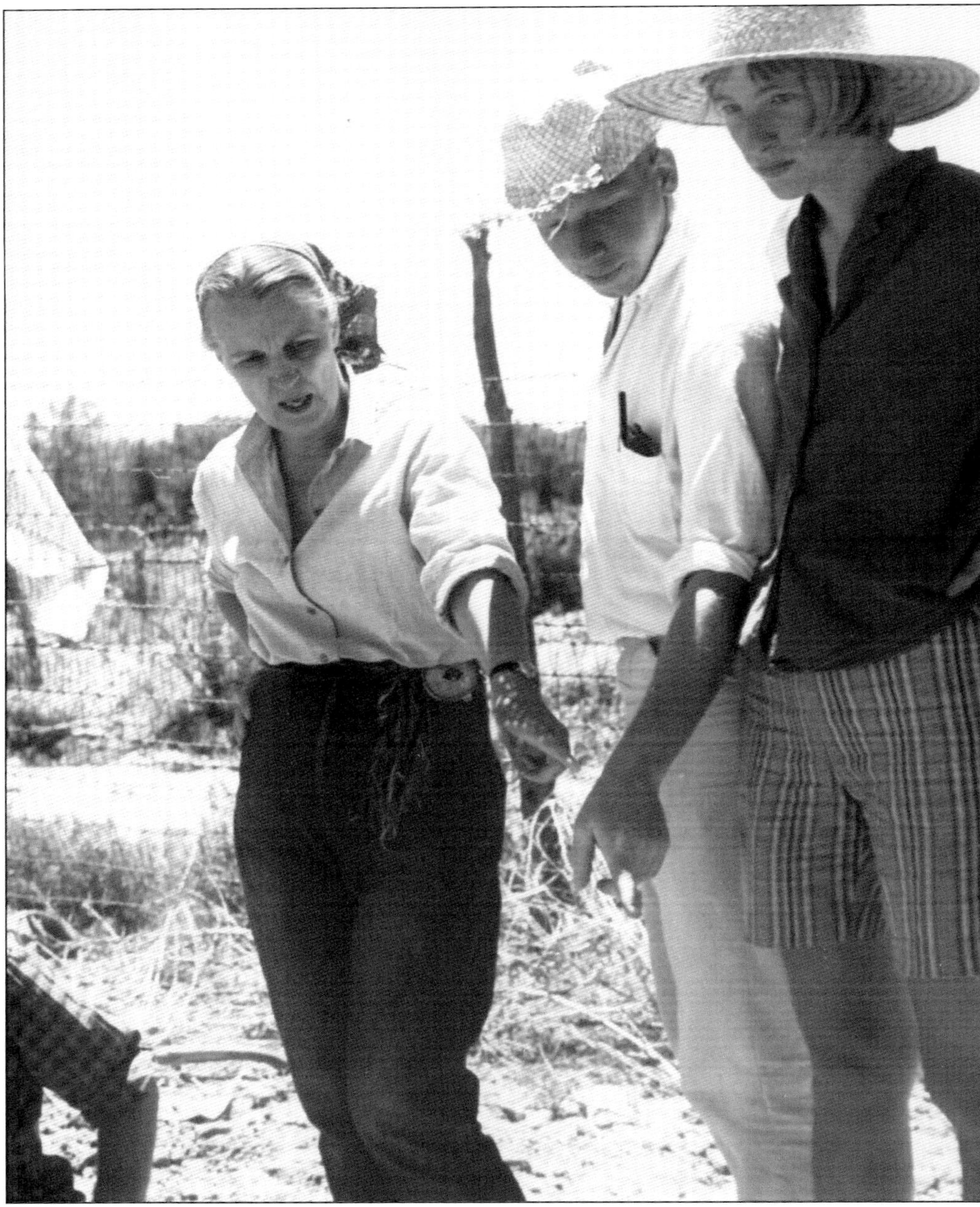

In the spring of 1959, Dr. Florence Hawley Ellis, of the University of New Mexico (UNM) archeology department, was invited by the governor of San Juan Pueblo to lead an excavation. Dr. Ellis—along with 50 students and a number of San Juan Pueblo helpers—began the dig at San Gabriel del Yungue. They uncovered some 100 rooms on three superimposed levels. Working within a narrow time frame, Dr. Ellis identified the first stage of the site, Yungue, as an enduring and successful Tewa pueblo. The second stage, San Gabriel, was in large part not reconstructed, but revised to alleviate some of the Spaniards' discomfort at living under unexpectedly difficult conditions. San Gabriel was settled 33 years after St. Augustine, Florida, and 22 years before English settlers established their colony at Plymouth Rock. (Maxwell Museum of Anthropology, UNM.)

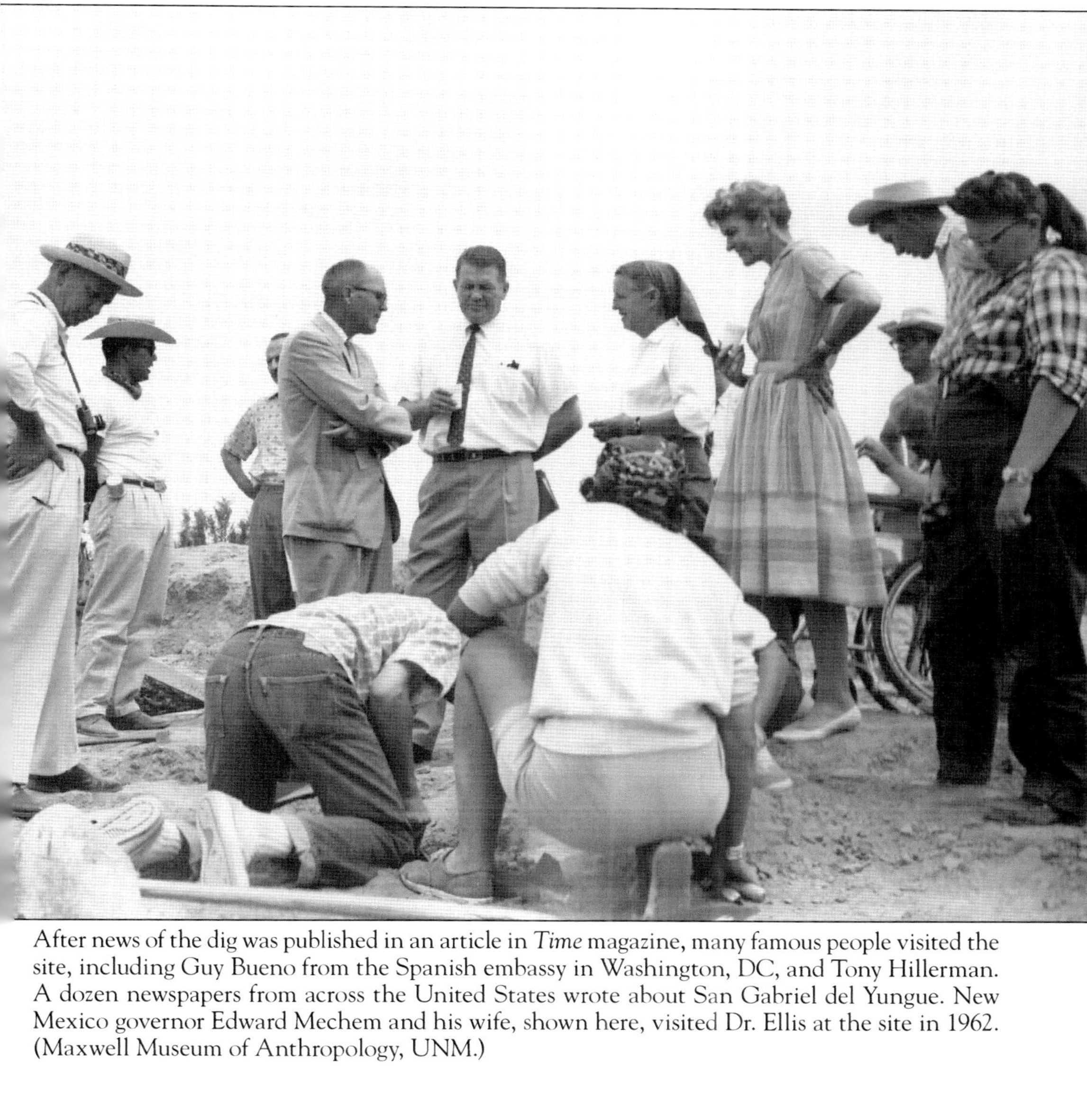

After news of the dig was published in an article in *Time* magazine, many famous people visited the site, including Guy Bueno from the Spanish embassy in Washington, DC, and Tony Hillerman. A dozen newspapers from across the United States wrote about San Gabriel del Yungue. New Mexico governor Edward Mechem and his wife, shown here, visited Dr. Ellis at the site in 1962. (Maxwell Museum of Anthropology, UNM.)

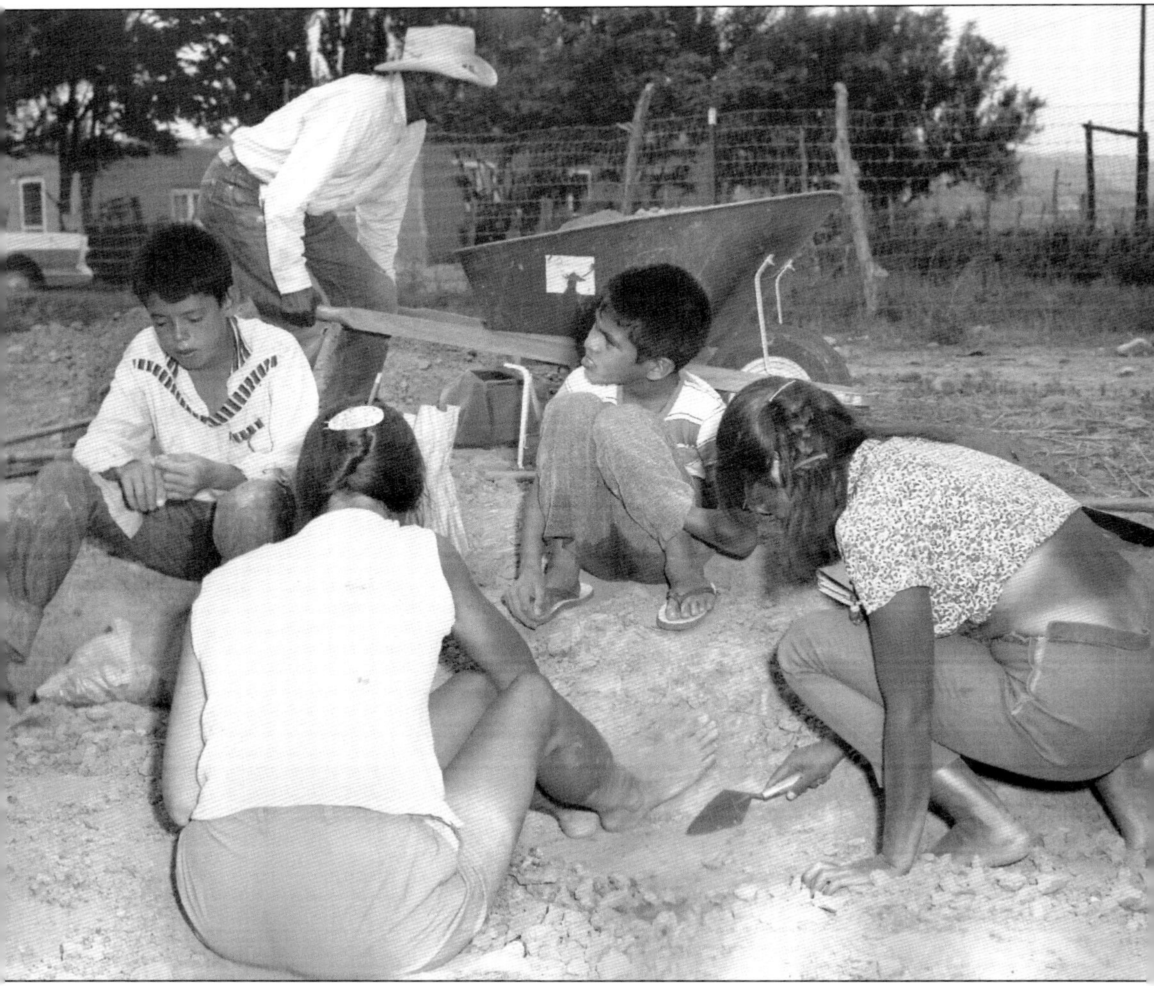

Residents of the San Juan Pueblo were employed by Dr. Ellis during the excavation. Men were assigned shovels and wheelbarrows, and the women were called upon as plastering consultants, as they are the traditional mud plasterers of the village. (Maxwell Museum of Anthropology, UNM.)

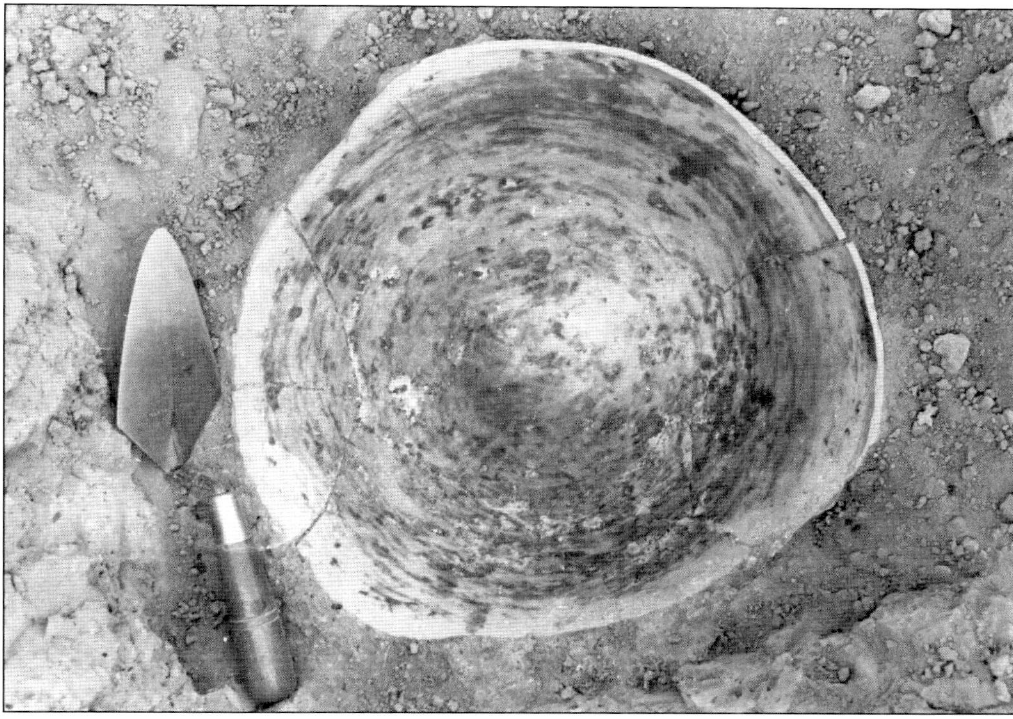

The standard tableware of the Spanish upper class living in Mexico during the 16th century was Majolica ware. Dr. Ellis found 23 examples of blue, green, yellow, brown, and orange-on-white Majolica pottery. Majolica was expensive, and its presence at Yungue suggests that some of the colonists were people of means who wanted the finer things of New Spain. This soup plate also illustrates the influence that Majolica ware had on the Rio Grande potters of this pre–Pueblo Revolt period. (Maxwell Museum of Anthropology, UNM.)

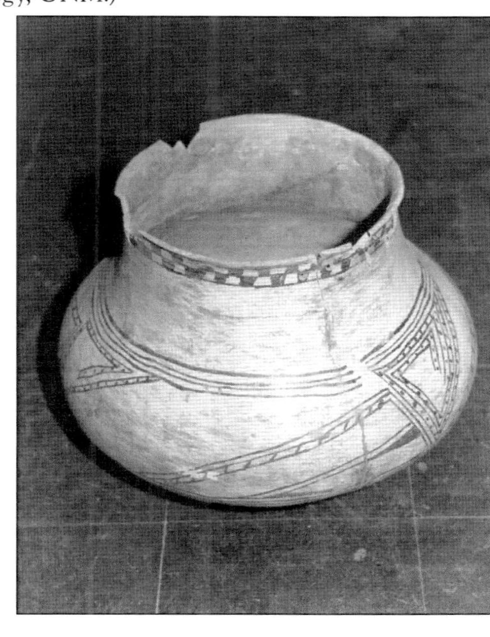

The earliest potsherds found by Dr. Ellis at San Gabriel del Yungue indicate occupation of this site dates back to sometime between 1200 and 1350. Most of the potsherds were identified as Abiquiu and Bandelier black-on-white, from about 1350–1550. Also found was Potsuwi'I incised pottery, dating to 1425–1525, and its usual companion, Sankawi black-on-cream, from around 1500–1600. Micaceous cookware dating from 1250 to post-1700 is also present, an indication that the Spanish occupants of San Gabriel were cooking in Micaceous pots. (Maxwell Museum of Anthropology, UNM.)

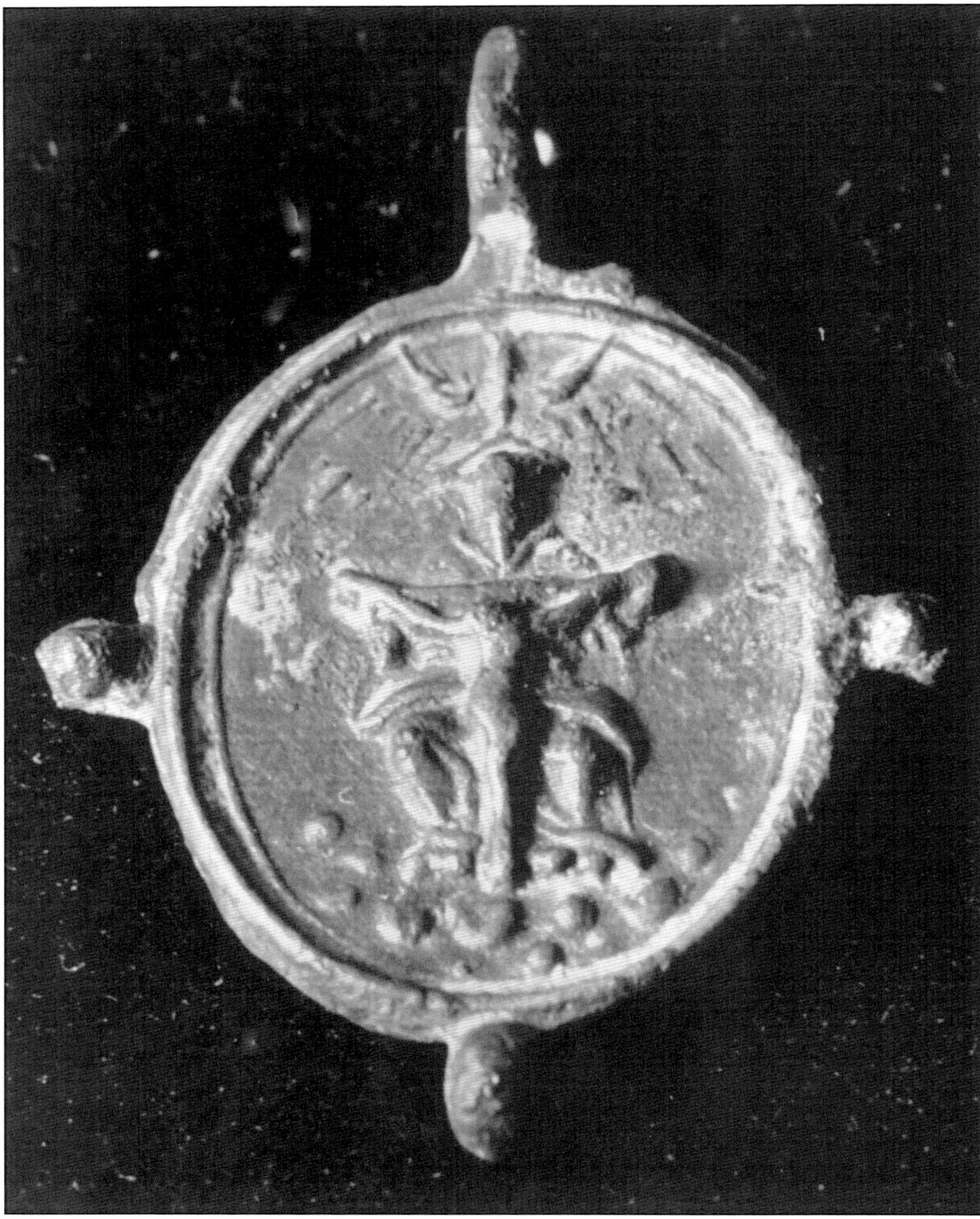

This small and exceptionally fine gilded 16th century medal, only about one inch high, was found by Dr. Ellis and identified by E. Boyd, of the Museum of New Mexico. The face of the medal shows the Holy Trinity as it was often depicted during the late Renaissance: God is seated with a dove above his head; the crucified Christ is propped between his knees. (Maxwell Museum of Anthropology, UNM.)

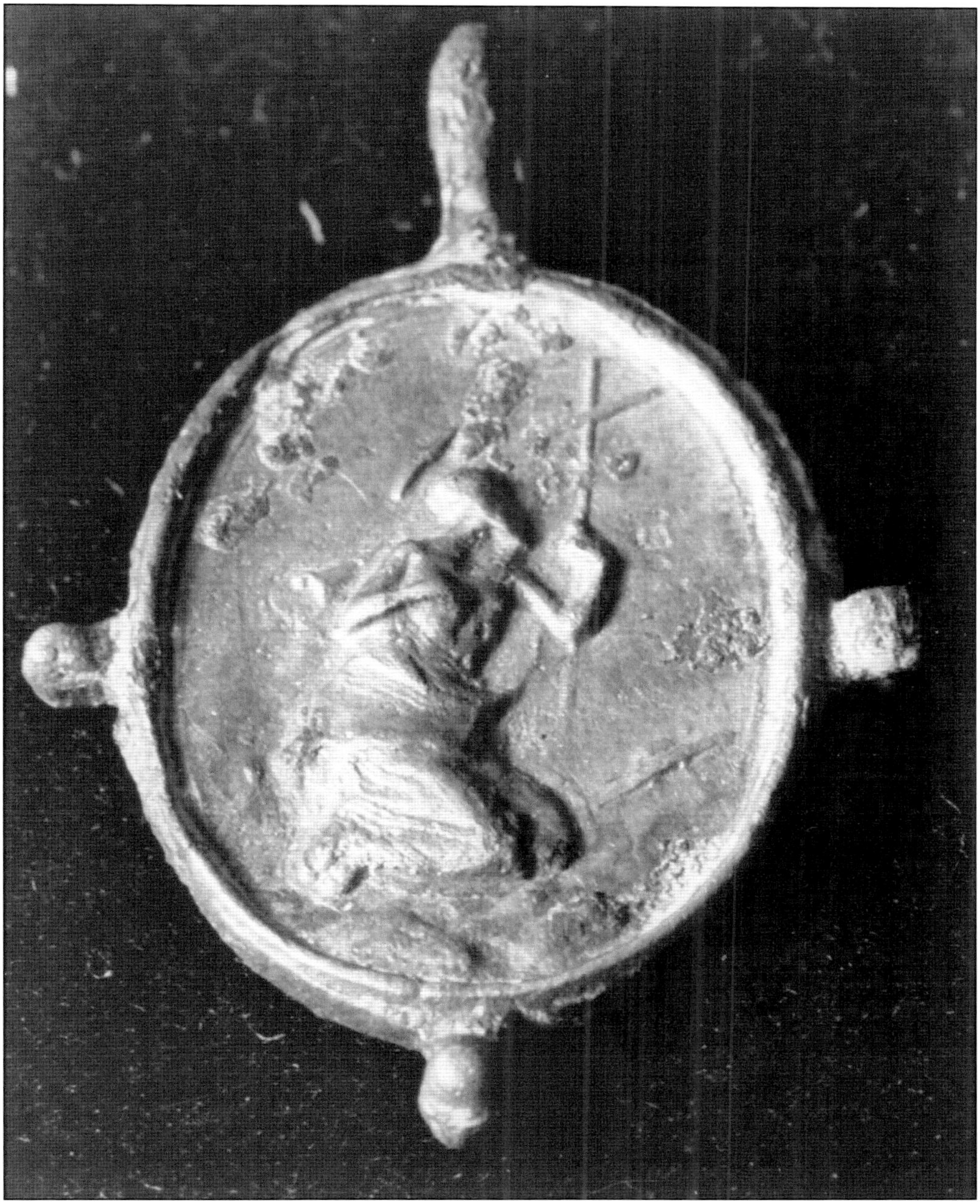
On the back of the medal is Saint Jerome kneeling in the desert, beating his breast. The symbolic lion associated with this saint lies at his feet. (Maxwell Museum of Anthropology, UNM.)

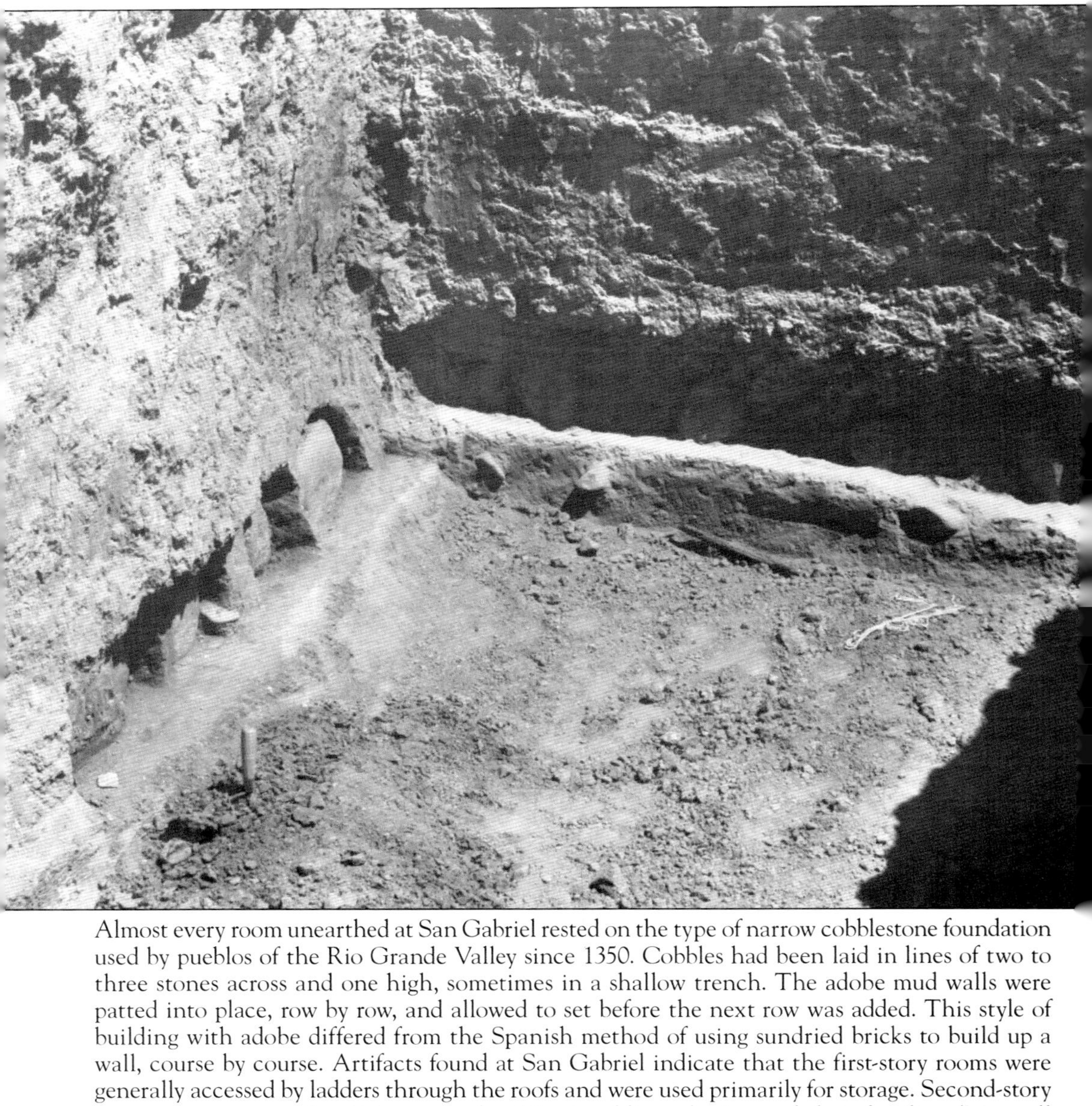

Almost every room unearthed at San Gabriel rested on the type of narrow cobblestone foundation used by pueblos of the Rio Grande Valley since 1350. Cobbles had been laid in lines of two to three stones across and one high, sometimes in a shallow trench. The adobe mud walls were patted into place, row by row, and allowed to set before the next row was added. This style of building with adobe differed from the Spanish method of using sundried bricks to build up a wall, course by course. Artifacts found at San Gabriel indicate that the first-story rooms were generally accessed by ladders through the roofs and were used primarily for storage. Second-story apartments were used as living space by Oñate's soldier-colonists and their families. (Maxwell Museum of Anthropology, UNM.)

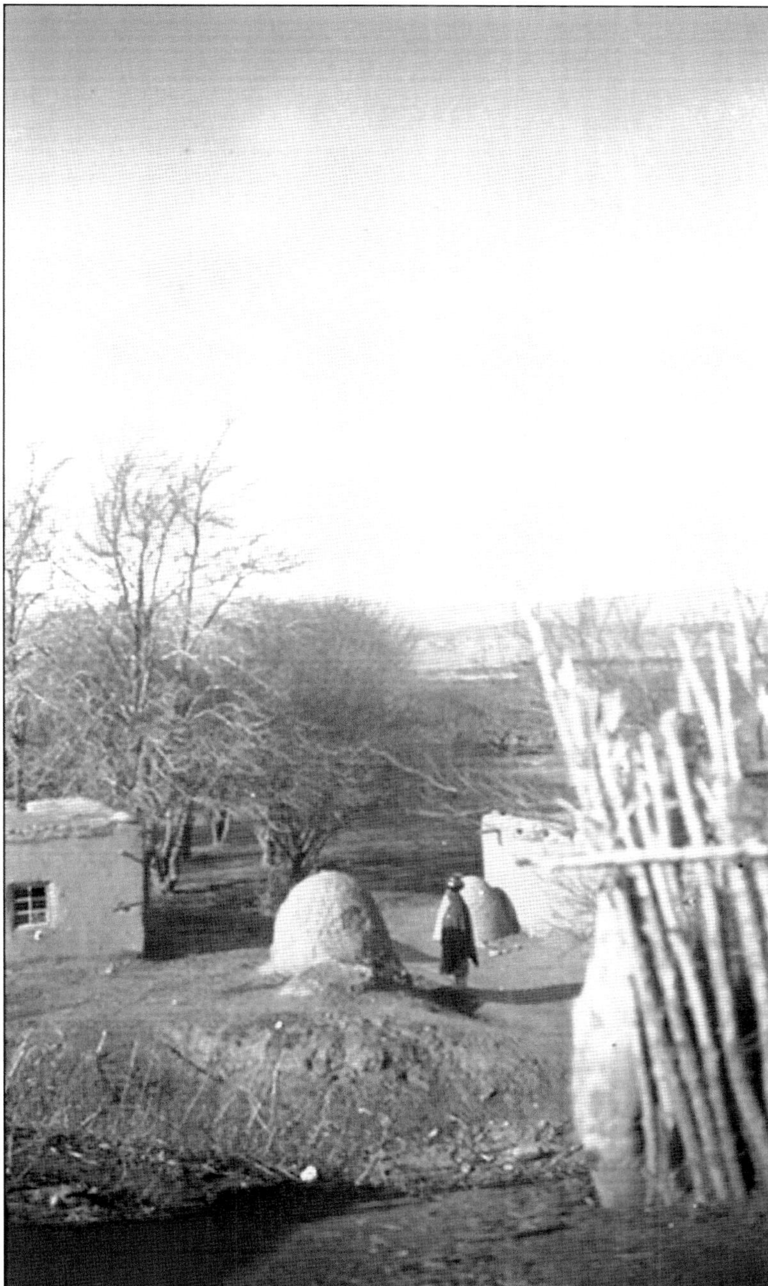

The first domed ovens in America for which evidence exists are the five examples uncovered at San Gabriel del Yungue. All five ovens, or *hornos*, had a base of stone mortared with mud plaster three to six inches thick and roughly four feet in diameter. The dome of the ovens probably stood three to four feet high. An arched opening was made at the bottom of the front of the dome, and a small circular opening would have been made in the upper dome to provide a draft. Two of the five ovens were still humped when found by Dr. Ellis at San Gabriel del Yungue. (Palace of the Governors Photo Archives, photograph by Edward S. Curtis.)

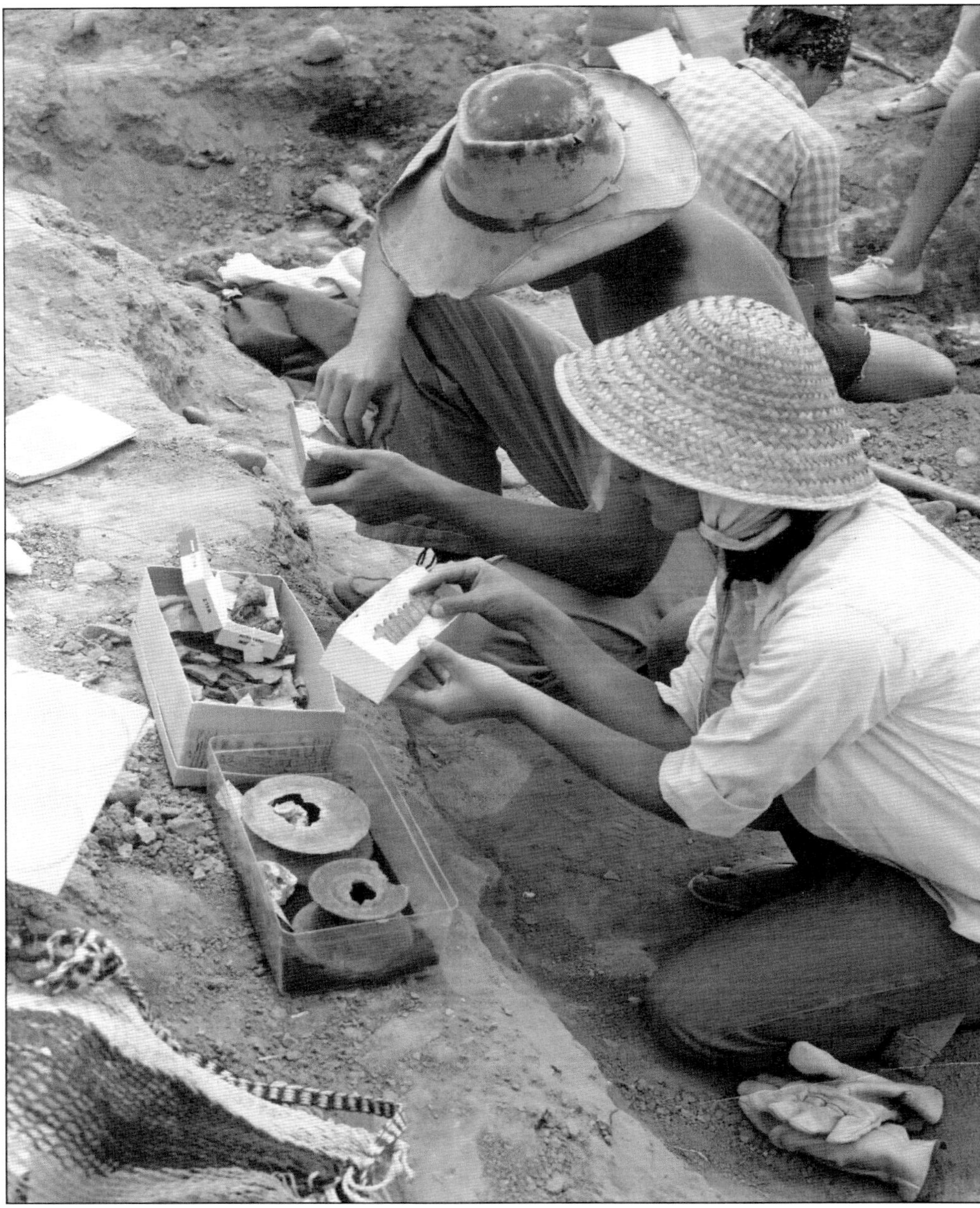

A scattering of chunks of volcanic tuff led Dr. Ellis to the church she had been seeking since the beginning of the project. Built in a cross-shape pattern, the old church of San Miguel had been split down its center by a modern dirt driveway. Local people had been driving up and down the nave of the oldest church in the United States without knowing it. Dr. Ellis was given permission to excavate the church, but had only one day to do so. Working frantically against the clock, she measured and plotted half of the church's outline before having to put the dirt back and restore the road. The clay candlesticks shown here were found at the base of the church's walls and were most likely made from locally quarried clay, by either Spanish or Native American potters. (Maxwell Museum of Anthropology, UNM.)

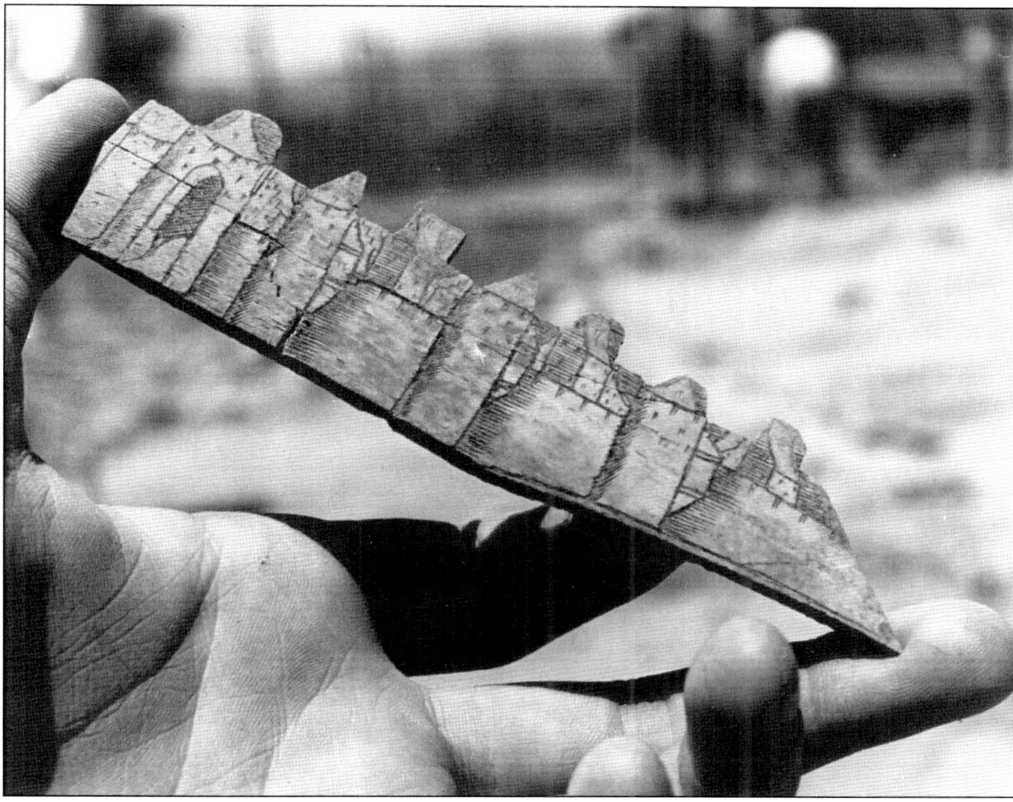

This inlay for a harquebus gunstock, carved from a femur of either a cow or horse, was found at the San Gabriel site. Weaving history with archeology, Dr. Ellis discovered that Rodrigo Velman, one of Oñate's men, was a native of Trimonia, a city in Flanders. She travelled to Belgium and found the medieval walls that are depicted on the carving. (Maxwell Museum of Anthropology, UNM.)

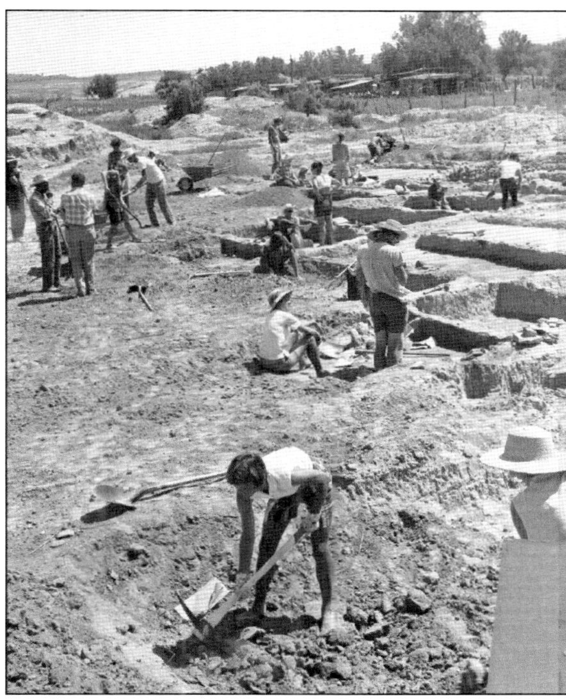

Approaching the end of her permitted timeframe for excavation, Dr. Ellis reluctantly closed the dig at San Gabriel del Yungue. Soaking the excavated rooms with kerosene, covering the floors with dirt, and laying new adobe bricks along the tops of the old walls, she protected the site as best she could. It was her wish that the site would one day be revisited. (Maxwell Museum of Anthropology, UNM.)

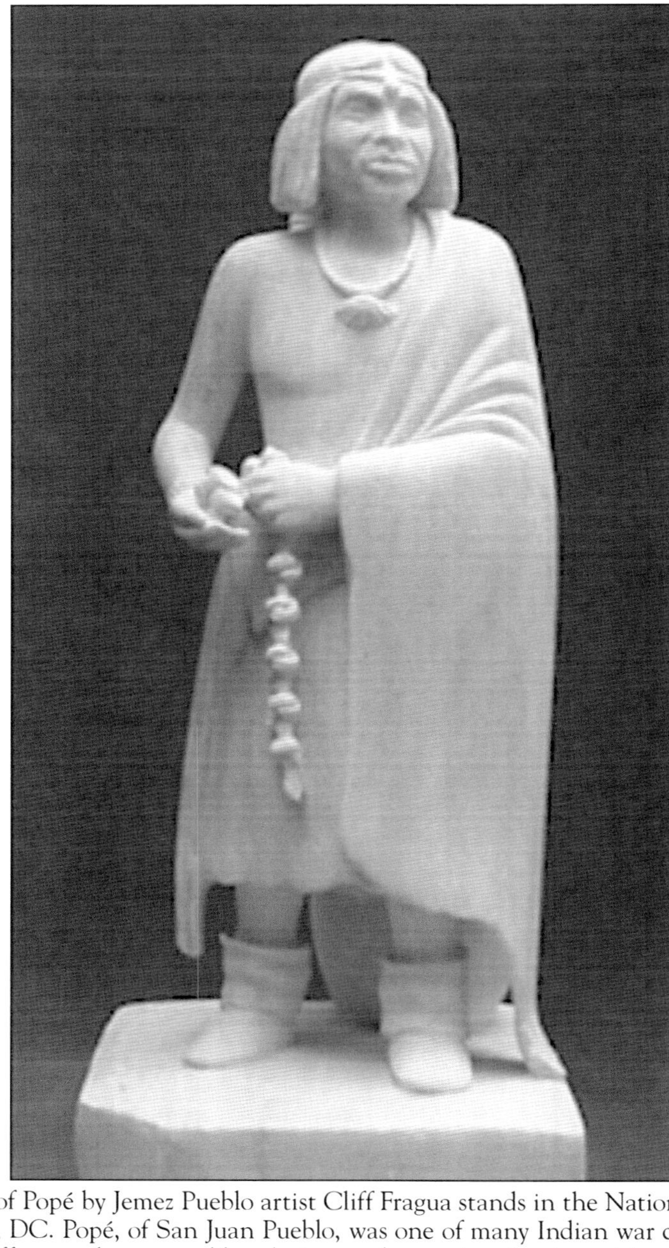

This sculpture of Popé by Jemez Pueblo artist Cliff Fragua stands in the National Statuary Hall in Washington, DC. Popé, of San Juan Pueblo, was one of many Indian war captains who met secretly in an effort to plan a possible solution to the overbearing imposition of a new religion and the suppression of indigenous religion by the Spanish during the 17th century. The revolt was so brilliantly planned that it struck just before the supply wagons from Mexico arrived, which happened only every three years. With such skill, Popé and his fellow leaders set into motion what was perhaps the most successful revolt by natives in the New World. The pent-up hatred for the Spanish soldiery, suppressed for so long throughout the Pueblos, was released. The Pueblo Revolt of 1680 accomplished the removal of the Spanish colonists from New Mexico for 12 years, until the Reconquista in 1692 when Don Diego DeVargas returned to Santa Fe. Another Pueblo revolt broke out in 1696, but was quickly put down. (National Statuary Hall.)

Two

Santa Cruz de la Cañada

In 1692, twelve years after the Spanish had been forced out of New Mexico by the Pueblo Revolt, Diego de Vargas reconquered the territory and once again claimed it for his king. Early the following year, he rode to the Villa de Santa Cruz with 66 colonist families, many of whom were returning to the sites where they had farmed and raised livestock prior to the revolt. When they arrived, they encountered Tano Indians, who, in the long absence of the Spanish, had occupied the land. De Vargas relocated the Tanos, established a military barracks upriver, and supervised the reoccupation of Santa Cruz.

At that time, the villa lay on the south side of the Rio Santa Cruz. Regular flooding of the river forced a decision, in 1732, to relocate the settlement to higher ground on the north side. An original land grant family donated a huge parcel to the governing Franciscan Order, allowing the villa to expand in all four directions.

Military power alone could not have made colonial settlement possible. Expansion of the villa also depended upon water. Slowly and steadily, the colonists dug a network of irrigation ditches—called *acequias*—an ancient communal irrigation technology with roots in Spain and Native America. In fact, 50 years before the United States was created in 1776, the acequia system was already a political, cultural, and agricultural institution in the Española Valley.

The building of the Santa Cruz Church took 15 years—from 1733 to 1748—one of the longest construction projects in the New Mexico of those times. Its original walls, which still stand, are the thickness of more than one *vara*, an early Spanish measure equivalent to about a yard. The church at Santa Cruz de la Cañada is a stunning example of New Mexican Franciscan mission architecture. Rather than import European statuary and paintings, parishioners of 18th- and 19th-century Santa Cruz turned to their own artisans (known as *santeros*), who produced a vast body of New Mexican religious iconography, wood and metal craft, and other work that, even today, remains a deep well of inspiration for contemporary Spanish Colonial artistic sensibility.

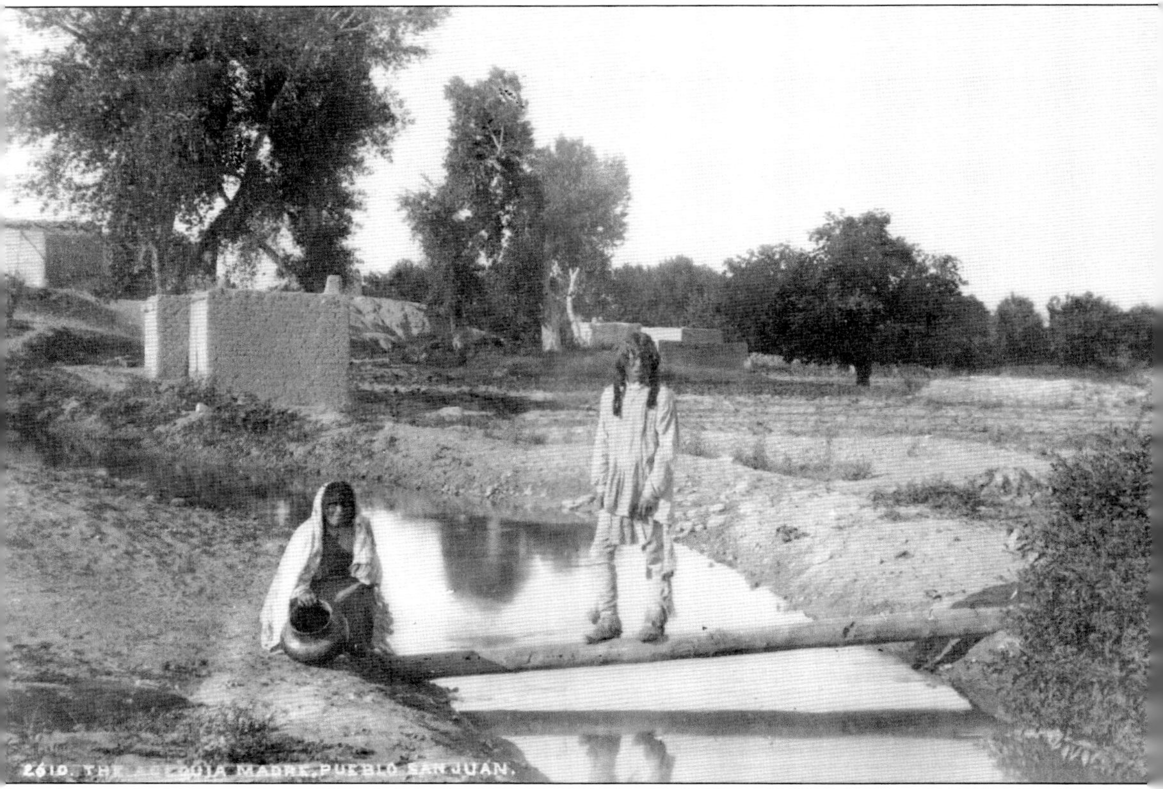

Before Oñate built the church of San Juan de los Caballeros at Ohkay Owingeh in 1598, he extended the existing acequia, or irrigation canal. Then, as now, water determined the abundance or scarcity of food. Taken in the 1880s, this picture shows the *acequia madre,* or mother ditch, at Ohkay Owingeh Pueblo, looking much as it did in the 17th century. The written record of acequias in the Santa Cruz Irrigation District begins with a 1787 deed that describes a lot, located behind the church and extending to an acequia, whose location matches that of the present-day Lomita ditch. (Palace of the Governors Photo Archives, photograph by William Henry Jackson.)

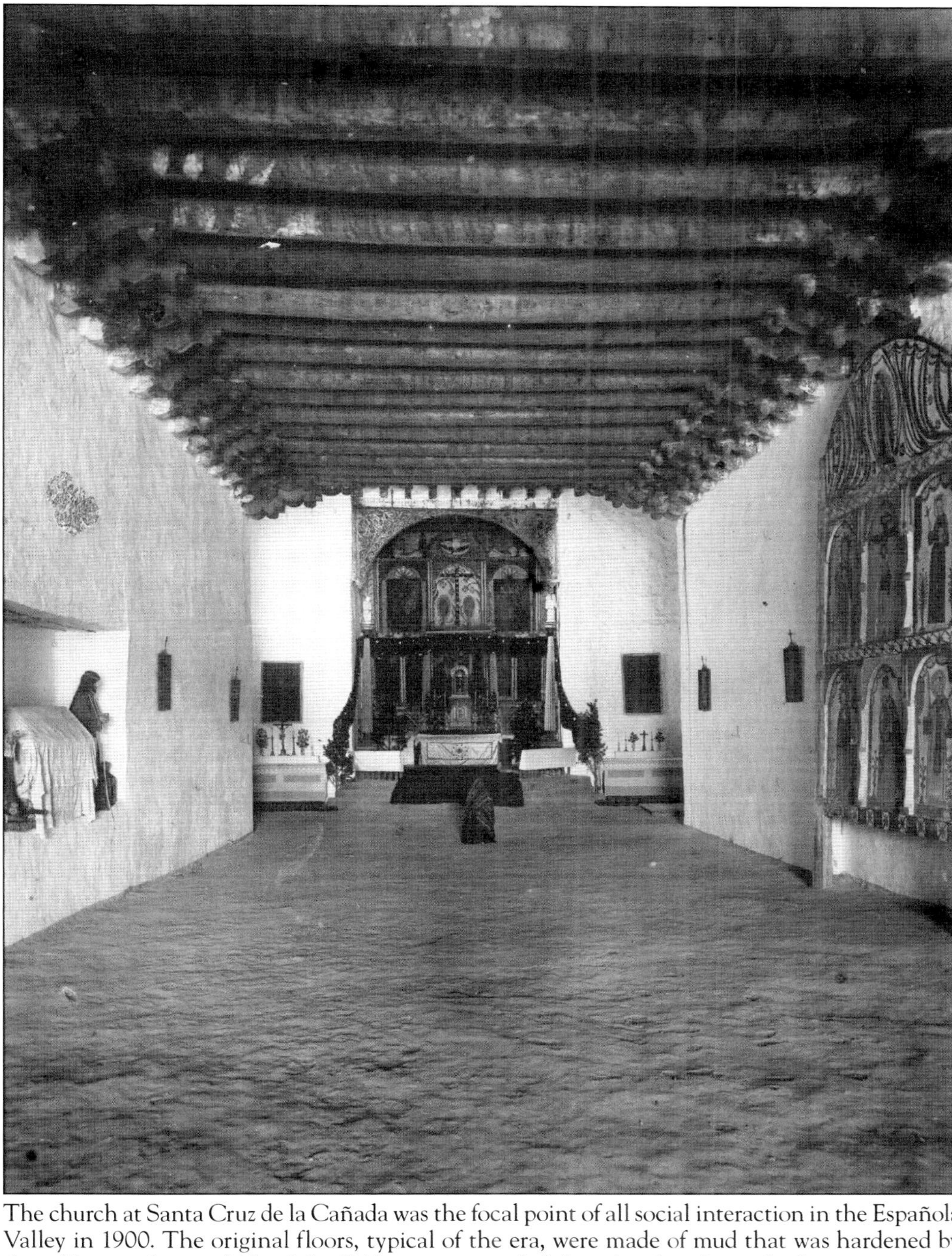

The church at Santa Cruz de la Cañada was the focal point of all social interaction in the Española Valley in 1900. The original floors, typical of the era, were made of mud that was hardened by the addition of animal blood. In 1748, it was recorded that the church was built at no expense to the Spanish crown. Following in that tradition, nearly all subsequent improvements to the church have been made by volunteer labor of the community. In the early 20th century, Eligio Madrid, a parishioner, replaced the mud floor with a wooden one. He used a team of horses inside the church to level the floor prior to placing the lumber flooring. (Palace of the Governors Photo Archives, photograph by William Henry Jackson.)

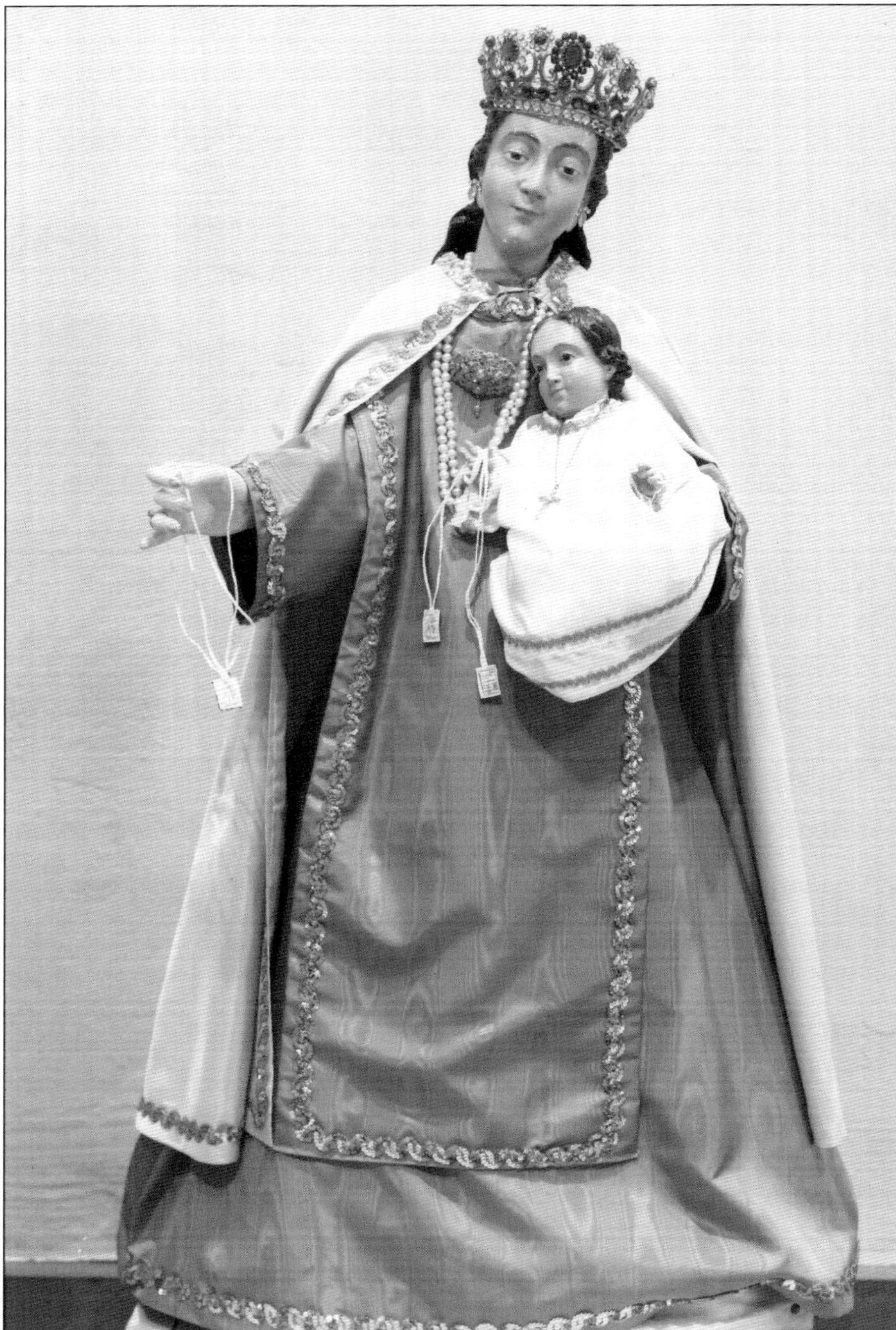

In 1867, the *santero* Jose Rafael Aragon created a *bulto*, or statue, of Nuestra Señora del Carmen—known in English as Our Lady of Mount Carmel—as prepayment for his burial in the north chapel of the church. Church records show that Aragon was buried twice; the first time was in the cemetery of the present village of Cordova; the second time—as Aragon had wished—under the floor of the chapel of Our Lady of Mount Carmel. (Santa Cruz de la Cañada Parish.)

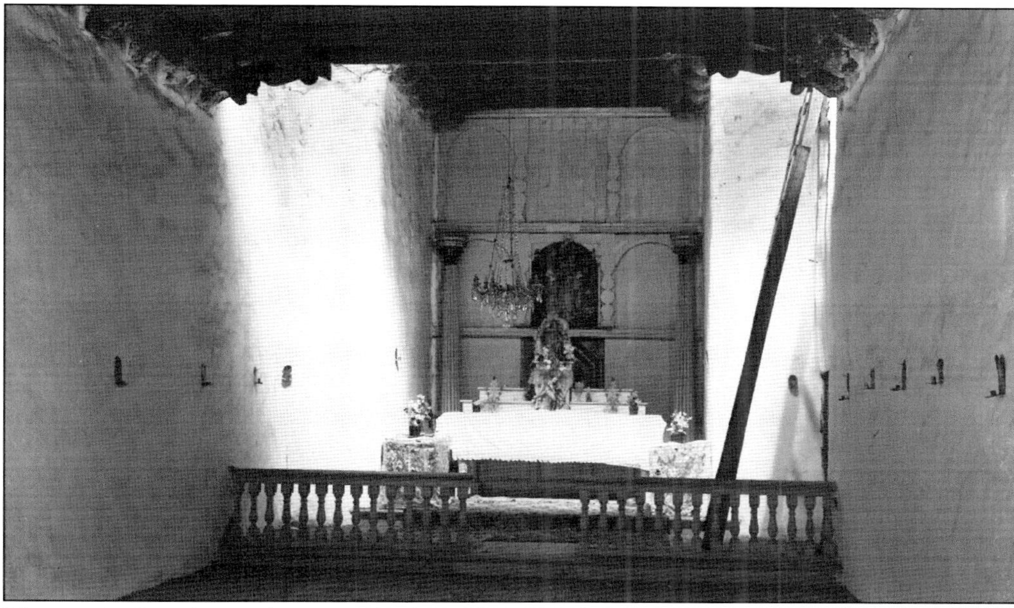

The north chapel, seen here, was built in 1748. By 1818, it had painted double doors, a single window to the east, and a choir loft. It also had a wood floor, unlike the rest of the church, which had mud floors. At the east side of the altar was a door to the sacristy, a small room that no longer exists. The slanting black object to the right of the altar is actually a freestanding altar screen, a *reredo*. At one time, there were seven such altar screens in the church. Three remain, permanently attached to the 40-inch-thick adobe wall. No one knows what happened to the others. The altar facing front is white, because in the early 1900s a mysterious person whitewashed it. Today, the altar is not visible at all; it has been plastered over completely. (Both, Palace of the Governors Photo Archives, photographs by Jesse Nusbaum.)

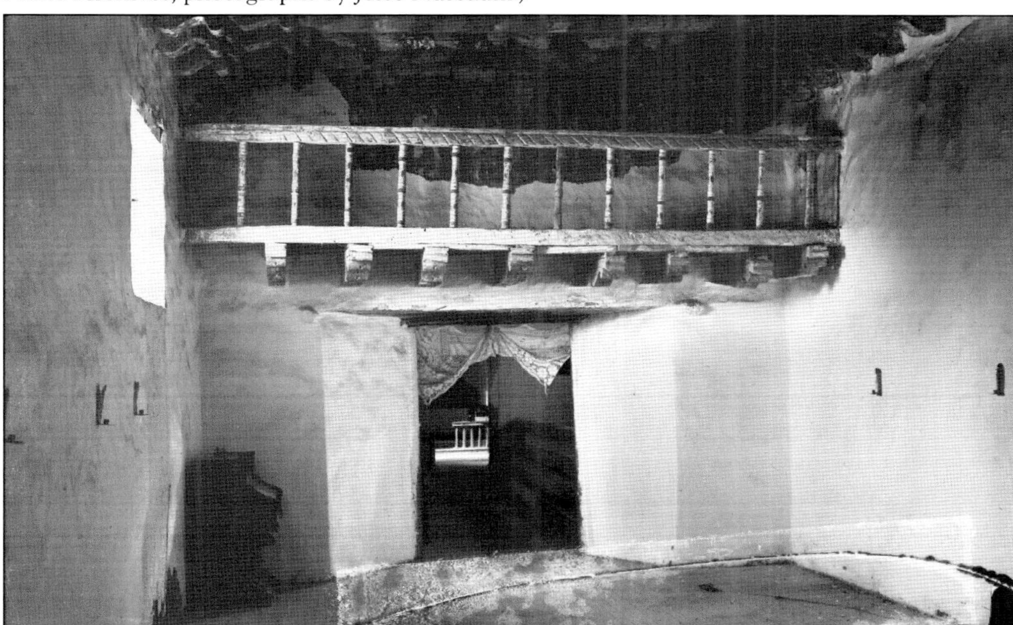

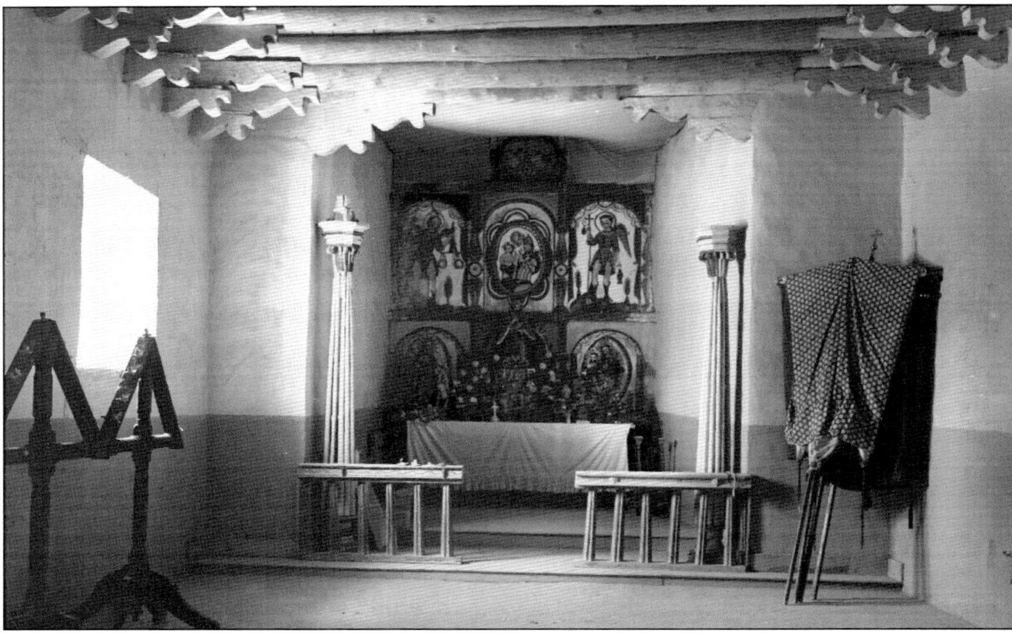

The south chapel, built around 1798, was dedicated to the Third Order of St. Francis. It is the first *morada* in the Southwest. Below are El Santo Entierro, Nuestra Señora de los Dolores, and Nuestro Padre Jesus Nazareno. For most of the 20th century, the almost life-size Padre Jesus was missing two fingers. In 1800, during a violent rainstorm, an *hermano*, or brother, broke off one of the fingers and threw it into the river; the raging waters retreated. In the late 19th century, an influenza epidemic killed many people throughout the Española Valley. A second finger was broken off and burned, and the ashes were applied to the foreheads of the people. Soon, the epidemic abated. Santo Entierro wears a crown of thorns, which has been known to sprout green leaves. Dolores depicts Christ's mother at the time of her son's death. (Both, Palace of the Governors Photo Archives, photographs by Jesse Nusbaum.)

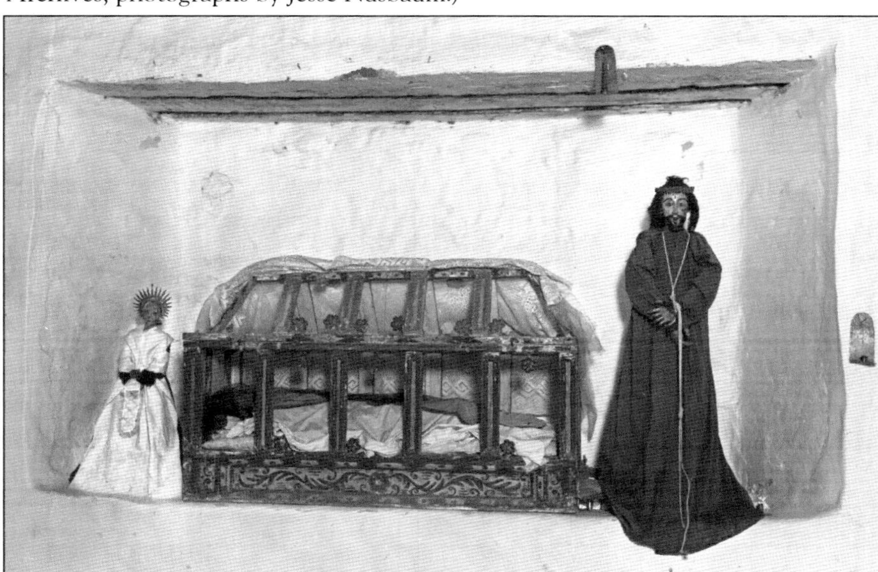

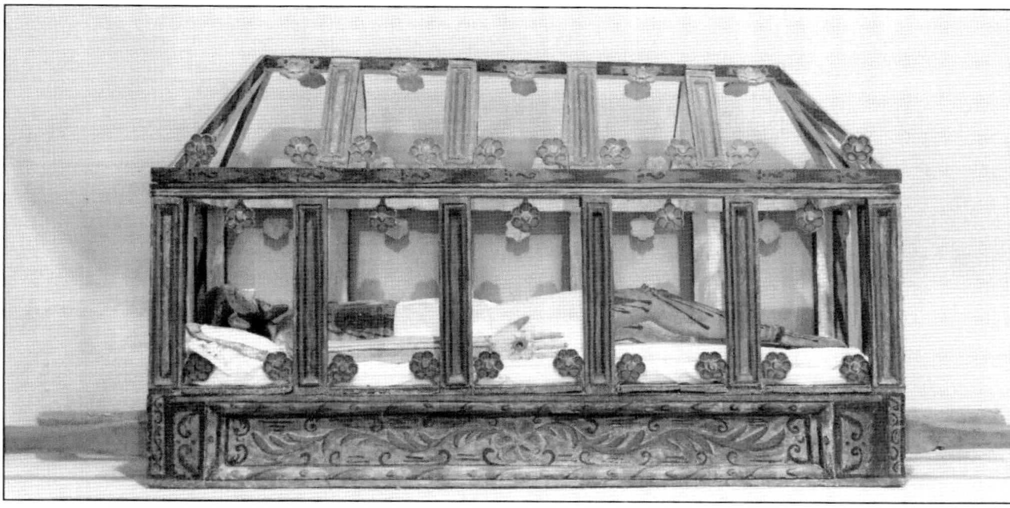

El Santo Entierro was created by Fray Andres Garcia, pastor of the church in the 1770s and an artist of genius. Garcia is the father of Spanish Colonial religious art in the United States. Much of the iconography in the church is by his hand, as is the original bell tower, which still stands. Below, men of the Cofradia de La Santisima Trinidad carry the Santo Entierro around the church plaza during Holy Week. Each *cofradia* keeps an antique *estandarte*, or banner, that leads the processions. When the *estandarte* passes, men remove their hats, and the women remain silent, as a gesture of respect. (Santa Cruz de la Cañada Parish.)

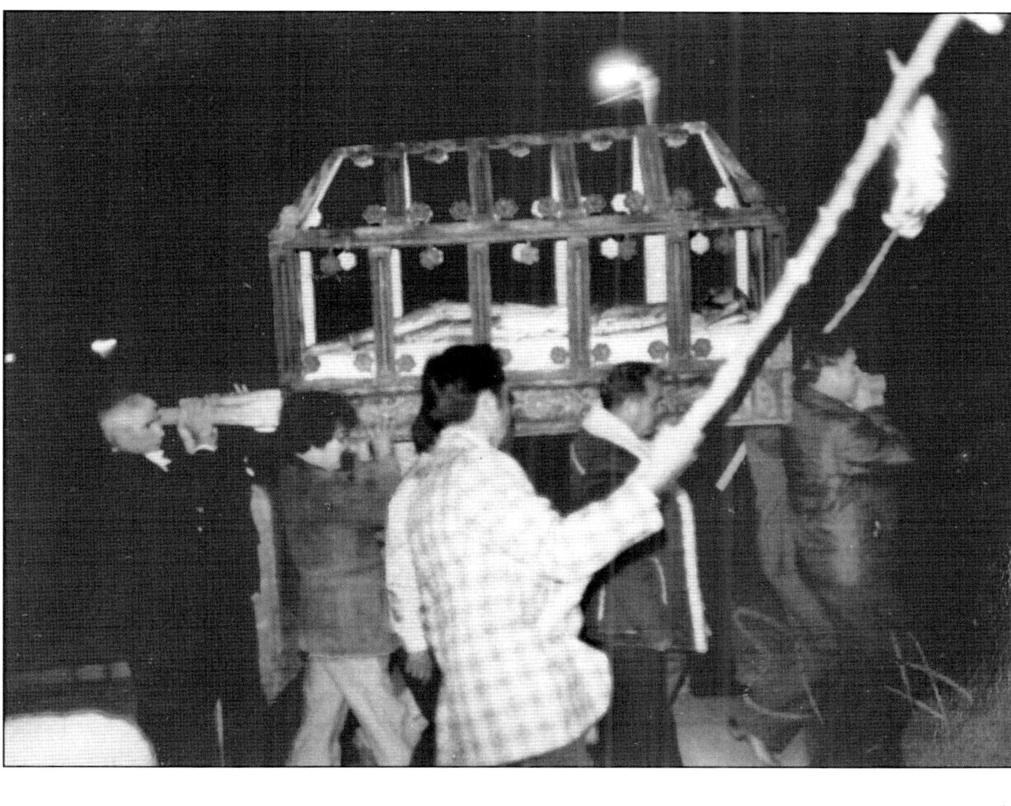

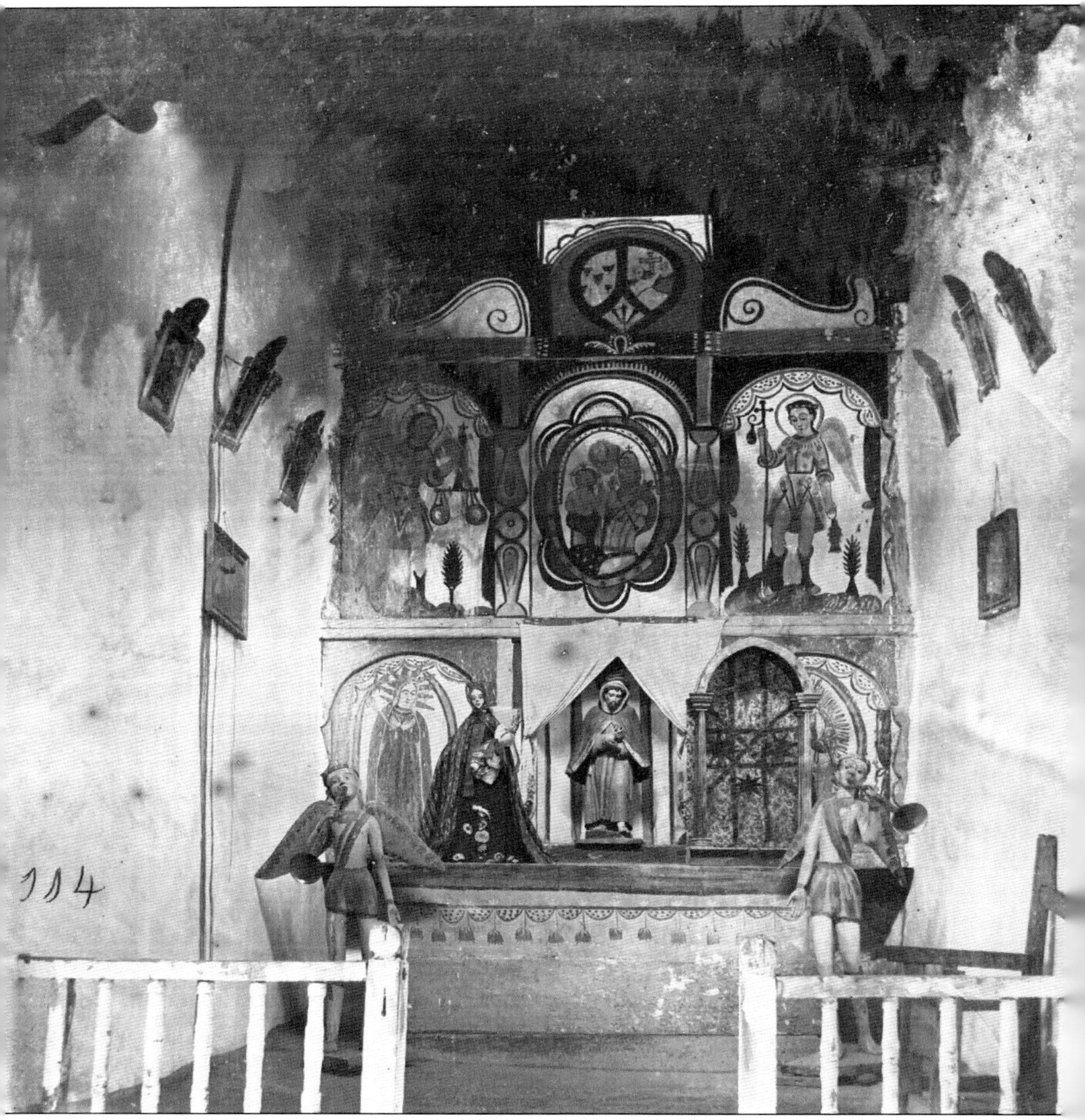

This beautiful old photograph shows the south chapel as it was in 1875. In the center of the altar is Saint Francis, the 13th-century Italian saint who experienced the first reported stigmata—mysterious wounds that imitate those of the crucified Christ. Next to Francis is the *bulto* of Our Lady of Mount Carmel that was carved by Jose Rafael Aragon. The large angels are believed to have been carved by Fray Garcia himself. (Palace of the Governors Photo Archives, photograph by H.T. Hiester.)

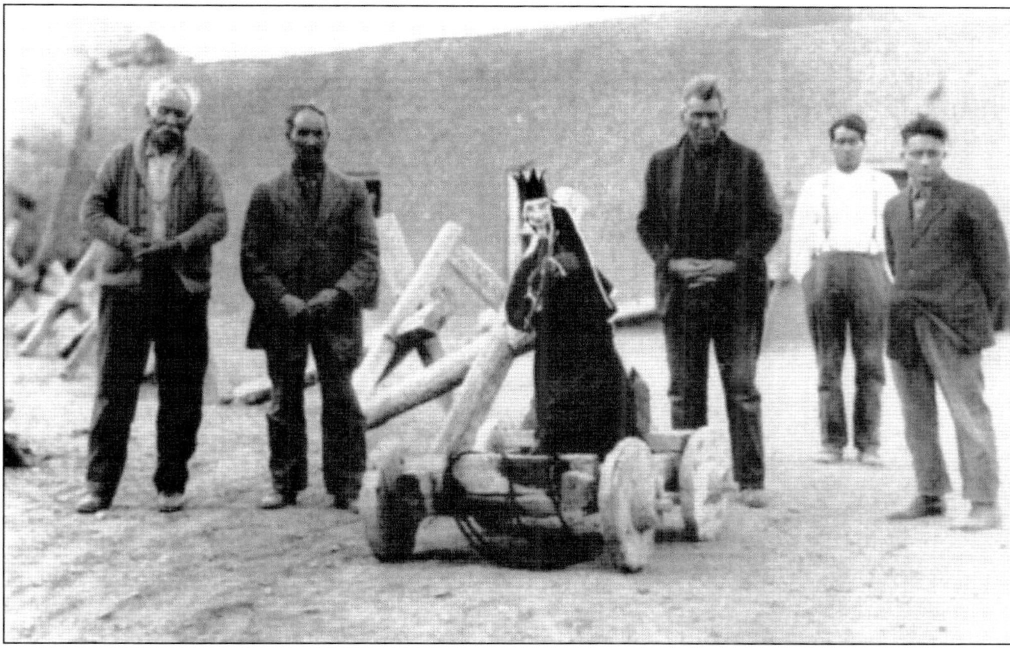

These Penitente *hermanos* of the early 20th century are shown outside their village *morada* during Holy Week. Behind them are the *maderos*, or heavy pine crosses, that the brothers willingly shoulder in sacrificial emulation of Cristo Jesus. Beside them is Doña Sebastiana, a sculpted interpretation of Death that accompanies the *hermanos*' vigilant prayer, reminding the community of the brevity of life and the certainty of death. The brotherhood survives to this day. Throughout the Española Valley, *los hermanos Penitentes* pray and fast in preparation for Easter. During Holy Week, their mournful singing calls through the canyons of time and reconnects Valley faithful to the beginnings of their culture. (Above, Alberto Trujillo; below, Leopoldo Trujillo.)

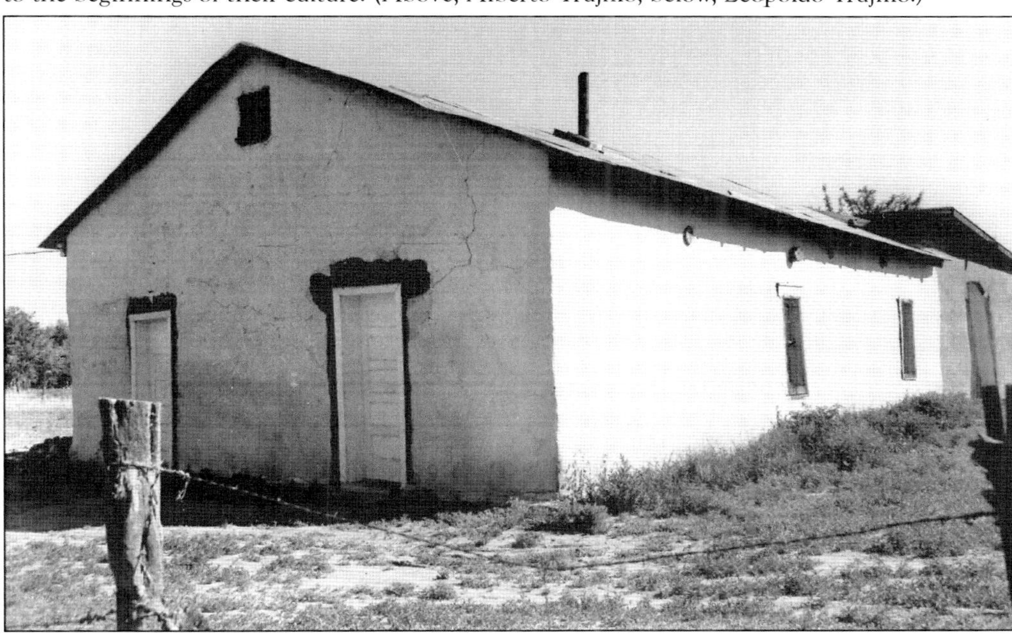

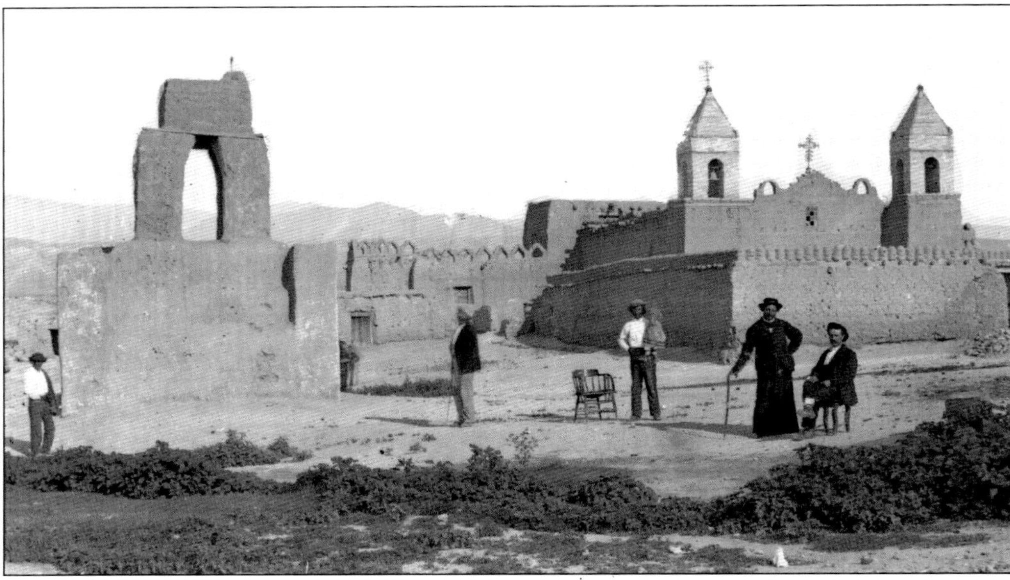

Fr. Jean Baptiste Courbon, the first of the French priests to serve Santa Cruz de la Cañada, is standing in the church plaza in 1897. The monumental church and the acequia running southward in front of it are indicators of what a thriving center of life the parish was. Below is Fr. Salvador Gené, the first priest from the Sons of the Holy Family, the Spanish order that still provides the parish with its priests. He is leading the annual procession of Corpus Cristi in June 1940. The Blessed Sacrament has been carried outside of the church, sheltered under a cloth canopy—or *palio*—as rose petals are strewn in its path. The attending priests will bless homemade family altars that grace the dirt plaza. (Above, Palace of the Governors Photo Archives, photograph by H.T. Hiester; below, Santa Cruz de la Cañada Parish.)

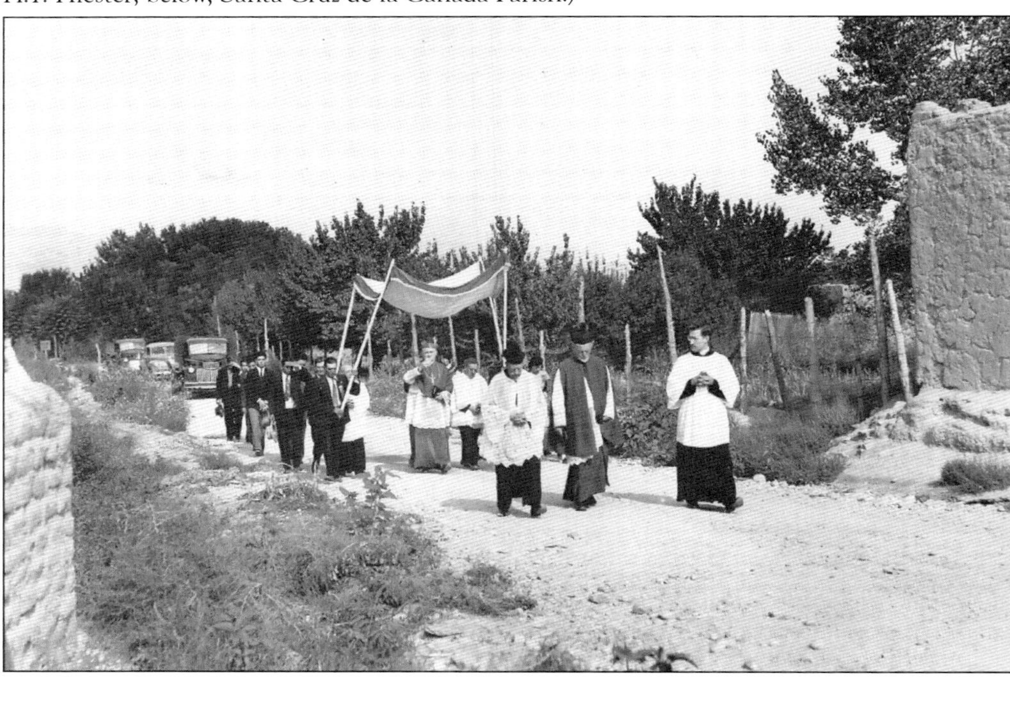

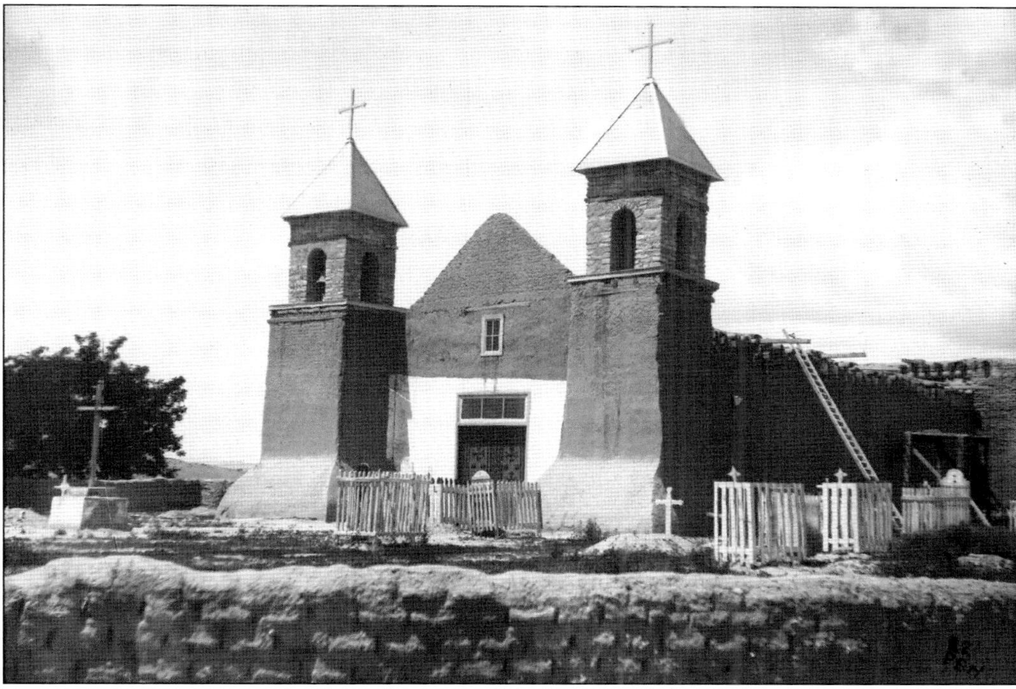

In 1897, a pitched roof with wooden shingles was built over the old flat roof. In 1918, Anastacio Lujan opened windows in the 40-inch-thick adobe walls. In earlier years, there had been no low windows because of the danger of Indian raids. Lujan also mud-plastered the exterior of the church. In 1919, Fr. Antonio Besset collected enough money from the parishioners to replace the split wood above the massive beams in the interior of the church. Under Father Gené's guidance, pews were built by Macario Quintana, wood burning stoves were replaced with butane heaters, the mud walls were hard-plastered, and the aging altar was painted over. In the 1930s, a tin roof replaced the wooden one. (Both, Palace of the Governors Photo Archives; bottom photograph by M.E.J. Colter.)

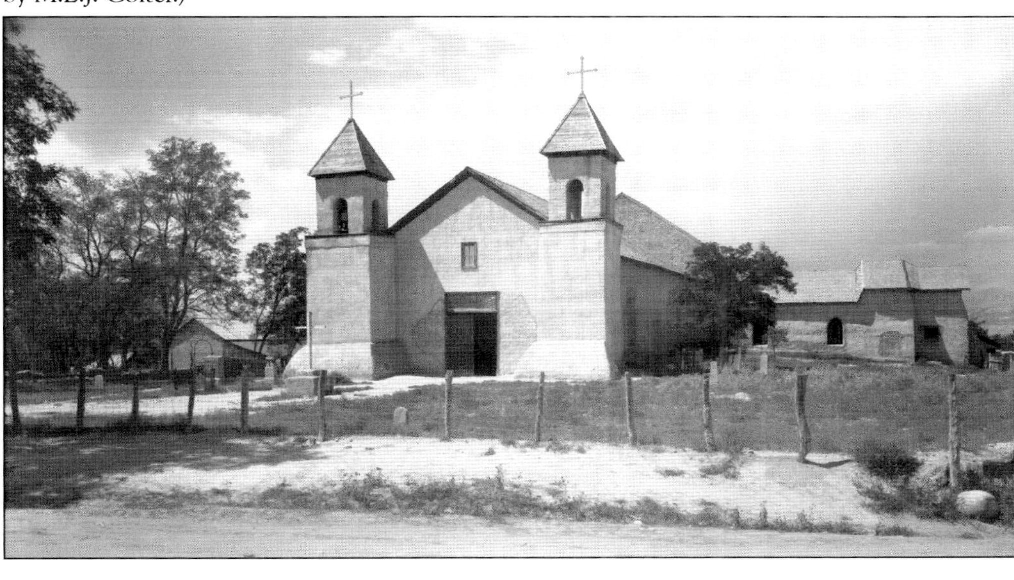

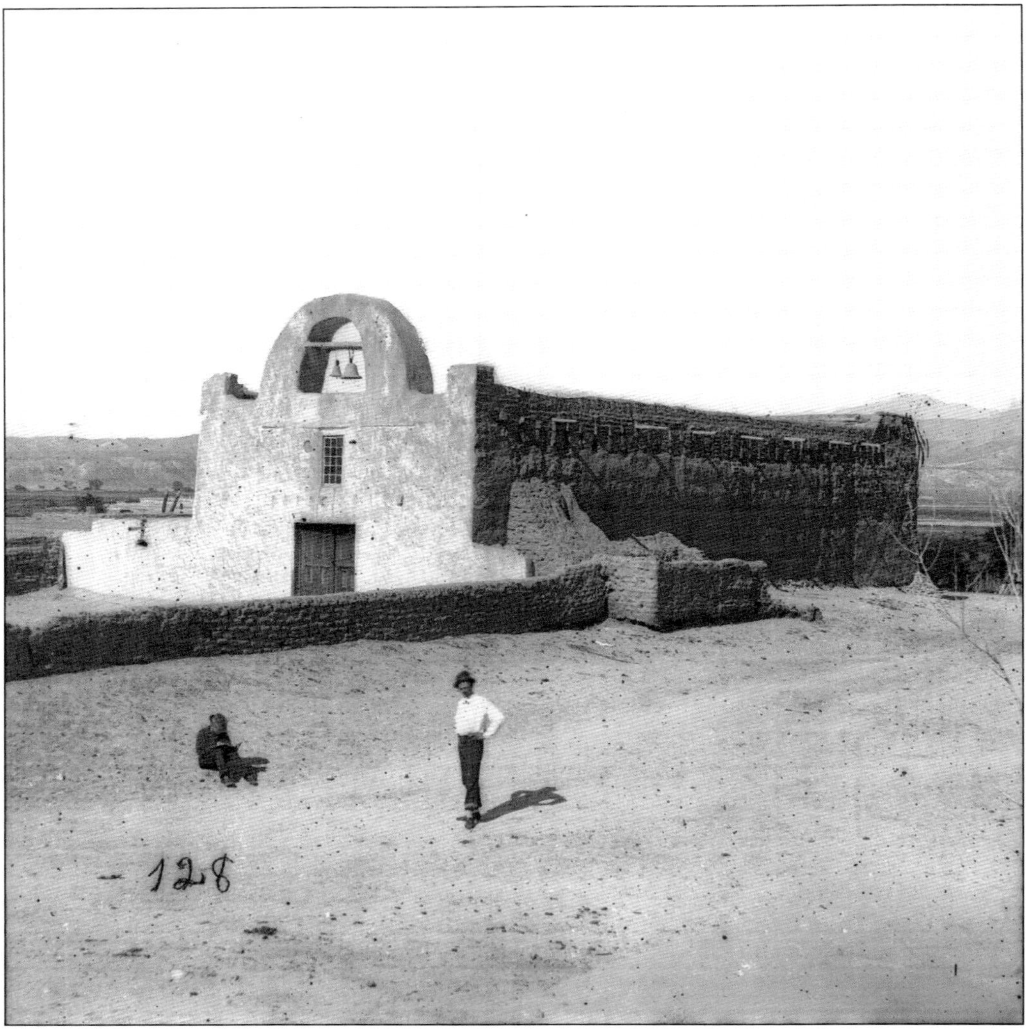

The mission church at San Juan Pueblo was built by the Franciscan friars who accompanied the Oñate expedition in 1598. This mission and all Pueblo Mission churches of that era were destroyed during the Pueblo Revolt, and all were rebuilt. In 1889, the newly assigned Fr. Camilo Seux built a small chapel dedicated to Our Lady of Lourdes across from the church, which soon became a pilgrimage site. The Mission-style church was replaced by Father Seux in 1913. Wishing to build a church similar to those of his native France, Father Seux demolished the old church with dynamite and replaced it with the one in use today. (Palace of the Governors Photo Archives, photograph by H.T. Hiester.)

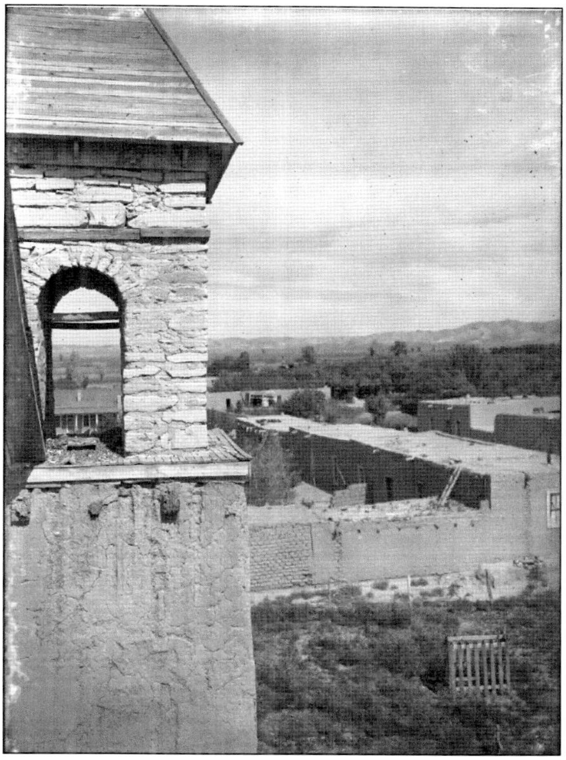

This early-20th-century photograph gives an idea of the extent of the parish, with its five missions and 19 chapels. Also visible are some of the 20 *placitas*, or courtyards, that surrounded the church. The first bell tower—the north one—was added to the church by Fray Andres Garcia in 1776. In this photograph, the tower does not have a bell. Cracked and lacking a clapper, the bell was sold, with the permission of the parish, to the Fred Harvey Touring Company in the 1930s. The south tower was added to the church by Fr. Juan de Jesus Trujillo around 1867. (Palace of the Governors Photo Archives, photograph by Jesse Nusbaum.)

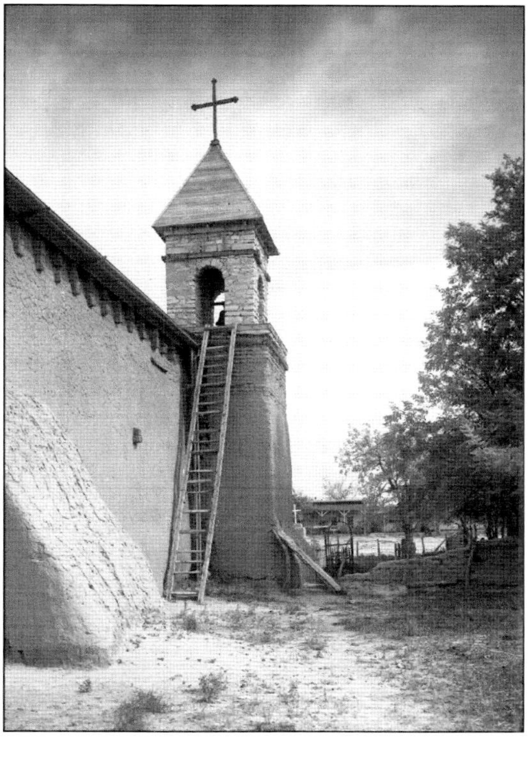

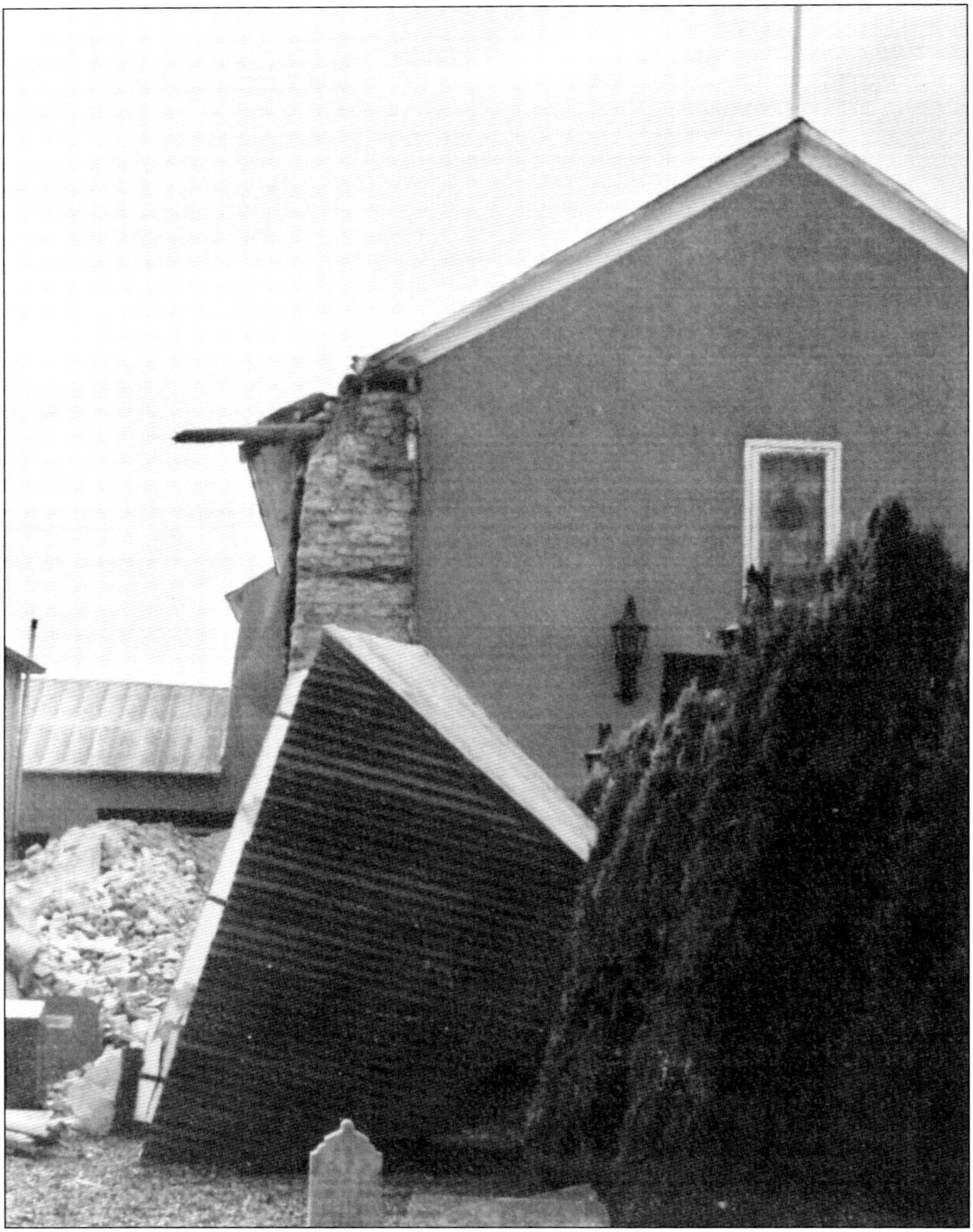

In November 1999, the south tower collapsed. The hard plaster and stucco that had been applied over the permeable mud plaster in the 1950s caused moisture to build up in the adobe. A huge pile of rubble fell over a wide area, but no one was hurt. The task before the parish was to build a new tower that was completely faithful to the old one. Parishioners consulted with professionals in and around the parish, and the new tower was designed. With materials and labor supplied by parishioners—as had been done by generations of their ancestors—work on the tower began. (Santa Cruz de la Cañada Parish.)

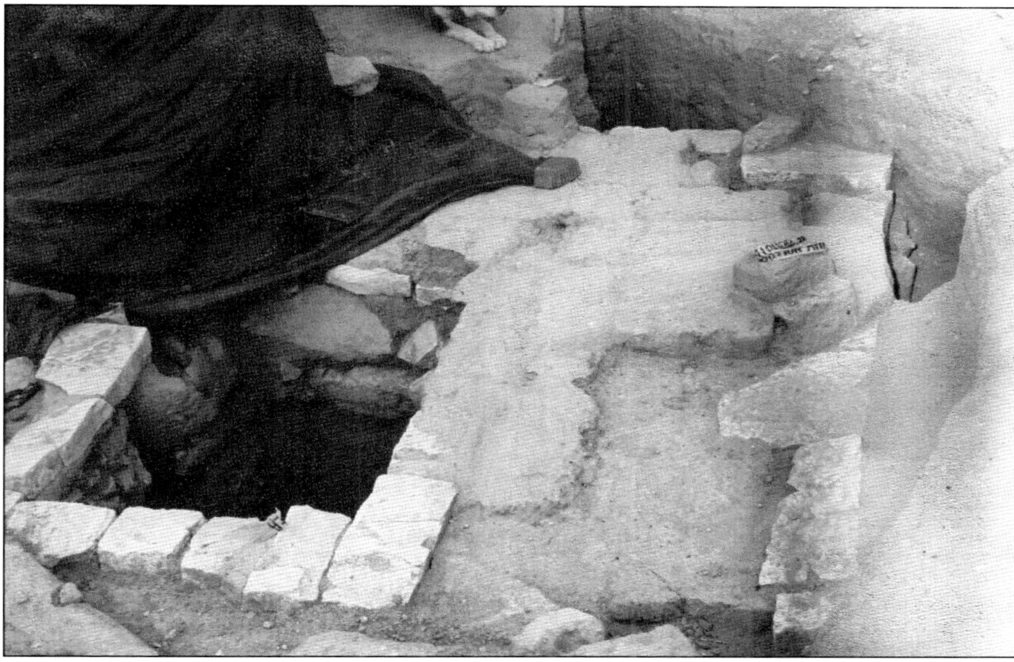

The south tower had been built by laying a massive adobe wall atop a stone foundation, a common practice of the day. When rubble from the fallen tower was cleared, an underground well was revealed, inside of which human remains were discovered. These remains were removed and reburied in the church's cemetery. The new tower was not built on stone, but on a concrete foundation strengthened with rebar. (Santa Cruz de la Cañada Parish.)

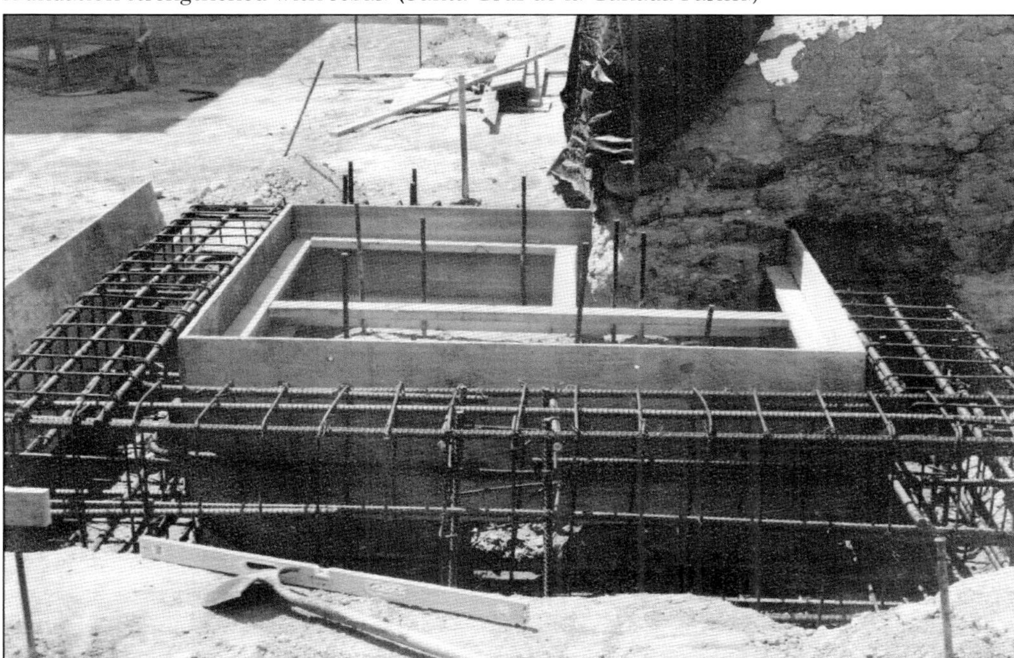

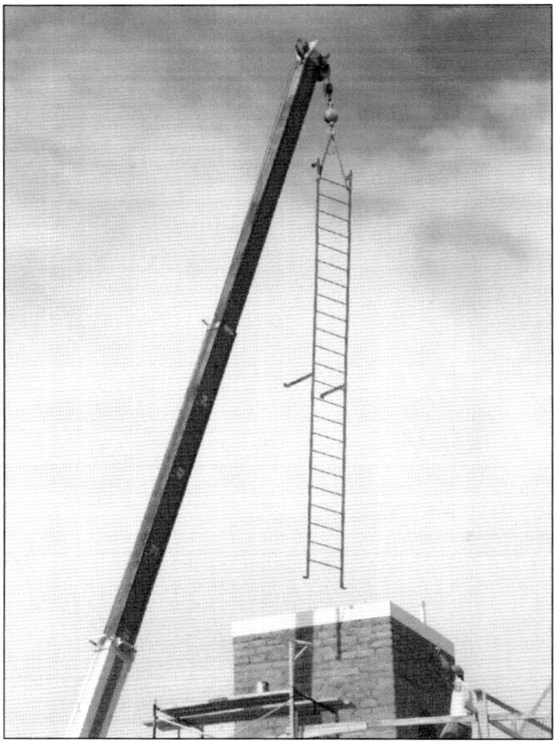

In former times, a wooden ladder was used to climb up to the bell tower's spire. For the new construction, before the spire was installed, a steel ladder was inserted into the tower from the top, using a crane. Because of the immense spiritual and cultural value of the Santa Cruz Church to the Española Valley, many people came from outside the parish to lend a helping hand. In age-old tradition, resources, labor, vision, and community joined to re-create the south tower. The rebuilding process took a year to complete. (Santa Cruz de la Cañada Parish.)

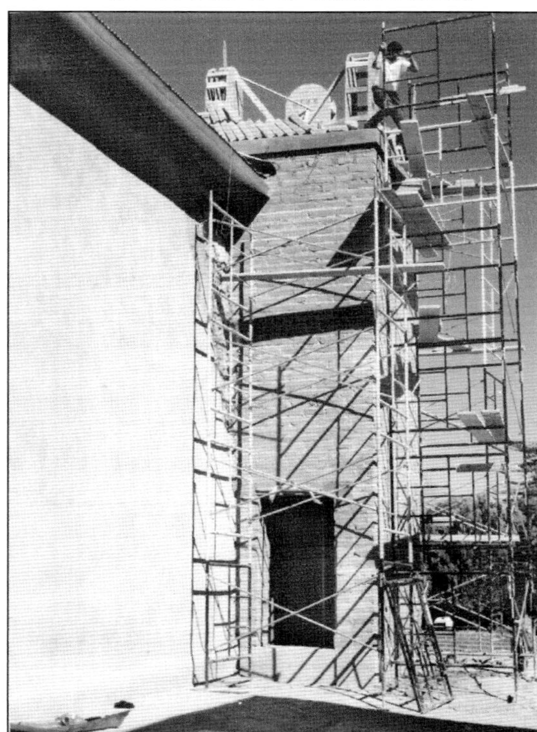

Santa Cruz de la Canada Bell Tower Project Participants

Name/Position	Organization
Father Ron Carrillo, Pastor	Santa Cruz de la Canada Parish
Father Jose Maria Blanche, Assistant Pastor	"
F. Xavier Garcia, Architect/Parishioner	"
James Hands, Engineer	Red Mountain Engineering
Rocky Fresquez, Contractor/Parishioner	Big Rock Builders
Norman Chavez, Angelo Padilla,	Personnel, Big Rock Builders
John Duran, Arturo Aranas, Jesus Leganda	"
Dennis Salazar, Jr. Leo Padilla.	"
David Snow, Archeologist	Private Archeologist
Tes Fresquez, Archeology	Santa Cruz de la Canada Parish
Marina Ochoa, Anthropology Research	Archivist, Archdiocese of Santa Fe
Charles Miller, Engineer, Soil Testing	Geo-Test, Inc.
Tom Velarde, Photo Documentation	Santa Cruz de la Canada Parish
James Espinoza, Video Documentation	Interested Citizen
Ralph Alarid & Ted Roybal, Elevation Survey	Santa Cruz de la Canada Parish
Moisture sampling/ analysis of Church Walls	
Mac Watson, Architectual Consultant	Cornerstones Foundation
Francisco Uvina, Architectual Coordinator	"
James Trott, Preservation Architect	US National Park Service
Jake Barrow, Preservation Architect	"
Rocky Fresquez, Parishioner/Contractor	Santa Cruz de la Canada Parish
Fred Rivera, Parish Council Chairman	"
Willie Atencio, Project Coordinator	"
Archdiocese of Santa Fe	
John Huchmala	Property Manager/Contract Adm.
Tony Maceroni	Insurance
Marina Ochoa, Chairperson, Commission for the Preservation of Historic Churches	
State of New Mexico, Office of Historic Preservation	
Elmo C de Baca,	Historic Preservation Officer
Alicia Abbot	Field Archeologist
United States, National Park Service	
Ernest Ortega, Historical Bulletin	Superintendent, US National Park Service

Sub-Contractors: Plastering: Rocky Mountain Lath & Plaster, Chris Sargent; Electrical: Houdini Electric, Donald Martinez.; Demolition Transport, Benjamin Quintana; Metal Welding, Ron Perraglio.

Donations. List of financial donations, ranging from $5.00 to one of $20,000.00, is on file in Parish Office. Parishioners have been very generous.

Work/Material Donations: Rocky Fresquez: New Metal Roof for North Bell Tower; Adobe Factory: 1,000 adobes; Benjamin Quintana, truck; Donald Martinez, electrical; Espanola Transit Mix, sand; Alpine Lumber, Santa Fe, Trim/wood.

From the files of the parish, this is a list of contributors to the tower project, a large number of whom were Santa Cruz parishioners. As present-day residents see the hands of their ancestors in their church, so will future generations. In the picture below, the tower project nears completion. Elsewhere in Northern New Mexico, where community enthusiasm and love for the old ways are not so pronounced, old Spanish churches have fallen into disrepair and disuse. But here, in the Española Valley, Santa Cruz de la Cañada remains protected, vital, and spiritually lively—a jewel in the Spanish American world. (Santa Cruz de la Cañada Parish.)

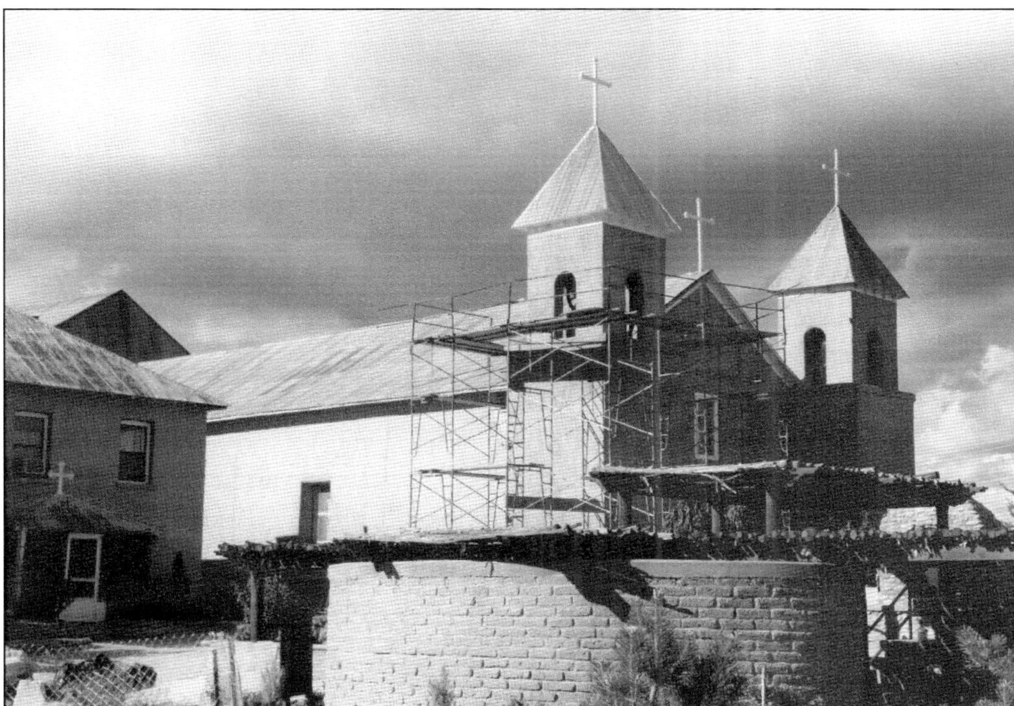

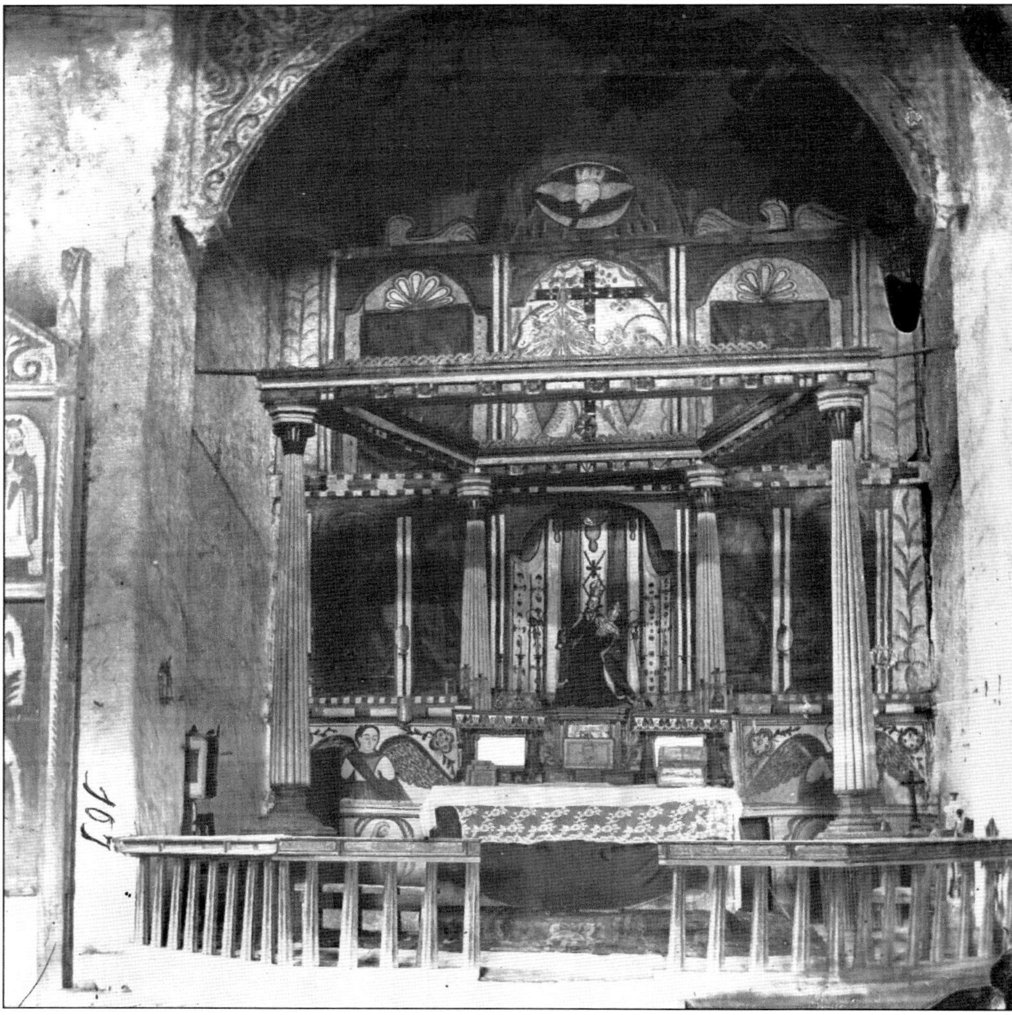

This photograph of the Santa Cruz Church, taken in 1872, caught the attention of parish priest Fr. Mario Vesga in 1978 and fired his imagination. He had a vision of the church restored to its Spanish Colonial glory. He shared his vision with his parishioners and with two brother-priests from Spain—Fr. Francis Gonzalez and Fr. Luis Picasso. Nathaniel Owings, an internationally renowned architect, and Alan Vedder, a representative of the Spanish Colonial Arts Society in Santa Fe, worked with a committee of dedicated parishioners on the eight-year effort to restore the interior of the church. (Palace of the Governors Photo Archives, photograph by H.T. Hiester.)

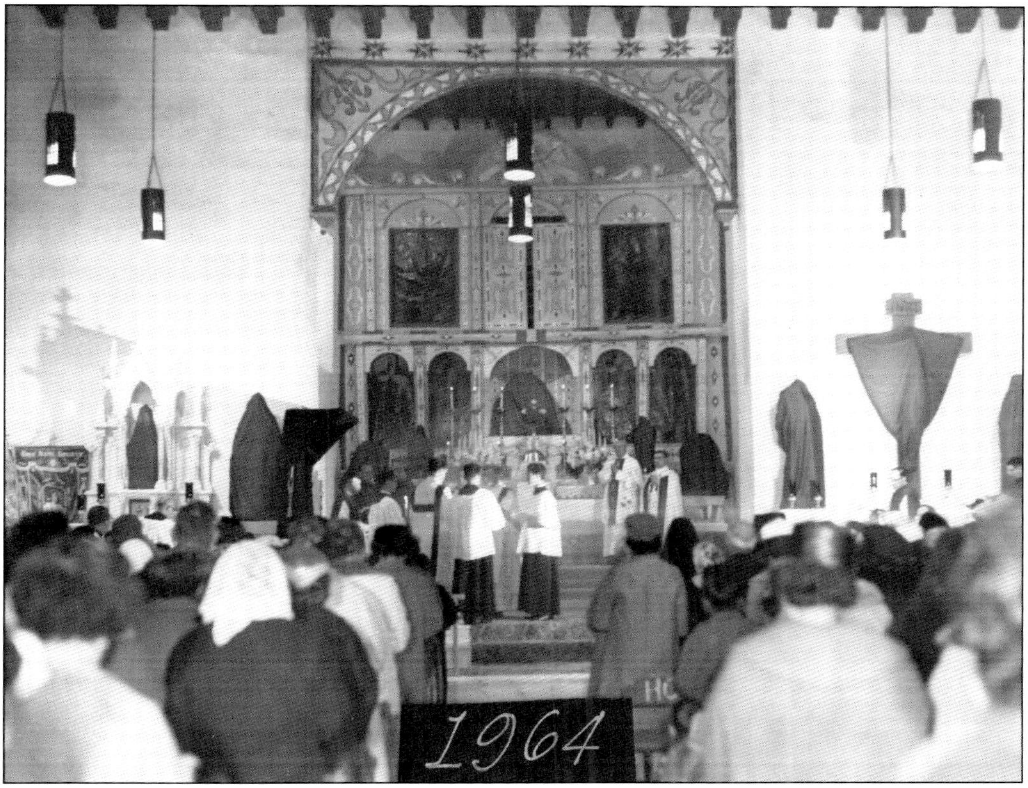

The decorations on the church altar in 1964 may seem appealing, but they are only a pale shadow of the profound beauty lying underneath the modern stenciling done during the tenure of Father Gené. However, not understanding the value of the original Spanish Colonial iconography, many parishioners resisted the restoration effort. "History will not forgive you if you fail to restore this great church," said Archbishop Roberto Sanchez as he launched the project. To restore the altar screen completely, oil paintings of several saints were removed. On the right, Arturo Quintana carefully lowers the painting of Santa Teresa de Avila. This painting and eight others were brilliantly restored by Iris Travaioli, a sixth-generation art conservator, residing in Alabama. (Santa Cruz de la Cañada Parish.)

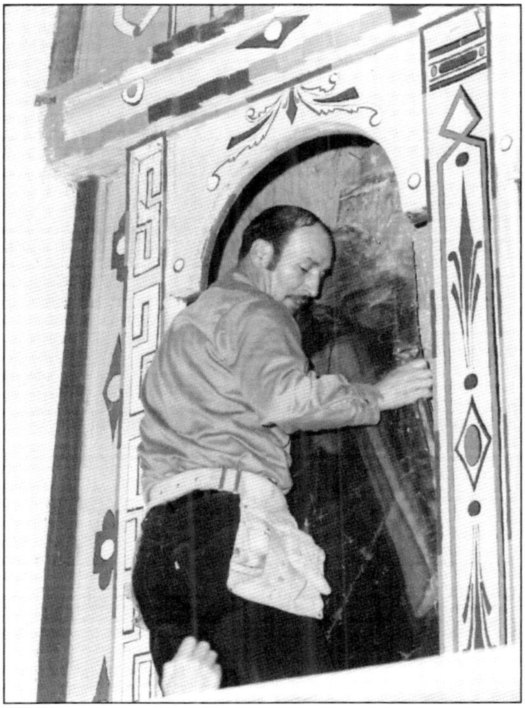

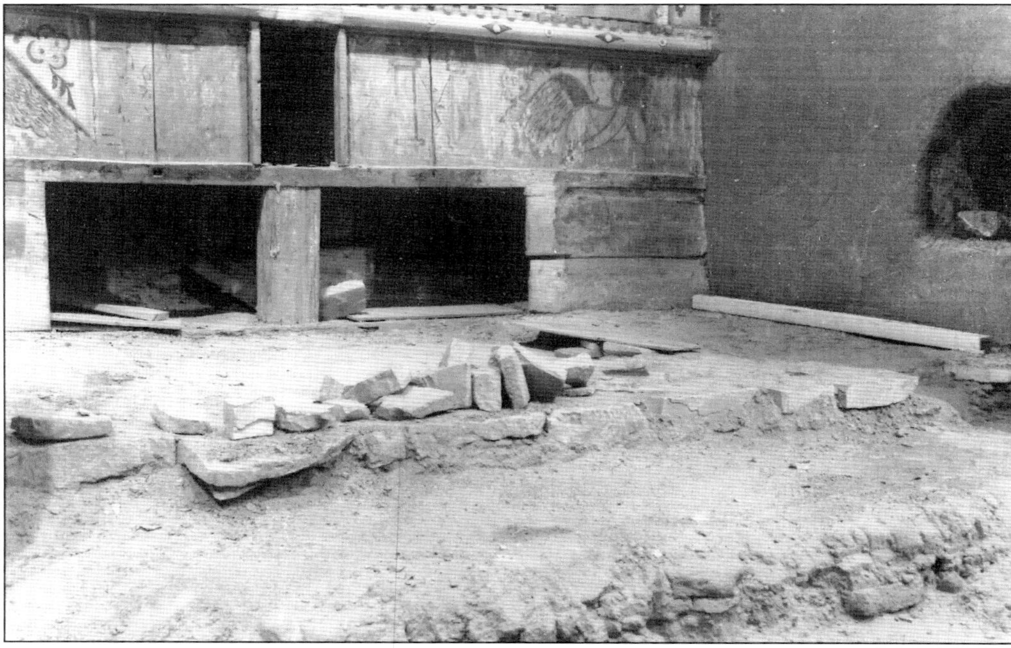

Another major job was lowering the floor of the sanctuary to its original level. Much damage had occurred to the old sandstone floor, and the entire altar floor was replaced with light-colored flagstone from Romeroville, near Las Vegas, New Mexico. The lowering of the floor also revealed more of the original altar screen. Restorers scraped the modern hard plaster from the interior walls, and three layers of natural mud plaster were applied, allowing the thick adobe walls to breathe again. Traditional *tierra blanca* clay was gathered from a hillside in Embudo; the layer of bright color provided the finish that returned the glow to the interior walls of the Santa Cruz Church. (Santa Cruz de la Cañada Parish.)

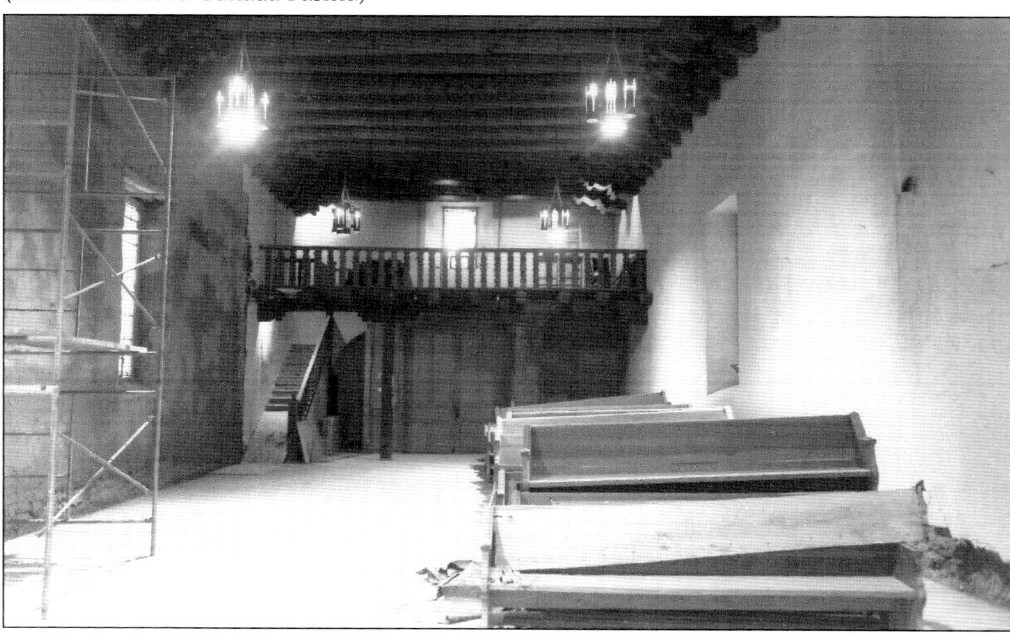

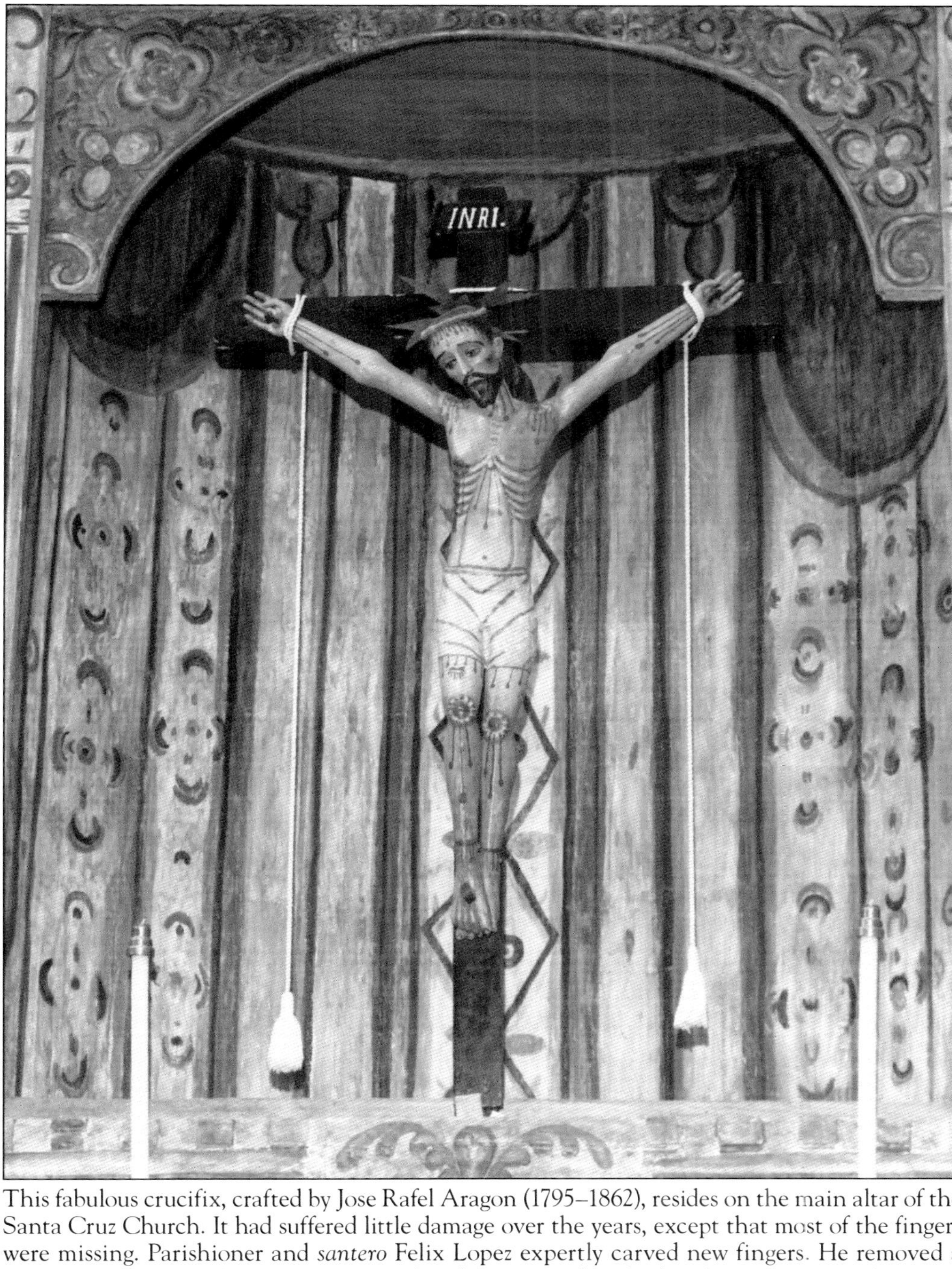

This fabulous crucifix, crafted by Jose Rafel Aragon (1795–1862), resides on the main altar of the Santa Cruz Church. It had suffered little damage over the years, except that most of the fingers were missing. Parishioner and *santero* Felix Lopez expertly carved new fingers. He removed a covering of oil paint that was not original to the piece and applied traditional gesso and paint to the *bulto*. (Santa Cruz de la Cañada Parish.)

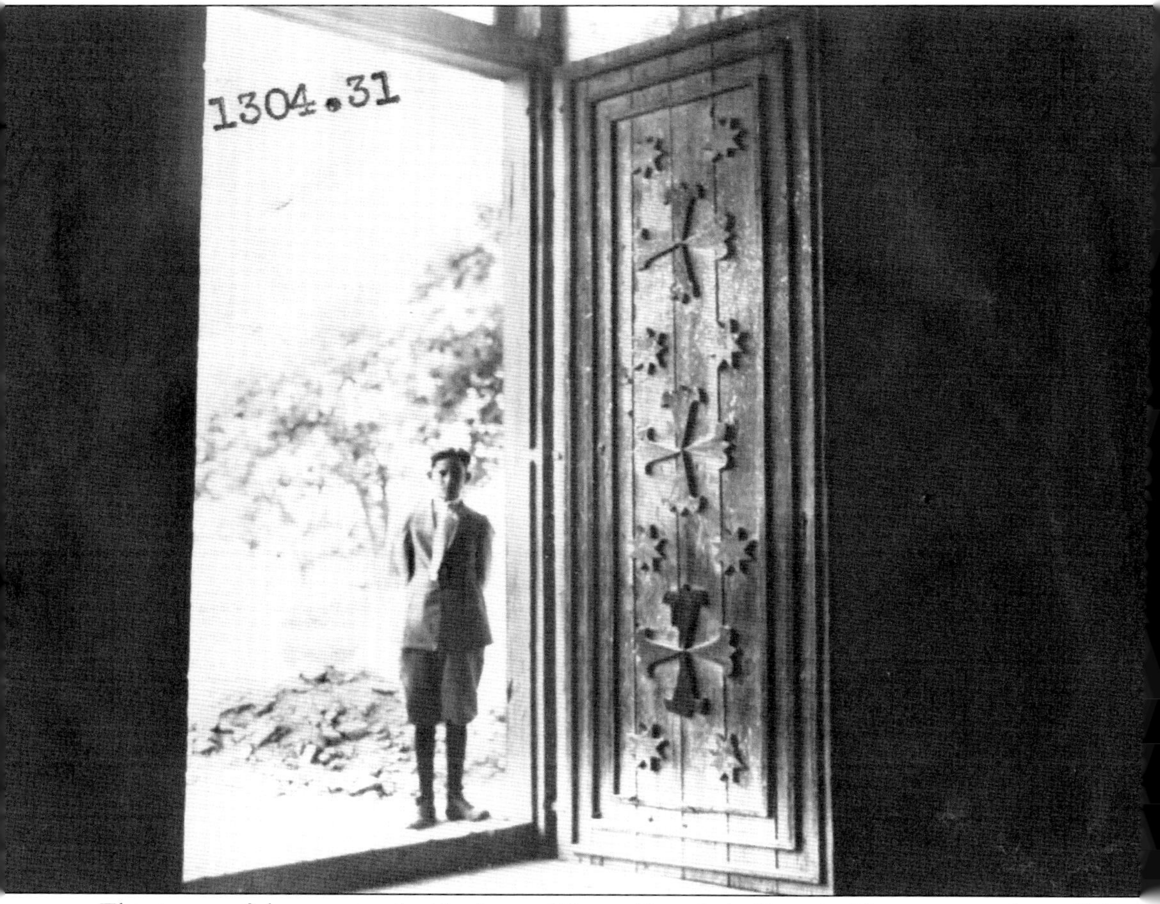

This is one of the massive double doors of Santa Cruz de la Cañada. They were made in 1880 by Guadalupe Garduño and family, of Nambé, and they still work perfectly. A boy stands in the doorway, wearing the clothing of the early 20th century. On one side of the threshold is the world that has changed and will change further. On the other side, the sanctuary of the Santa Cruz Church remains, fundamentally, much as it has been since the mid-1700s. (Palace of the Governors Photo Archives, photograph by Wesley Bradfield.)

Three

Faith and Resistance

The 19th century was a time of expansion for the United States of America. While Mexico was gaining its independence from Spain in 1820, the United States was laying the groundwork for the occupation of the Southwest.

It is hard to imagine that the military invasions by Mexico in 1837 and by the United States in 1847 would be well received by the residents of the Villa de Santa Cruz de la Cañada. In 1836, men of Santa Cruz and Taos formed the Santa Cruz Militia. Protesting an increase in taxes by the Mexican government, the militia repelled Mexican governor Albino Perez and his army, in what is known as the Battle of La Mesilla.

The Santa Fe Trail had opened in 1821, bringing financial opportunities to a few wealthy businessmen of Rio Abajo, near Belen. One of those wealthy men was Manuel Armijo, who in 1837 led a volunteer army that included business associates and American traders, against the Santa Cruz rebels. Serving both the Mexican and American governments, Armijo was instrumental in paving the way for the subjugation of Santa Cruz.

Stephen Watts Kearny and the American army occupied New Mexico eight years later. Once again, the Santa Cruz Militia and the Taos rebels protested the intrusion of a foreign government. Newly appointed governor Charles Bent was killed in Taos. In response, Col. Sterling Price led a strike force from Santa Fe to Santa Cruz de la Cañada.

The Battle of Cañada took place on January 24, 1847. Colonel Price and his 400-man army approached the Santa Cruz Plaza from the south, where they were met by 1,500 rebels. Price's mounted infantry, equipped with rifles and 12-pound howitzers, scattered the rebels. Price pursued them to Taos Canyon, where the Battle of Embudo ensued. The Santa Cruz and Taos rebels suffered enormous losses. Price's army was victorious.

The Treaty of Guadalupe Hidalgo, signed in 1848, ended the Mexican-American War with the assurance that all previous Spanish and Mexican land grants would be respected and legally maintained.

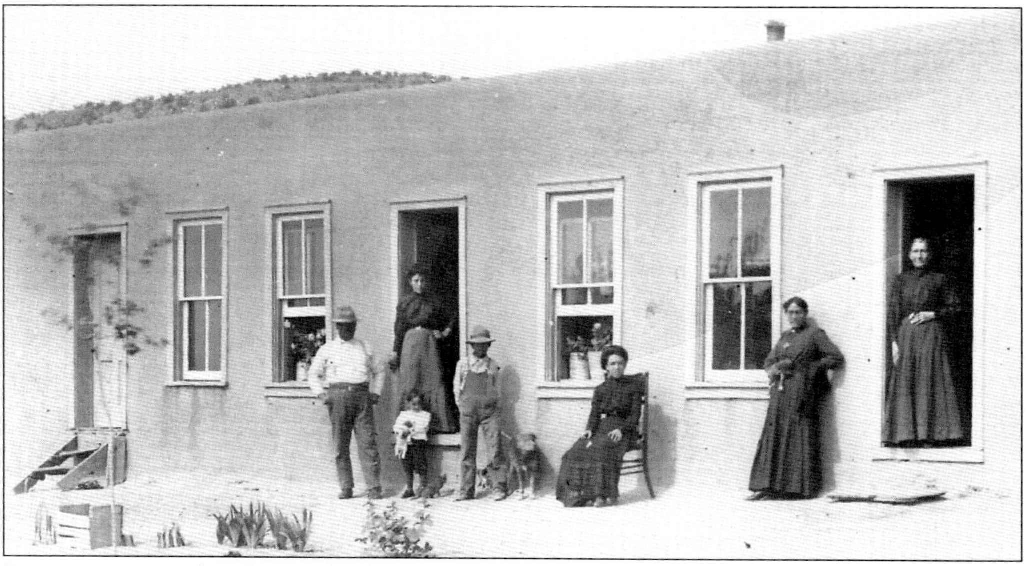

It is not surprising that the people of Santa Cruz were resistant to domination and innately rebellious against both Mexico and the United States. Their cultural style—which had developed in relative isolation since 1700—was no longer European, nor was it Mexican or American. It had become something entirely its own. There is no photographic record of what people of the parish looked like in 1830, but it was not very different from these late 19th century ancestors of Eloisa Maestas of Angostura. Intimate contact with the Pueblo way of life over many generations marked these people and set them apart. They developed religious traditions and religious artistic expressions that were unique in the Americas. A sublime manifestation of their soul is the Capilla de Nuestro Señor de Esquipulas, more commonly known as El Santuario de Chimayo. It was purchased by the Spanish Colonial Arts Society in 1929 and donated to the Archdiocese of Santa Fe. (Above, Ofilia Quintana de Valdez; below, Holy Family Parish, Chimayo.)

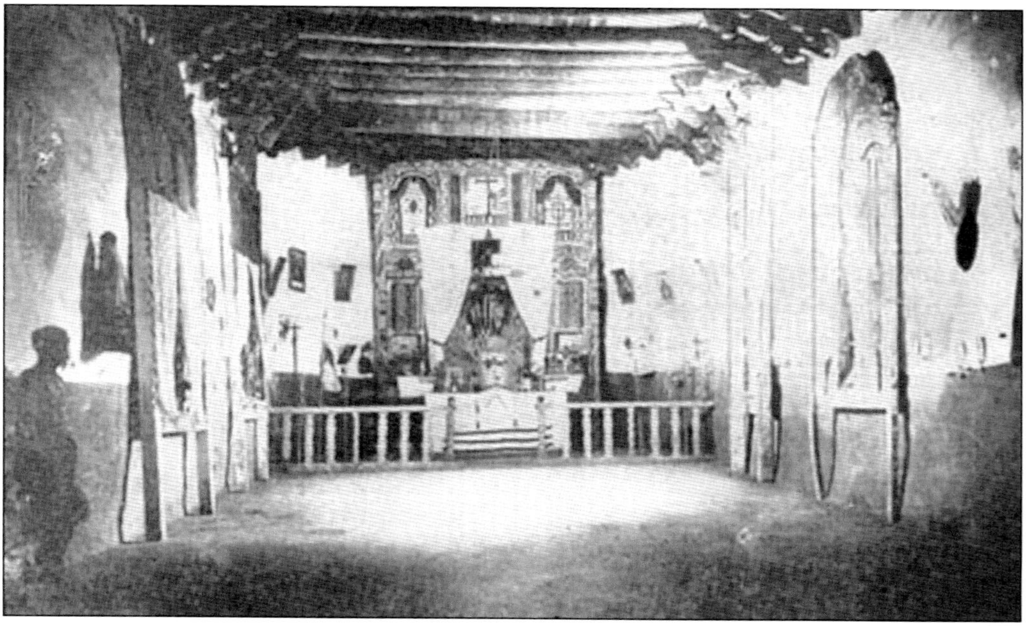

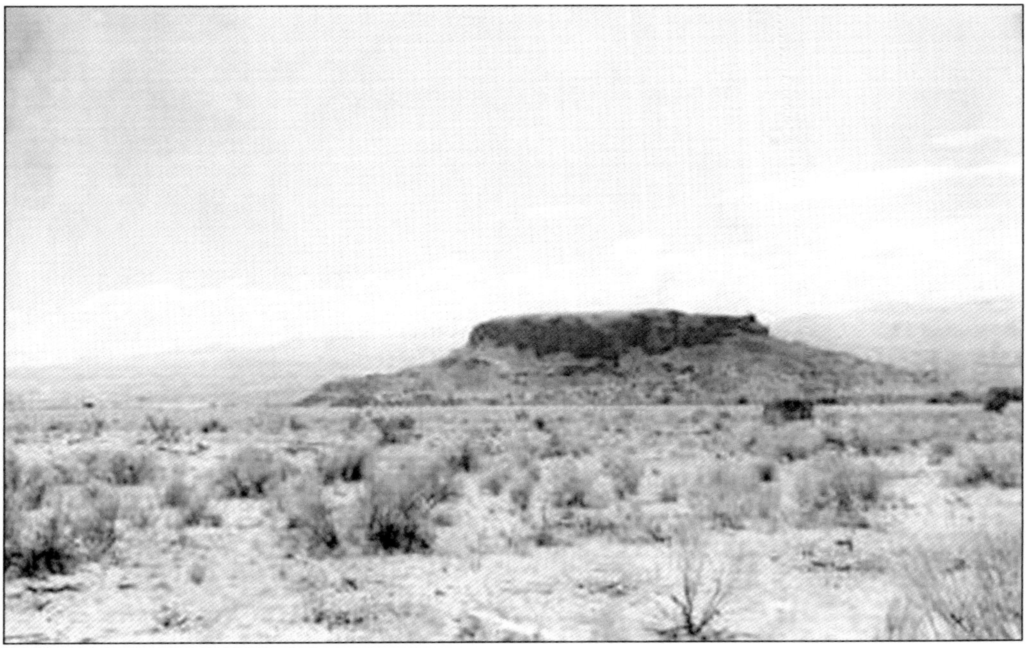

The transition from Spanish rule to Mexican was met with resistance and frustration from the residents of Taos and Santa Cruz. In 1837, in response to a military visit from newly appointed Mexican governor Albino Perez, the Santa Cruz Militia overpowered Perez at La Mesilla. Perez fled south and was killed. Later that same year, Manuel Armijo, a wealthy businessman from Rio Abajo, led a volunteer army against the Santa Cruz rebels. Pablo Montoya, one of the rebel leaders, gave Armijo four other rebel leaders in exchange for his own freedom. Armijo executed the four leaders. By 1838, rebel governor Jose Angel Gonzalez was apprehended and executed at Santa Cruz. Armijo replaced Gonzalez as governor. (Above, San Gabriel Historical Society; right, Sandoval County Historical Society.)

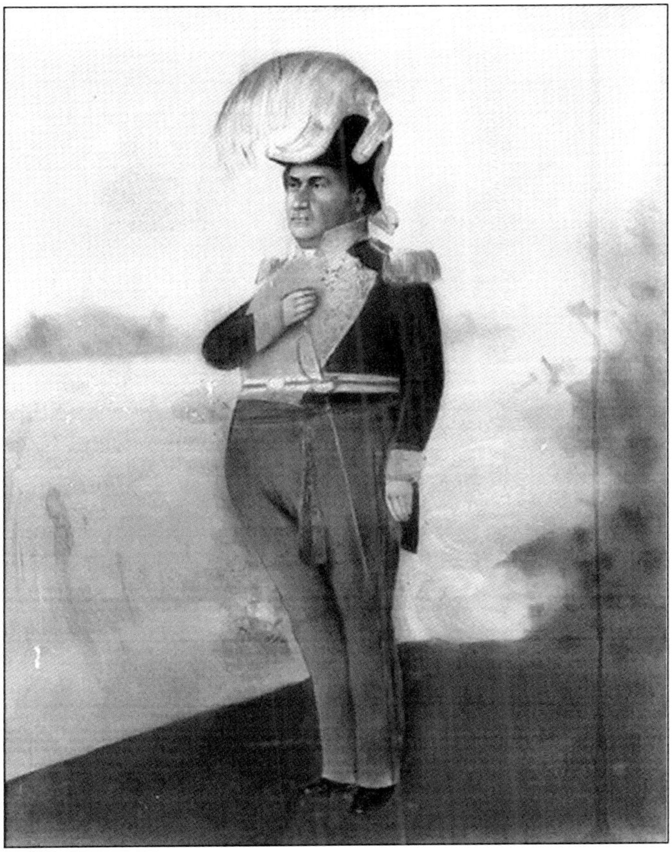

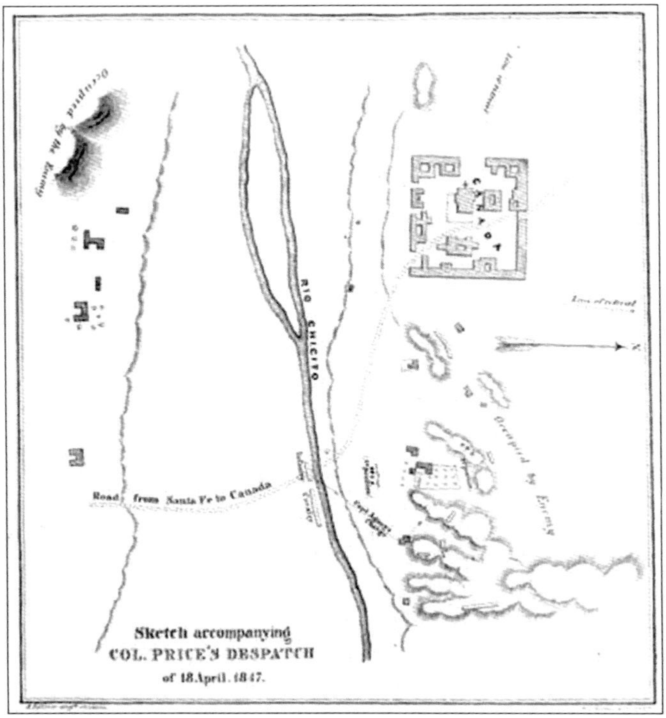

Stephen Watts Kearny's military occupation of New Mexico in 1846 was met with little resistance from the treacherous Governor Armijo. But citizens of Taos and Santa Cruz assembled a militia to block the American army. This map illustrates the strategy employed by Col. Sterling Price at the Battle of Cañada in January 1847. Battles at Embudo, Mora, and Las Vegas quickly followed. Rebels were apprehended at Taos Pueblo and executed, including chief rebel leaders Pablo Montoya and Tomàs Romero. The Plaza, seen from the Santa Cruz Church bell tower, shows the Camino Real, the road taken by Price's army. (Left, Santa Cruz de la Cañada Parish; below, Palace of the Governors Photo Archives.)

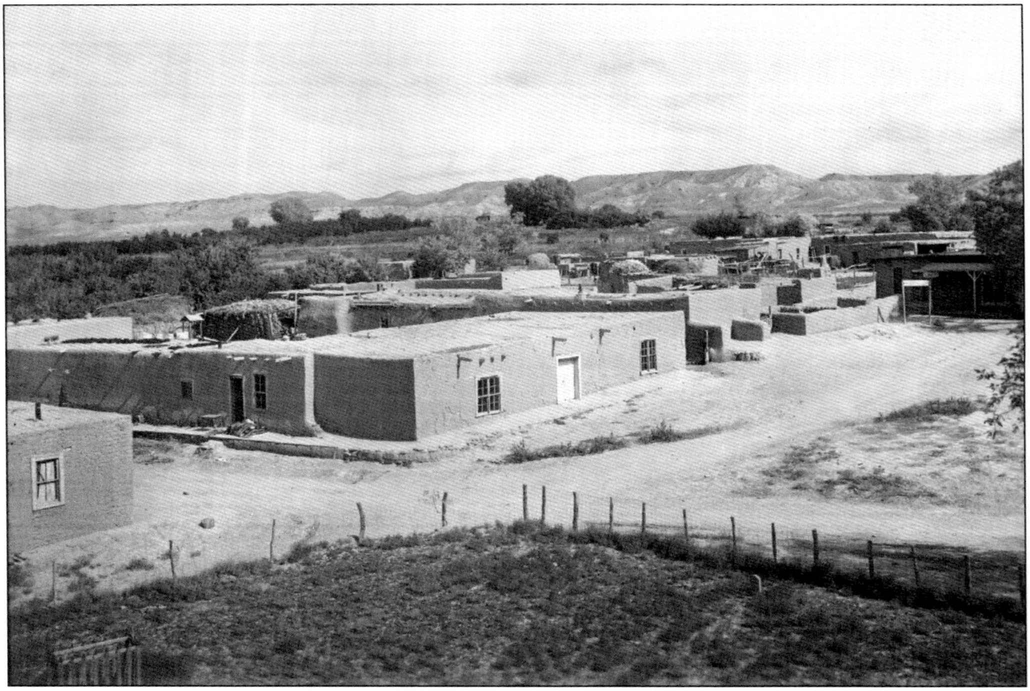

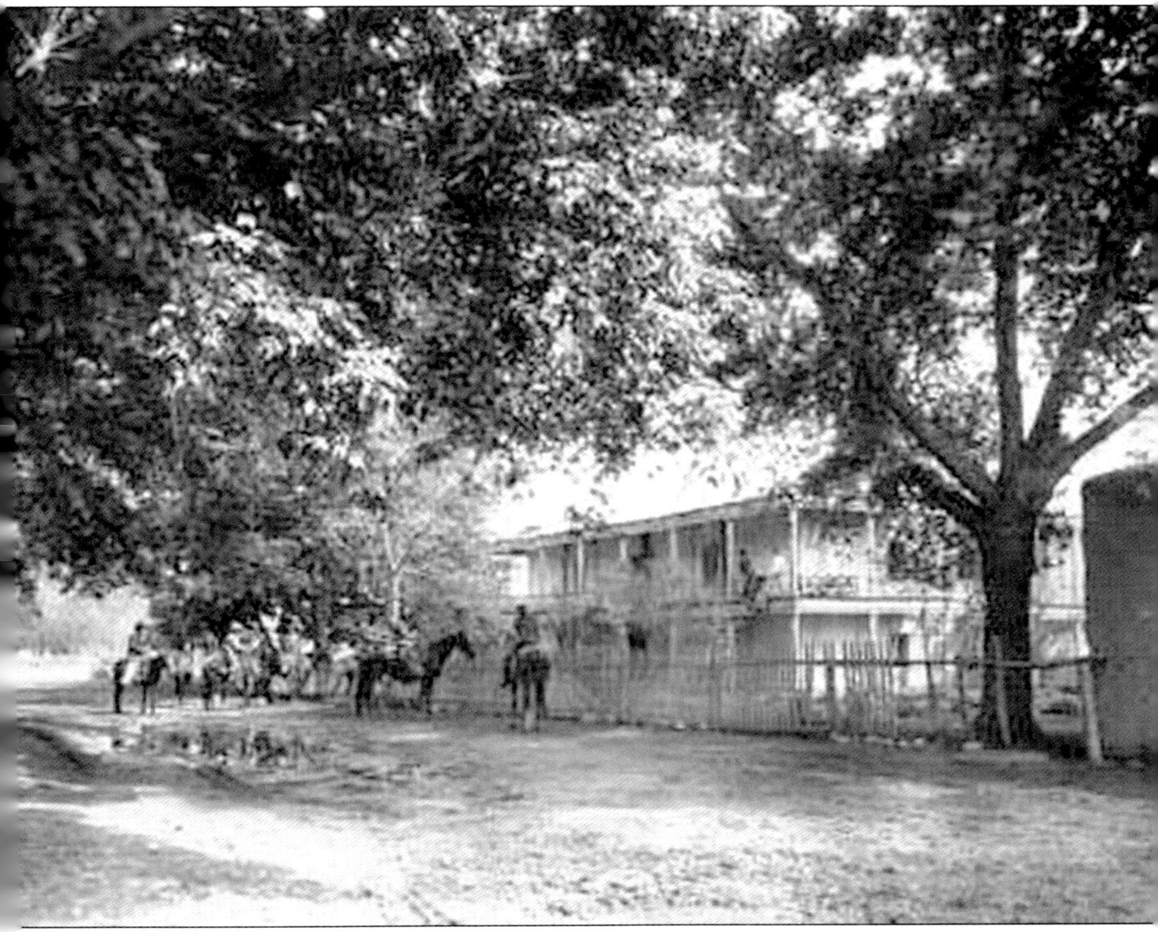

From 1848 to 1851, the first American county seat for Rio Arriba was north of Ohkay Owingeh, at Julian Lucero's home at Los Luceros, shown in about 1900. In those times, rooms were sometimes rented from private homes to be used as courtrooms in Territorial Court sessions. The county seat was moved to Chamita in 1852, and then to Alcalde. In 1880, the first county courthouse was established 90 miles north of Española, in Tierra Amarilla, where it remains today. (San Gabriel Historical Society.)

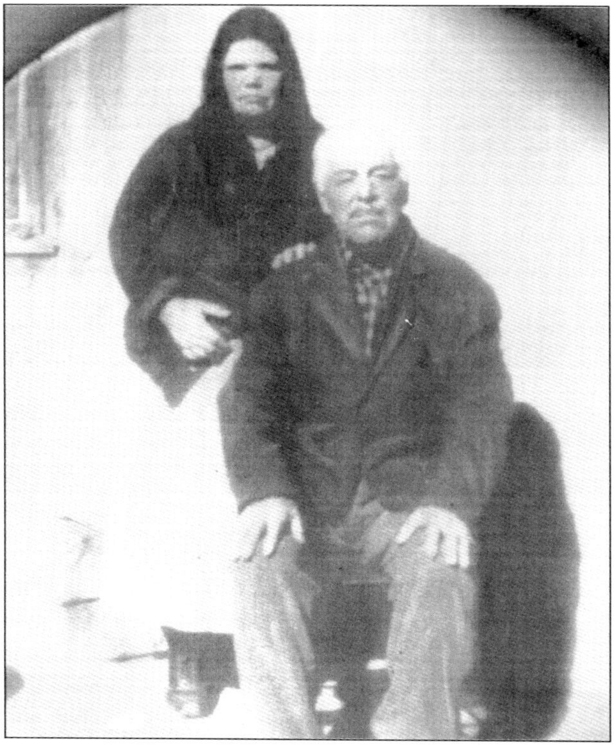

Juan Luis Garcia was born in 1850. While herding sheep near the family home on the west side of the Española Valley, he was taken by Navajos and sold to a Navajo family near Fort Wingate. After three years, at age 11, Juan Luis escaped and was making his way back home. When asked, "Where do you live," he replied, "La Vega de los Vigiles," the name of the area that would become Española. Garcia raised two families. The first was with his wife, Leonora. After she died, his second wife, Donaciana (left) raised his first nine children and their own six. Because Garcia was the first person to homestead the Pajarito Plateau in 1882, he is considered the first resident of Los Alamos. Aurelio, Juan Luis's first son from his second marriage, is shown below with his parents, in about 1900. (Both, Tony and Jesse Borrego.)

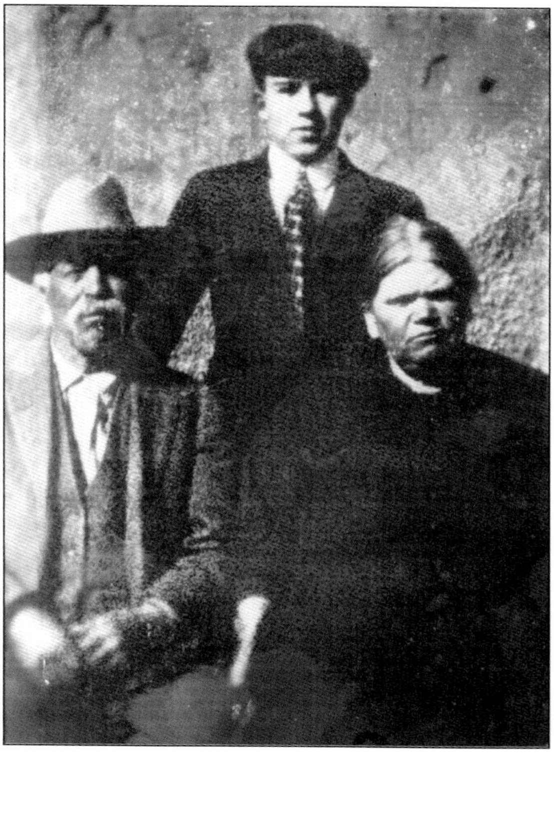

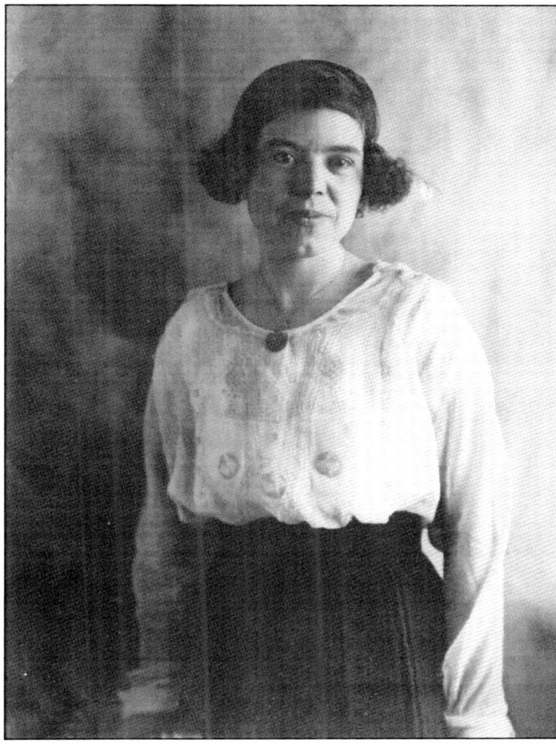

Elinea Garcia was the oldest daughter of Juan Luis and Donaciana Garcia. She was born in 1905 in Guachupangue. In 1925, she married Luis Borrego from Ranchitos. Elinea and her siblings and stepsiblings became heirs to the Garcia Canyon homestead, which Juan Luis had settled. Garcia Canyon would eventually be consolidated into the Los Alamos National Lab holdings. Elinea's big brother Jose Aurelio Garcia married a woman named China, from Kentucky. In 1923, they moved to Leadville, Colorado, and raised a family. China, wishing to help her husband integrate into American society, persuaded him to change his name legally to Joseph Garcy. They are shown below with their daughter Goldie in 1935. (Both, Tony and Jesse Borrego.)

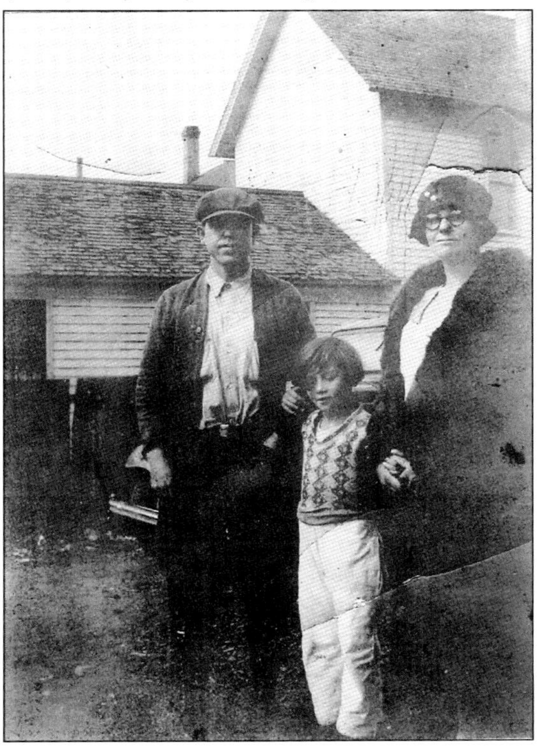

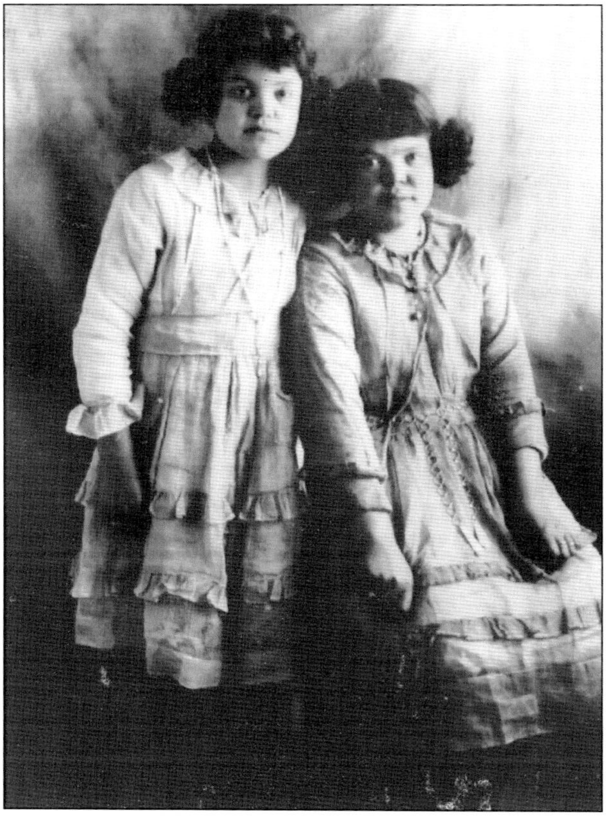

Teresina and Sarita (left) were the youngest of Donaciana and Juan Luis Garcia's six children. The girls were born and raised in Guachupangue in the 1920s. Across the Rio Grande from the Garcia home, in the village of San Pedro, the Francisco Montoya family was thriving. Third from left below, standing near his mother, Loretita, is Adolfo, born in 1897. Adolfo would eventually work for the Los Alamos Ranch School, coaxing beautiful and bountiful plants from the school's garden. Adolfo's brother, Flavio, fifth from left, would grow up to marry Petronila Vigil, the Garcias' neighbor in Guachupangue. On the far right stands "Tia Reyes," a Navajo servant who was raised by the Montoya family. Tia Reyes died the night Flavio and Petronila were married, in January 1907. The young bride was asked to sew the black cloth cover for Tia Reyes' casket—a great honor. (Left, Tony and Jesse Borrego; below, Sam Montoya.)

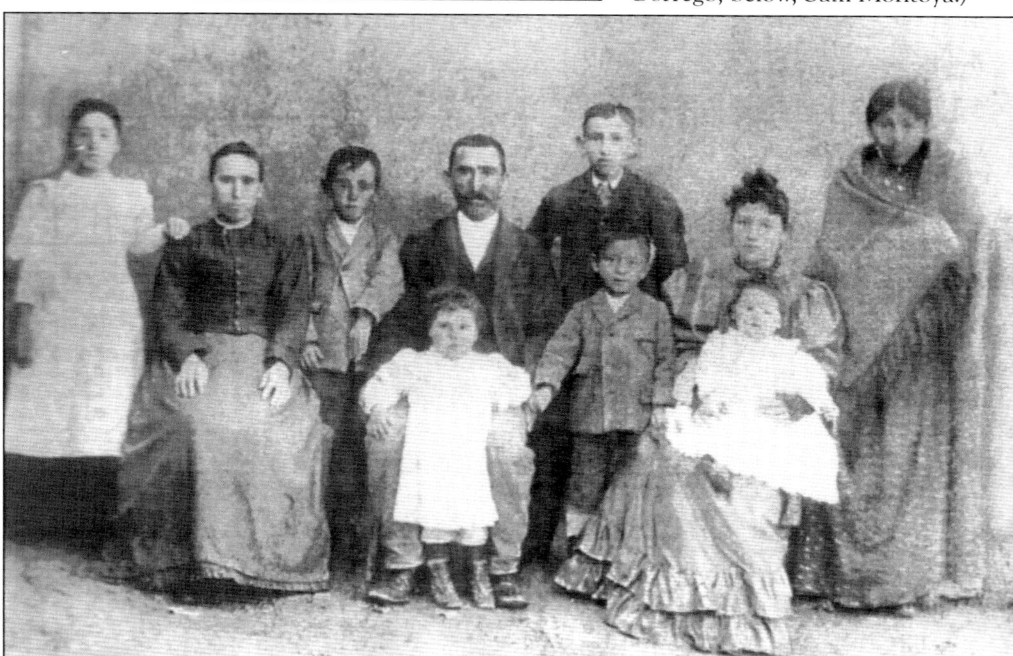

Abelino Moya was born and raised in La Gallina, north of Española. His family was very poor. He is shown at right shortly after his graduation from the Santa Fe Indian School, where he was sent when he turned 12. Shown below is Moya's mother, Cecilia. A Navajo Indian, she was taken as a child from her home in Cañon Largo, near the Jicarilla Apache Reservation, and raised by a Spanish family. Abelino's daughter Frances married Max Vigil from San Pedro. Max Vigil's grandparents were Manuel Reyes and Cleofitas Vigil, of a prestigious family from Guachupangue. Their property, La Vega de Los Vigiles, would become Española. Their daughter Petronila married into the Montoya family. The Montoyas donated the property on which the San Pedro chapel was built in 1875. The chapel was rebuilt in 1938, and is still in use. (Both, Max and Frances Vigil.)

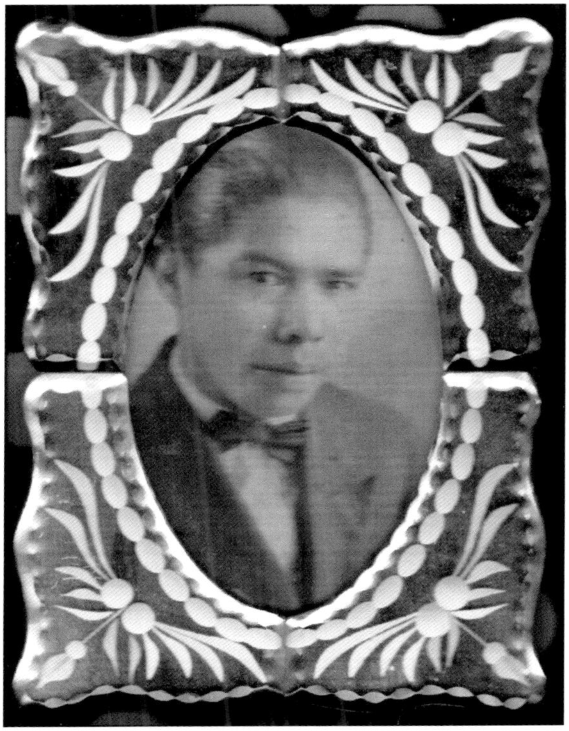

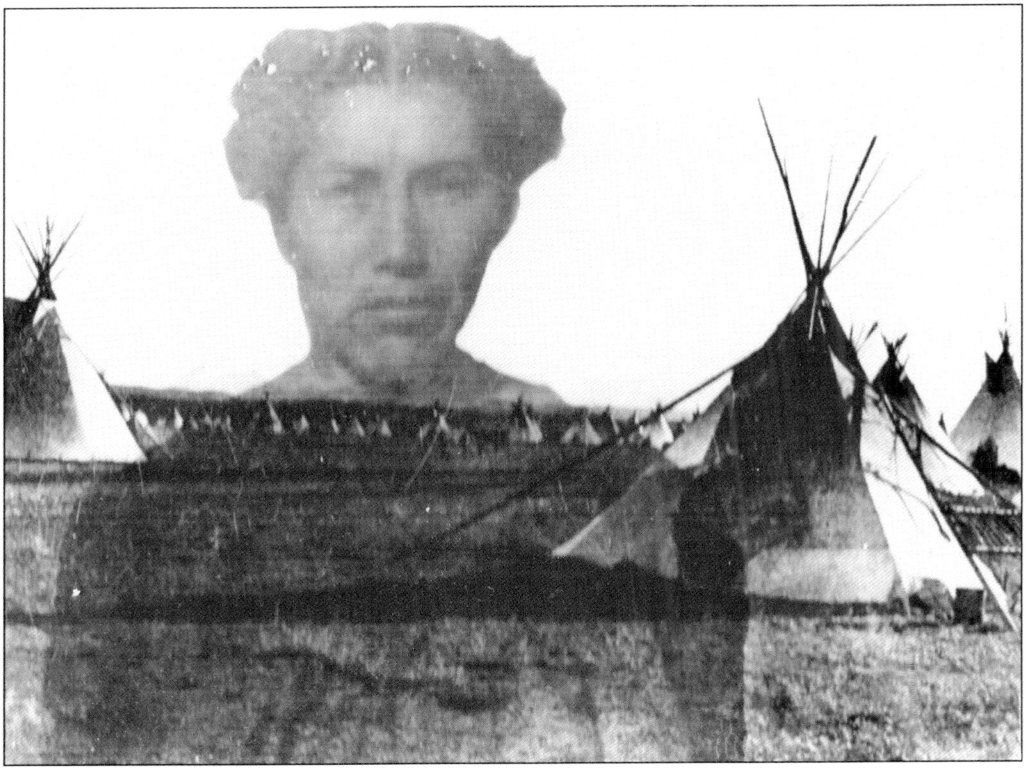

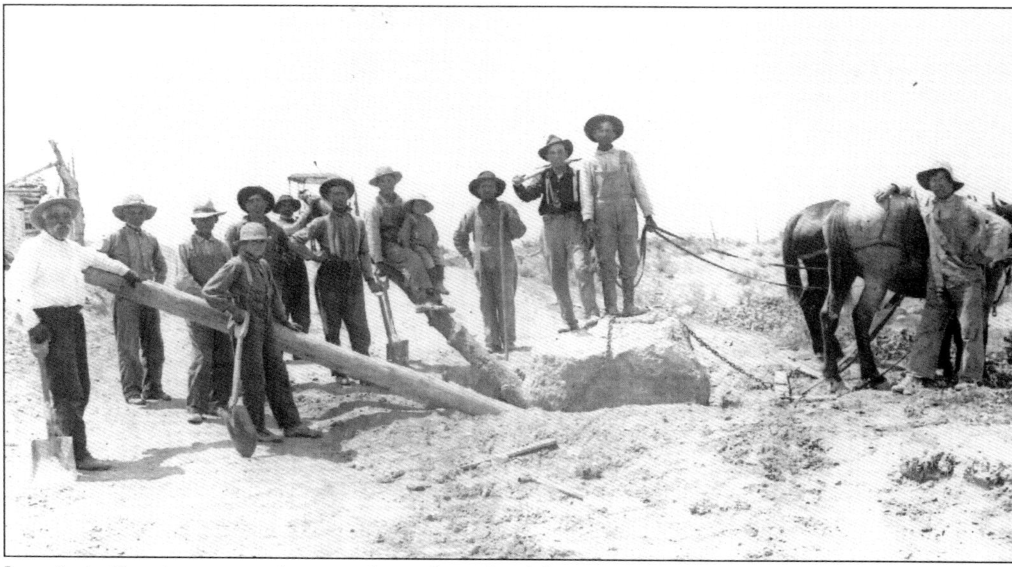

Juan Luis Garcia remained active throughout his lifetime. Standing at far left above, he assists in the removal of a boulder. Juan Luis's heirs continued to build seasonal homes in Garcia Canyon through the 1950s. Homesteaders of the New Mexico Territory could maintain their 160-acre parcels by farming, ranching, foraging, and living part-time on their property. By improving the land in this manner, the homesteaders were granted patents by the federal government. These patents secured ownership of the property against any and all other claims. The Pueblo Land Reform Board began evicting squatters from Indian land in the 1930s. Ohkay Owingeh, shown below, and the other Tewa villages of Santa Clara and San Ildefonso, regained some of their lands that had been lost to Spanish colonization in the 18th and 19th centuries. (Above, Tony and Jesse Borrego; below, Palace of the Governors Photo Archives, photograph by Carlos Vierra.)

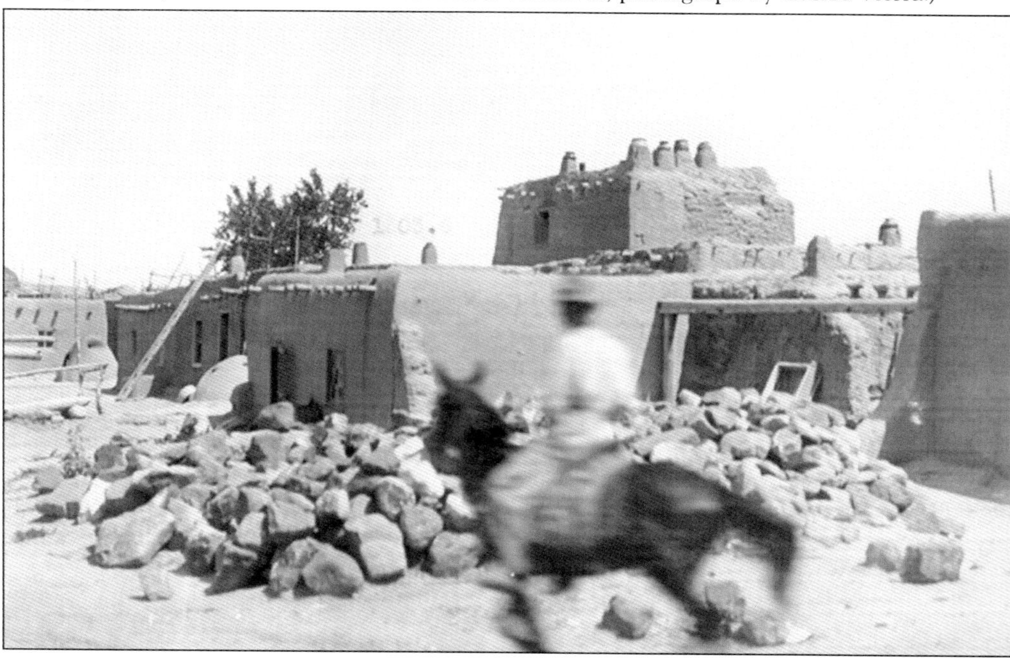

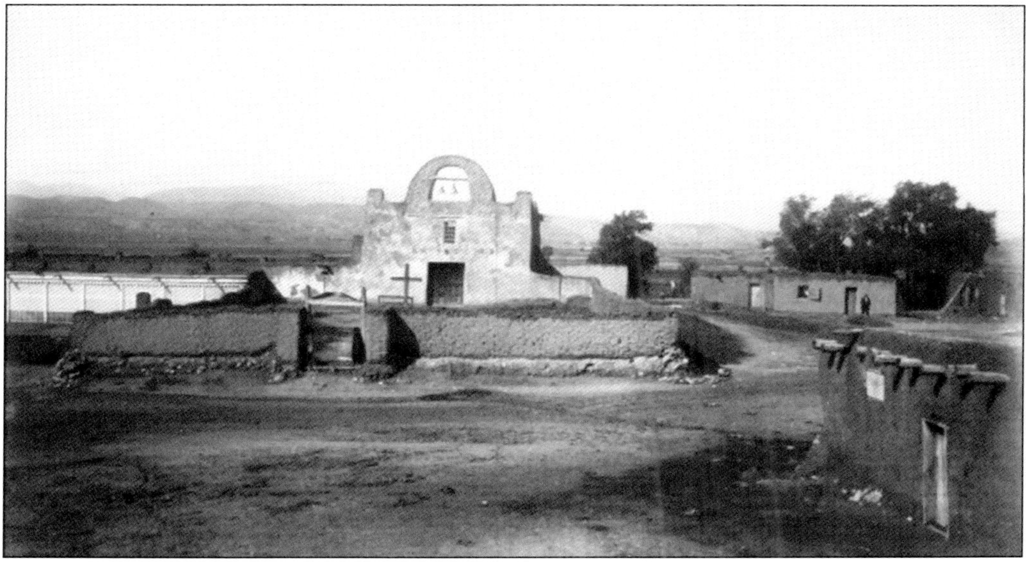

Santa Cruz de la Cañada continued to minister to its mission churches for most of the 19th century. San Juan Pueblo Mission, seen above, was rebuilt by Fr. Camilo Seux in 1912. Father Seux served at San Juan for 54 years, and is buried under the floor of the Lourdes Shrine, across the street from the church. El Santuario de Chimayo, seen in the 1915 photograph below, is the only designated pilgrimage shrine of the Archdiocese of Santa Fe. Thousands of people visit this famous shrine yearly. Many miraculous healings have been attributed to the holy dirt that comes from El Santuario. The shrine is located 12 miles east of Española. During Lent, and especially during Holy Week, the road to El Santuario becomes a footpath for pilgrims seeking favors, or fulfilling a vow. (Above, Palace of the Governors Photo Archives, photograph by W.H. Rau; below, Holy Family Parish, Chimayo.)

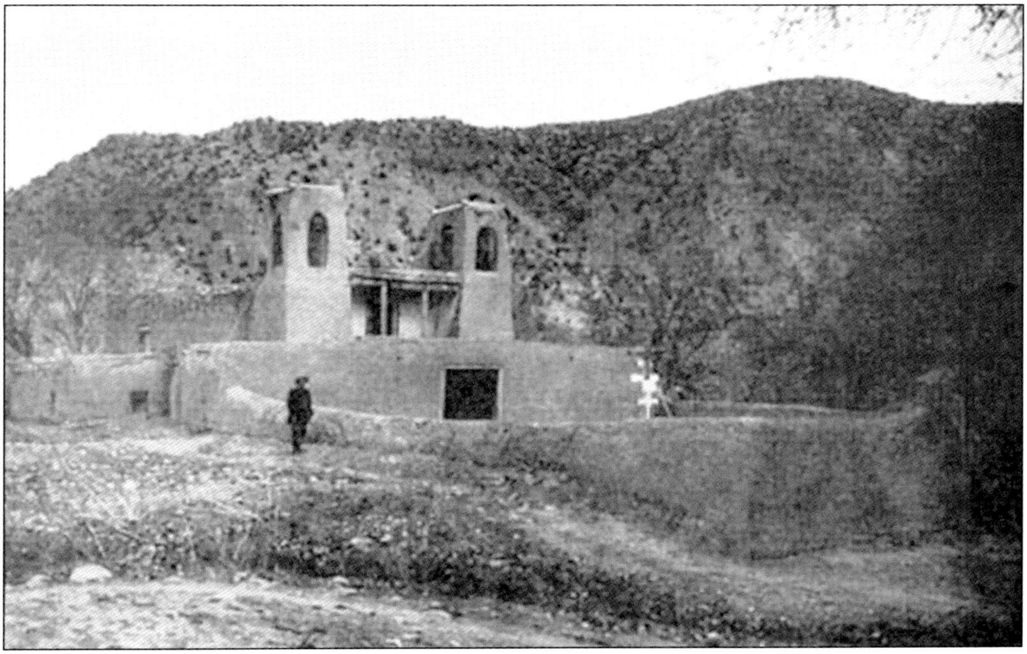

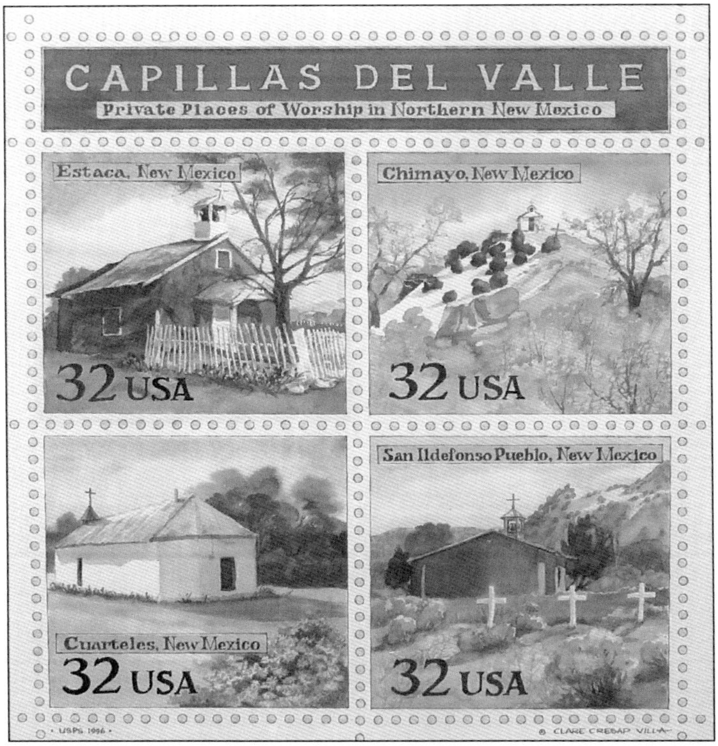

The Parish continues to maintain its family-built village *capillas* (chapels) throughout the Valley. Clare Villa's watercolor pays homage to four of them. Leroy Martinez painted La Capilla de la Sagrada Familia as it was before restoration in 1990. In the 1880s, the community of Pajarito built the chapel near Black Mesa, sacred landmark of the Tewas. Cecilia Roybal and her husband, Telesfor Vigil, from Guachupangue, completed it in 1924. By 1937, non-Indian residents had been relocated, most settling in the Española Valley. (Left, Clare Cresap Villa; below, Leroy F. Martinez.)

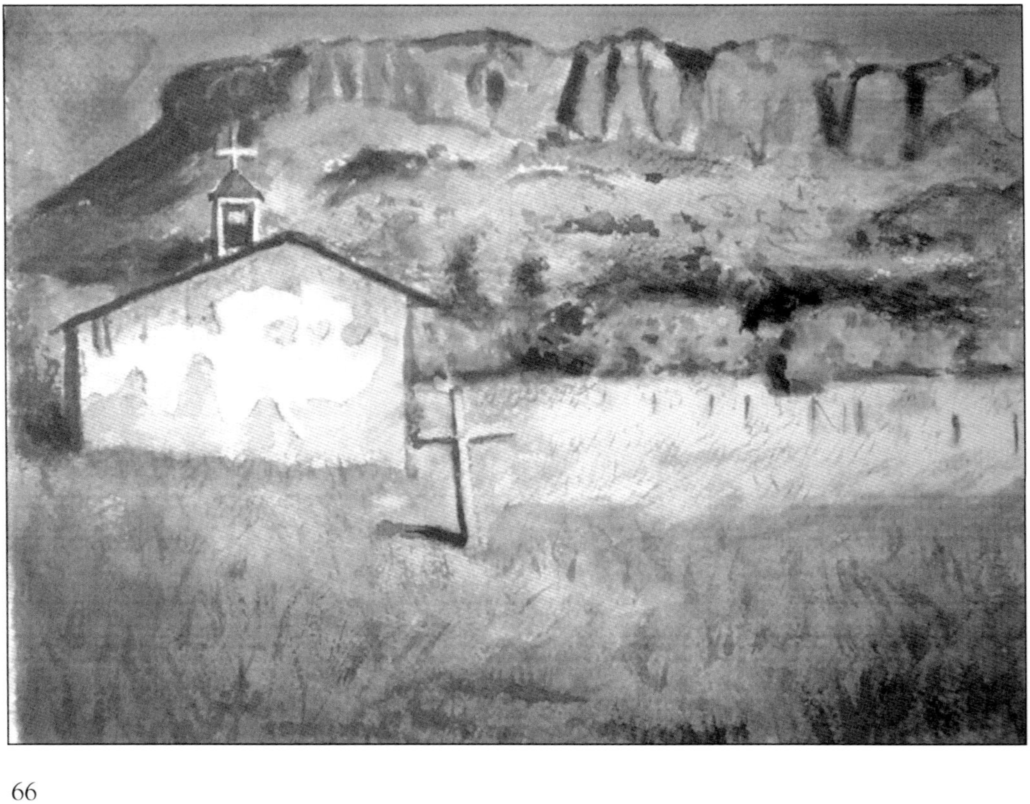

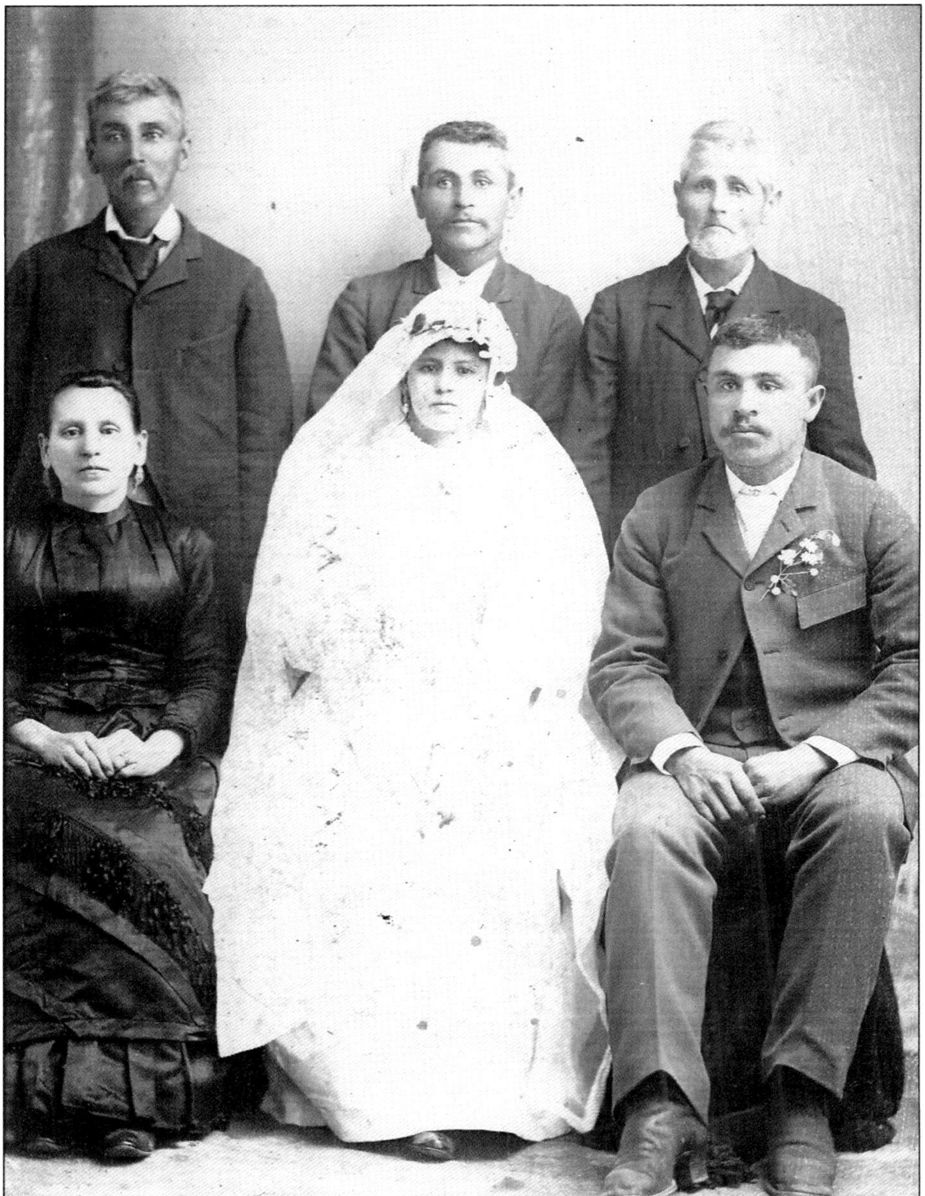

Shown on their wedding day in 1870, Raquel and Jesus Jacobo Vigil are surrounded by their family. Raquel's sister Cleofitas, left, was married to Jesus Jacobo's brother Manuel Reyes, standing behind Raquel. The sisters' father, Jose Francisco Vigil, and the brothers' father, Juan Francisco Vigil, were first cousins. The two sisters married their second cousins, not uncommon in the 19th century. All those pictured were descendants of Jose Ramon Vigil, who in 1857 purchased the 31,000-acre land grant that is named after him. Vigil paid Antonio Sanchez two oxen, 36 sheep, one ram, and $20 for the land, which extends from the Jemez Mountains, all the way to the Rio Grande, including the Valle Grande and present-day White Rock. In 1879, Jose Ramon sold his land to the priest at Santa Clara Pueblo for $4,000. In 1884, Fr. Thomas Aquinas Hayes sold it for $100,000. (Águeda Trujillo.)

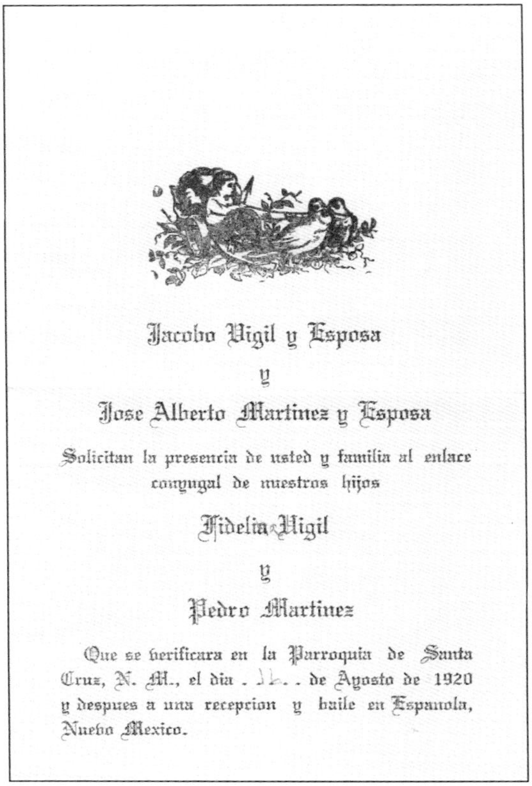

Jacobo Vigil y Esposa

y

Jose Alberto Martinez y Esposa

Solicitan la presencia de usted y familia al enlace conyugal de nuestros hijos

Fidelia Vigil

y

Pedro Martinez

Que se verificara en la Parroquia de Santa Cruz, N. M., el dia ..16.. de Agosto de 1920 y despues a una recepcion y baile en Espanola, Nuebo Mexico.

A formal invitation announces the wedding of Raquel Vigil's daughter Fidelina to Pedro Martinez. While visiting his family in the village of Corral de Piedra, Pedro was introduced to Fidelina, whose family lived on the adjacent property. In the 1830s, Pedro Martinez's family had moved from Santa Cruz to Rociada, located near Mora, but still maintained family ties in the Española Valley. Pedro and Fidelina were married at Santa Cruz de la Cañada Church on August 16, 1920, and built their home near Guachupangue. Their daughter Águeda Isabel Corina married Anselmo Trujillo, a well-known teacher in the Española Valley. (Águeda Trujillo.)

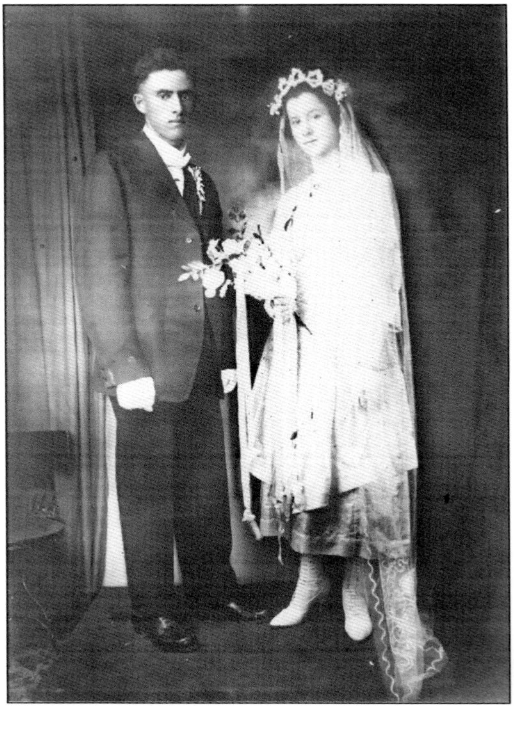

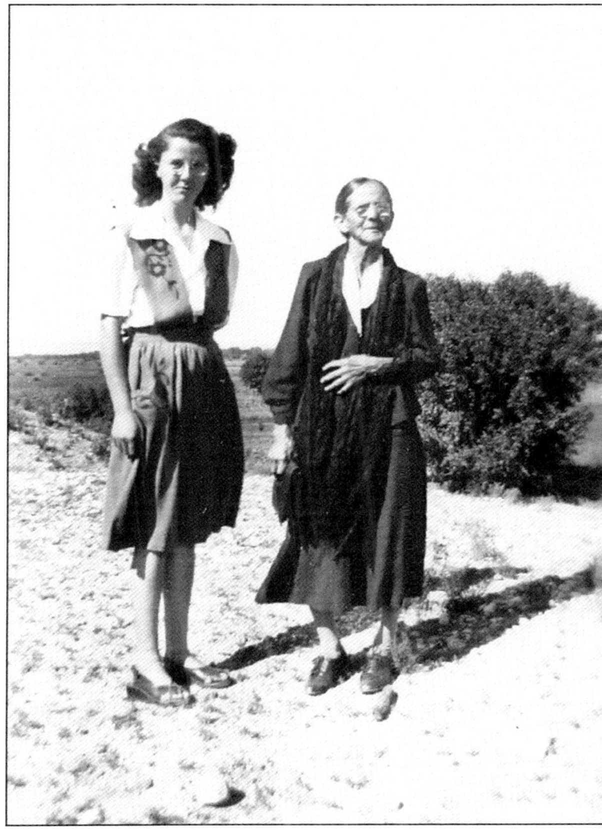

In 1942, 72 years after her wedding, Raquel Vigil and her granddaughter Lucy Martinez stand above Española, at what is today the back of Española City Hall. Looking past them, over their shoulders, readers can gaze eastward to the river bottomlands and the Bosque along Railroad Avenue. Beyond the Rio Grande are the foothills of El Llano. At this time, the Vigils still owned a vast tract of land that went from the West Side LotaBurger to Angelina's Restaurant. Below, Lucy's mother and father, Fidelina and Pedro, their little son, and their mule stand on another high point on the family's holdings. The spot looks isolated and remote in this photograph from 1925, but this is the site of Northern New Mexico Community College's administration building. (Águeda Trujillo.)

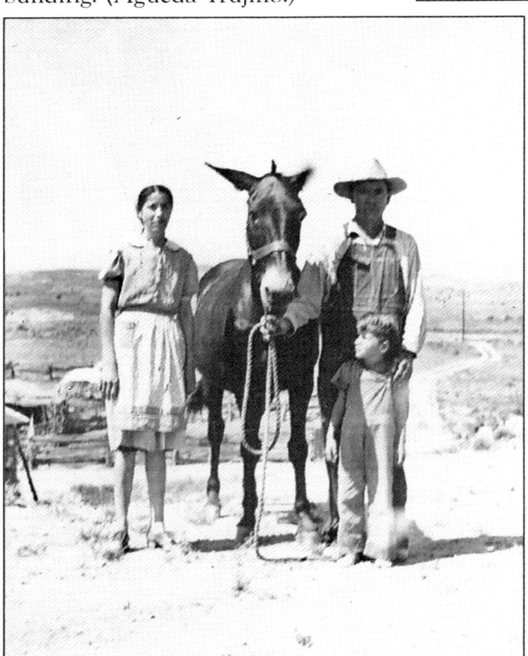

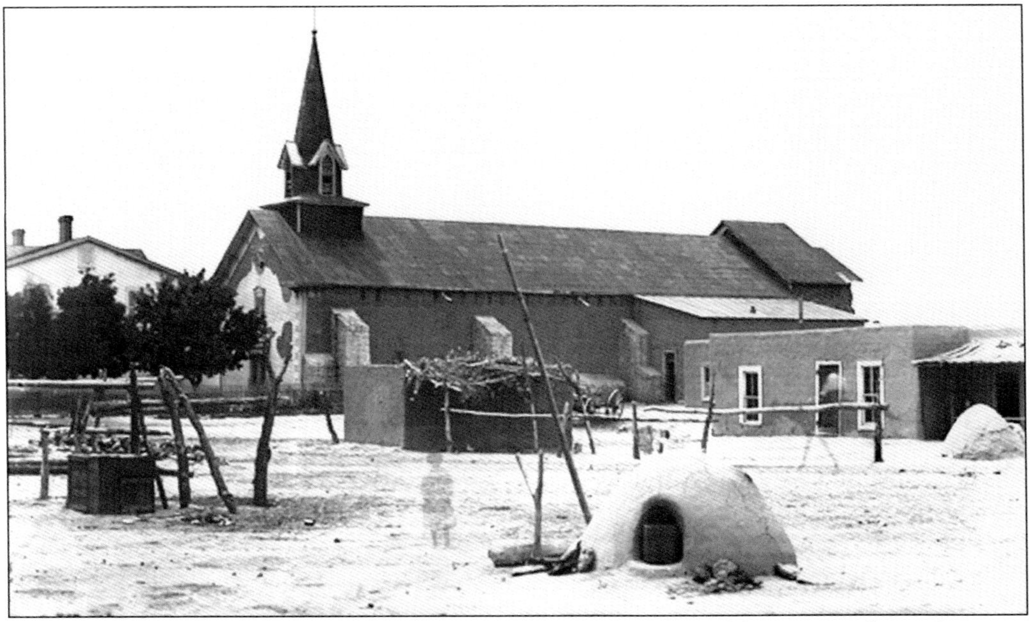

Looking at the San Juan Pueblo Church from the north plaza of Ohkay Owingeh, readers get a feel for the quiet vitality of the Pueblo people in the early 1900s. The adobe bread ovens that were introduced by the Spanish colonists have taken hold in Tewa village life. Still too early for cars, hitching posts for horses are the garages of the day. This photograph includes two "ghosts"—one of a child and one of a horse and rider. There is an excited atmosphere to the picture below. It looks like a summer day, and the author wonders if the well-dressed visitors are attending the Pueblo's June 24 Feast Day. Or perhaps the recently finished church is being re-dedicated by pastor Camilo Seux, who has paid for its construction. (Above, by Carlos Vierra; both, Palace of the Governors Photo Archives.)

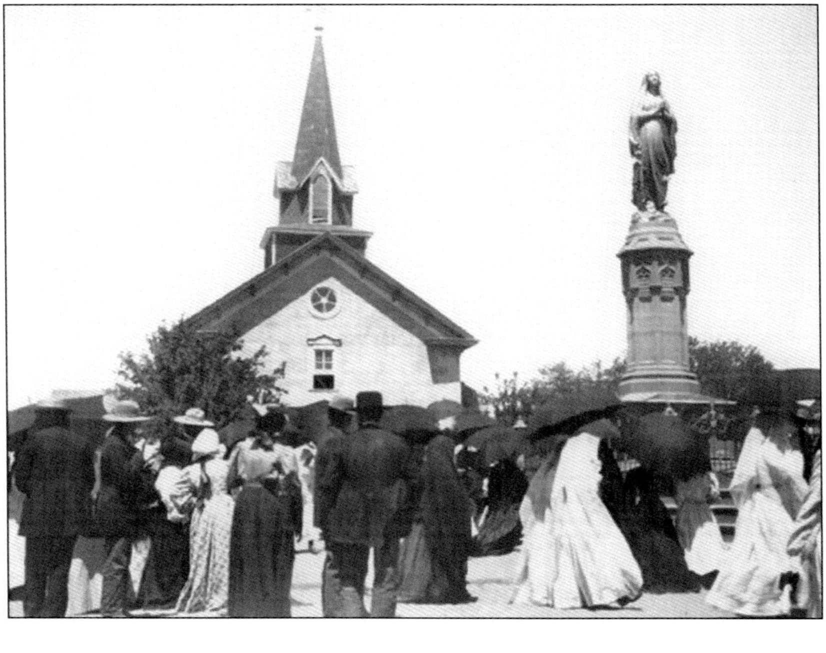

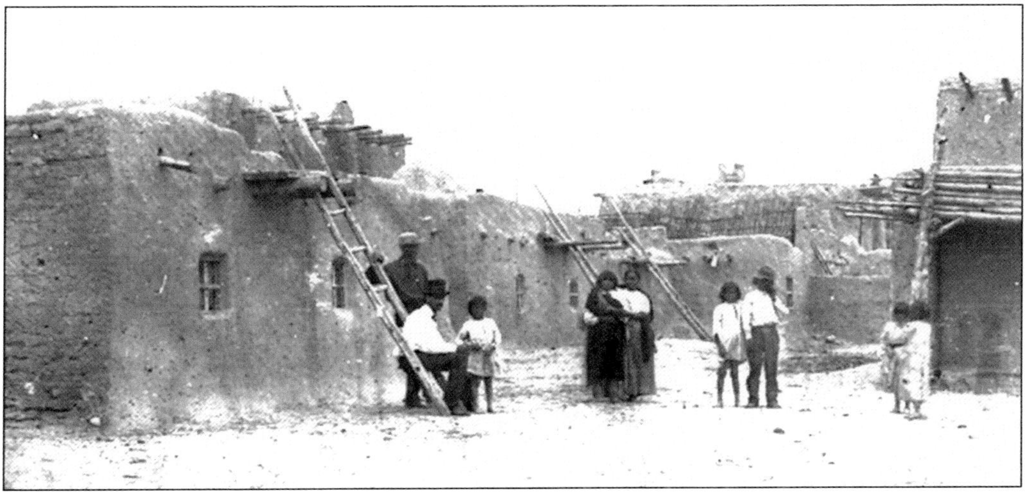

Native traditional attire meets Spanish Colonial dress and an American top hat in the 1875 photograph above. The presence of the Rio Arriba County seat in nearby Alcalde at this time would make for a steady flow of visitors to Ohkay Owingeh. The Spanish village of Chamita, located across the Rio Grande from the pueblo, is one of the oldest settlements in the United States. Viewed as a "snapshot" of the era, Ohkay Owingeh comfortably embraces the past, present, and future of the Española Valley. A somewhat more formal mood at Ohkay Owingeh is created in the 1904 Edward S. Curtis photograph below. Preparations for a traditional mud plaster, the familiar church across the plaza, and a graceful woman speak of an ancient community poised to enter the 20th century. (Above, Palace of the Governors Photo Archives, photograph by H.T. Hiester; below, Palace of the Governors Photo Archives, photograph by Edward S. Curtis.)

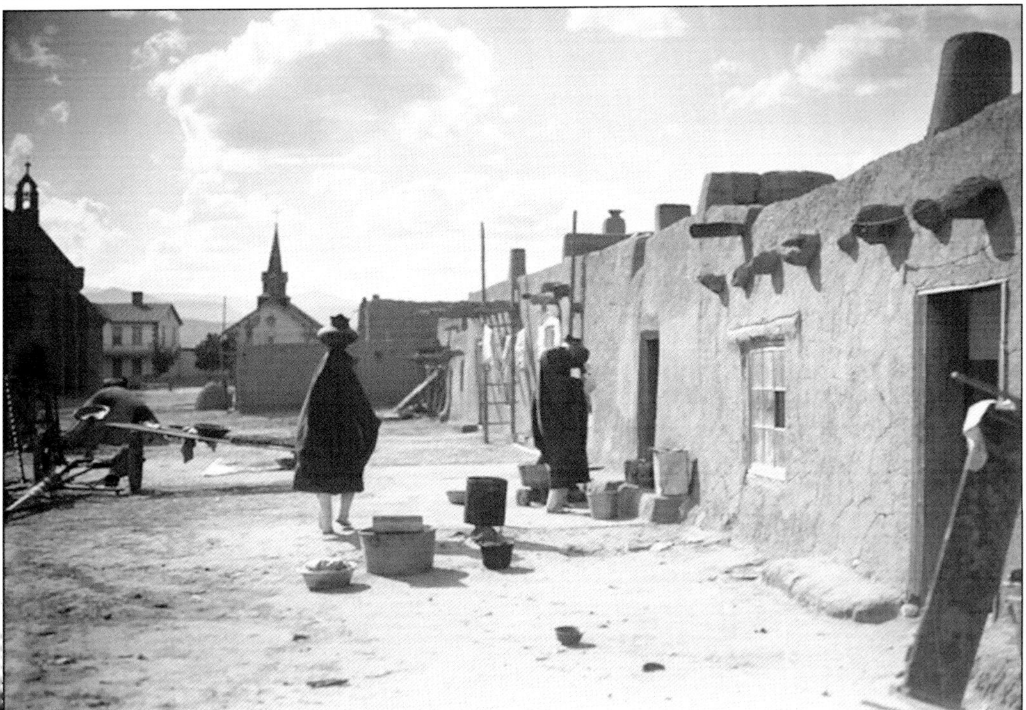

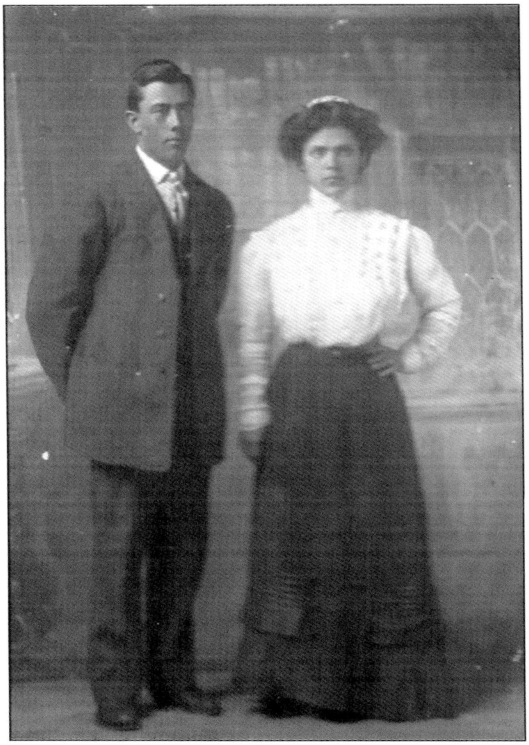

Celestina Maestas and Pedro Quintana (l) were married in 1904. After Pedro's death, Celestina left their Upper San Pedro home to their three sons, Manuel, Amadeo, and Juan. Celestina remarried, and made a new home on Lower San Pedro with her second husband Jose Montoya. Their son, Jose Montoya Jr., still maintains that home. Celestina's grandchildren and great-grandchildren continue to live in San Pedro and maintain the fabric of village life within the Española Valley. Julian Lucero II, pictured below with his bride in 1912, is the grandfather of Richard Lucero, three-time mayor of Española. Richard runs Country Farm Supply on Riverside Drive. (Both photographs courtesy of Martha Archuleta.)

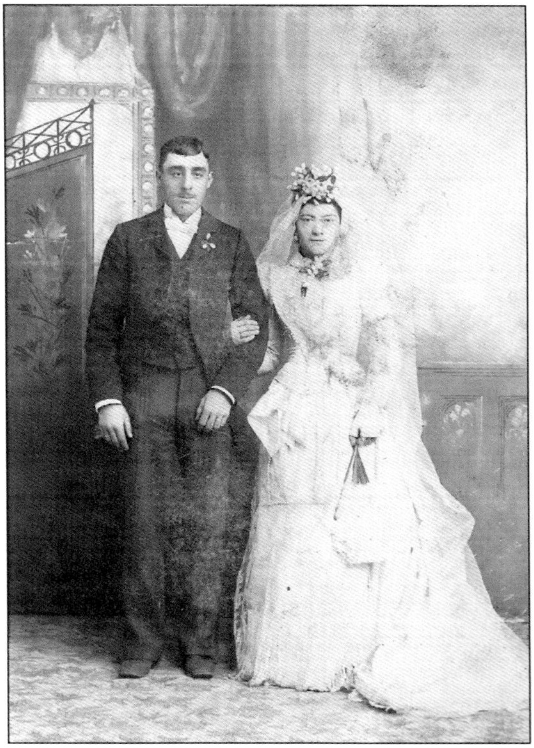

Four

El Nuevo Estado

When Ofilia Valdez, the grandmother of the author's daughter, moved to Española in the early 1920s, she was four years old. She had a big sister, Herminia; a little sister, Olivama; and a baby brother, Eliseo Jr. Their mother had died, and their father, Eliseo, was bringing the family from Tierra Amarilla to Española to make a new life near the southern terminus of the Chili Line, a narrow gauge railroad. Eliseo, a passionate Republican, was one of the few people in New Mexico who had a printing press. He had been publishing a newspaper called *El Nuevo Estado*. When he came to Española from the High Country, Eliseo changed the name of his newspaper to *La Voz del Rio Grande*.

There was much to write about in Española. Public education was spreading throughout the region. The Chili Line was carrying goods out of the Española Valley—apples, sheep, pine nuts, wool—a sign of commerce and prosperity. The railroad brought lumber from La Madera, where men from the Valley were finding work in the lumber camps, helping to meet the demands of a swiftly growing nation. The Chili Line transported soldiers leaving to serve in World War I.

Influential people from the outside world were coming to Española. Mellie Perkins, of the United Brethren Church, arrived by the Chili Line. When Fr. Salvador Gené arrived in Española by train in 1920, the rains had caused flooding and the trestle bridge had washed away. Father Salvador was transported across the river by rowboat. A horse and buggy waited on the other side to take him to Santa Cruz.

Traveling south on present-day Railroad Avenue, which runs behind Northern New Mexico College, the pastures on either side of the street remain much as they were in 1880, when the Chile Line first chugged into Española from Colorado.

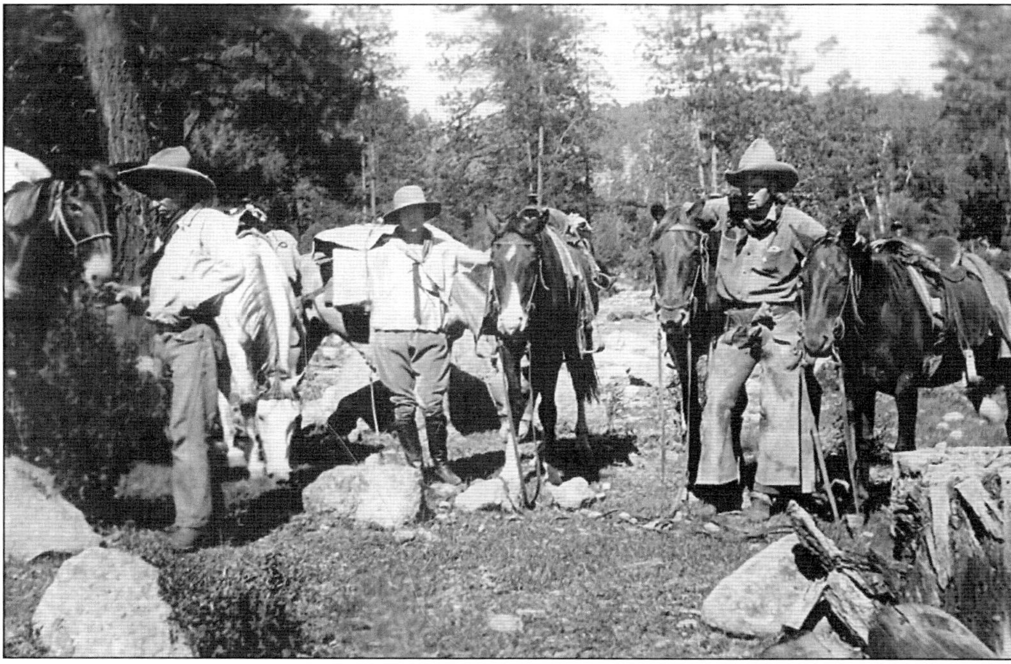

Maximiliano "Max" Vigil was the son of Cleofitas and Manuel Reyes Vigil. Born at the turn of the century, he naturally developed the deep familiarity with the mountains and valleys that made him a sought-after guide. Visitors arrived in Española by the Chili Line. Vigil would take them north to Colorado and then west to the Grand Canyon. Such treks lasted many weeks. In the top photograph, taken in the 1920s, Vigil (left) attends to a group of adventurers. In his later years, Vigil managed Mary Cabot Wheelwright's ranch in Los Luceros. In the bottom photograph, he is sitting in the front seat of the wagon; his sons Gilberto and Max Jr. follow on horseback. Wheelwright and her colorful guests enjoyed camping trips to the Valle Grande in wagons such as this one. (Both, Max and Frances Vigil.)

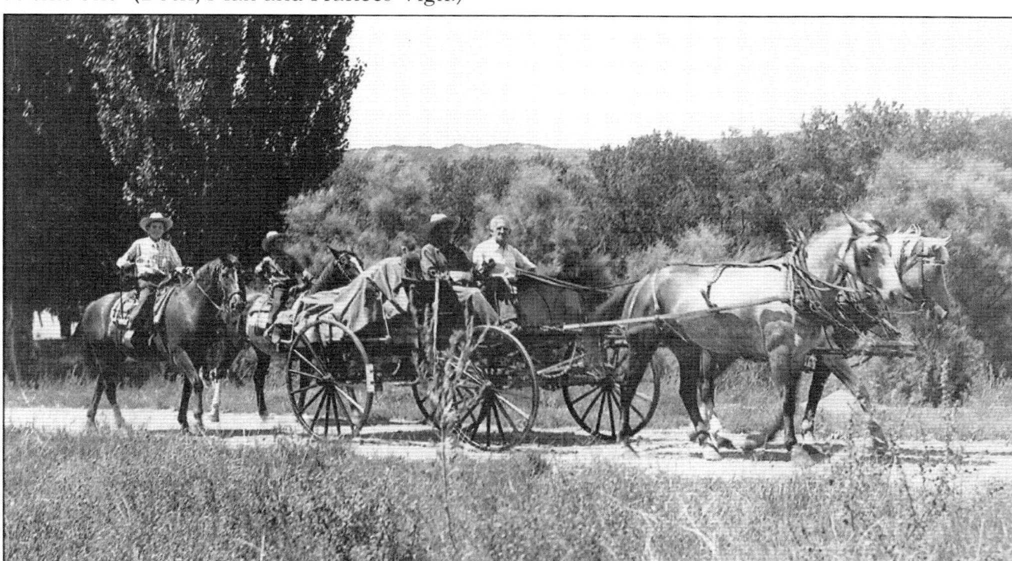

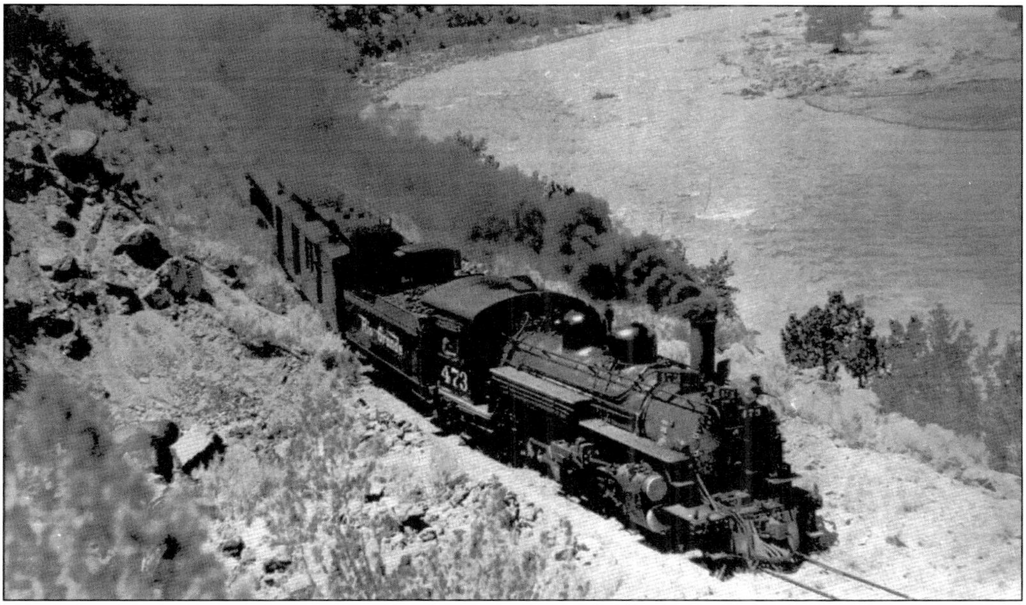

By December 1880, the Denver & Rio Grande Railroad had laid track from Antonito, Colorado, to Española. In 1887, the Texas, Santa Fe & Northern Railroad's route through Buckman Flats was completed. This connected the Chili Line from Española to Santa Fe. Above, engine No. 473 heads south along the river to Española; it is possibly carrying lepidolite from Embudo, mica from Tres Piedras, or quartzite from Glenwoody. Farther south, past Santa Clara, tracks lead to Otowi Station, made famous by Edith Warner, a frail young woman who had come to New Mexico seeking healing. She wrote, "The landscape's nudity surprised me—everywhere bare rock clothed only in a shift of shadows, sand pooled deep in dry stream beds, wide gravel washes, deadwood caked with dust, cracked mud, silt ankle deep in drifts beside the rusted rails." (Both, Los Alamos National Lab Archives.)

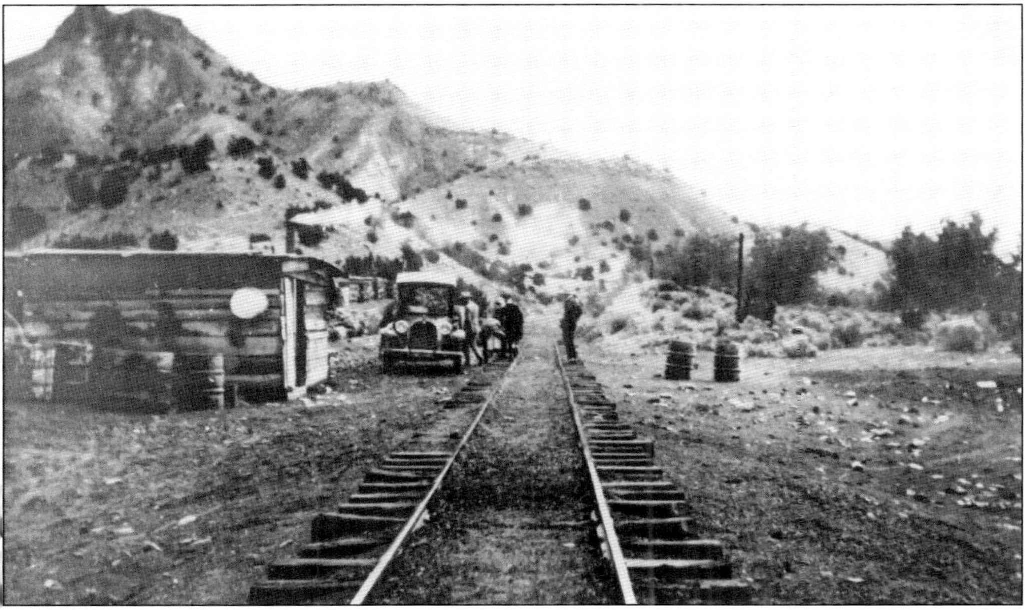

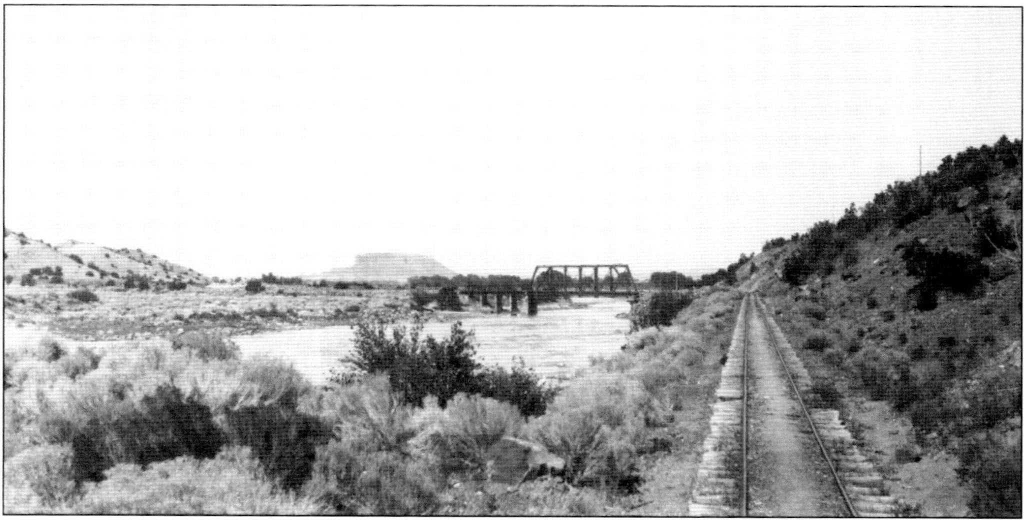

In the 1920 photograph above, taken a little south of Otowi, one of many trestle bridges on the Chili Line crosses the Rio Grande. In the short distance from Otowi to Buckman, the train crossed five trestle bridges over deep arroyos. This particular bridge does not exist today. Buckman Station, as seen below, looks solitary and abandoned but in former days was the site of a huge mill that sawed thousands of trees into lumber destined for Albuquerque. This area, the Caja del Rio Grant, was originally part of San Ildefonso Pueblo. To the north is the sacred Black Mesa of the San Ildefonso people. (Above, Palace of the Governors Photo Archives, photograph by Wesley Bradfield; below, Los Alamos National Lab Archives.)

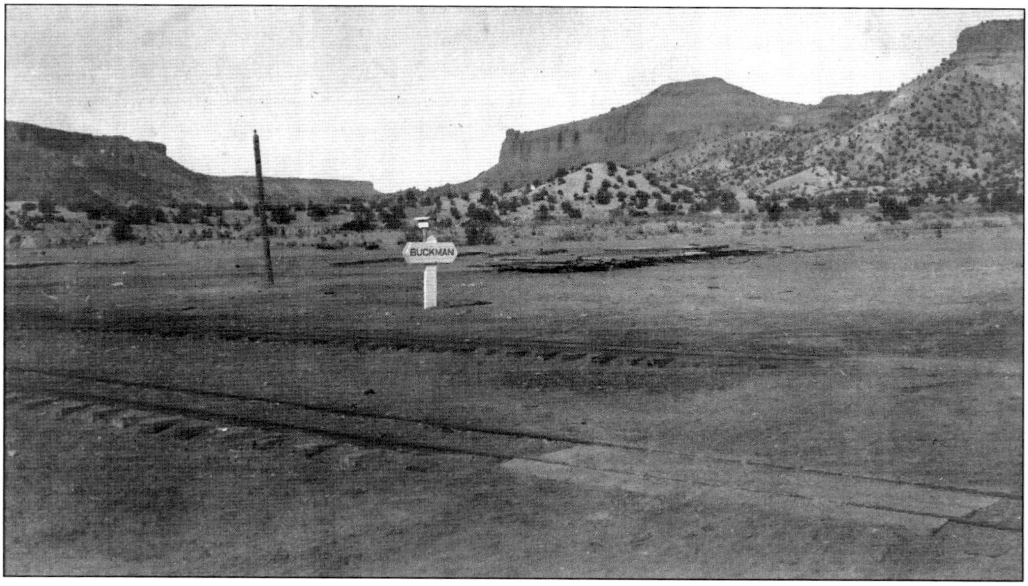

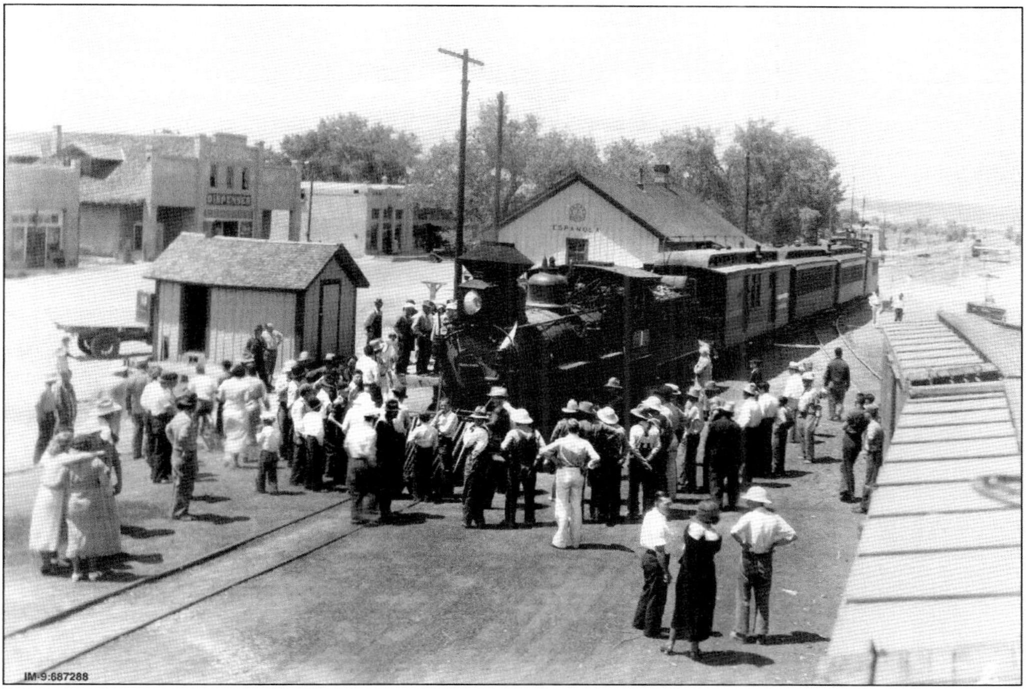

The train brought new people to the Española Valley, such as this crew of actors and extras waiting to shoot a scene for the 1936 movie *Texas Rangers*, starring Fred McMurray. The engine has been embellished with a carbide lamp and a fake smokestack to make it look older. The site is present-day Railroad Avenue, about a half mile south of the Convento. The Chili Line also brought work to the area. Shown at right is Luis Borrego, a member of a crew that maintained a section of track near Velarde—an important job, because the sandy soil on which portions of the line had been built could give way, causing 12-ton engines to topple. Borrego is the grandson of Juan Luis Garcia, who was taken by Navajos as a boy and eventually found his way home. (Above, San Gabriel Historical Society; right, Tony and Jesse Borrego.)

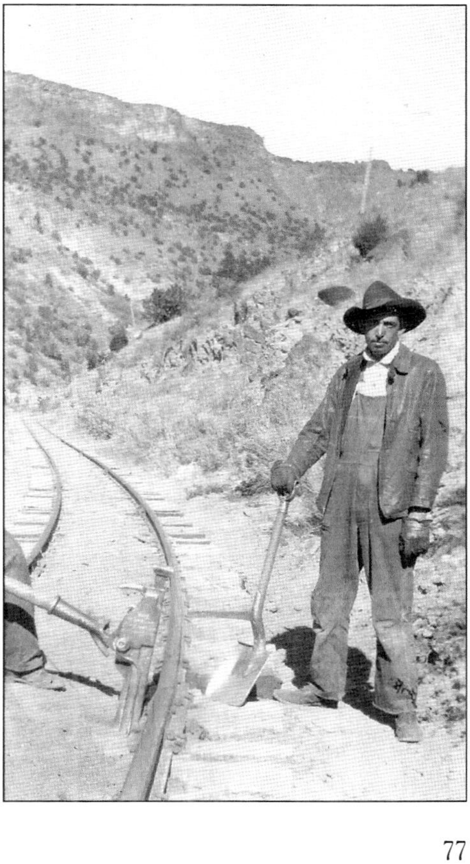

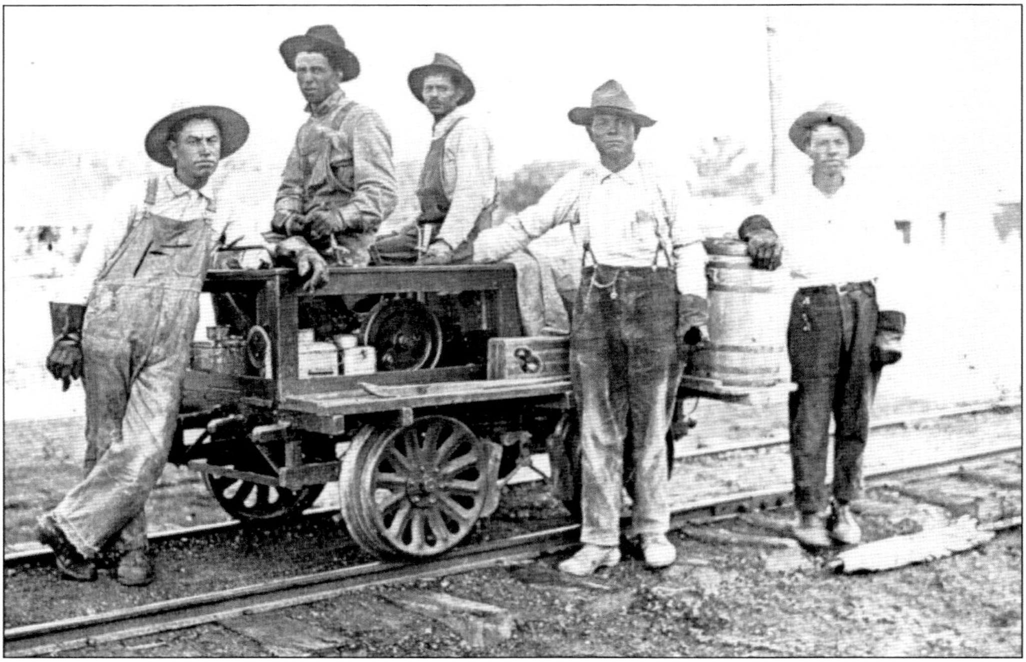

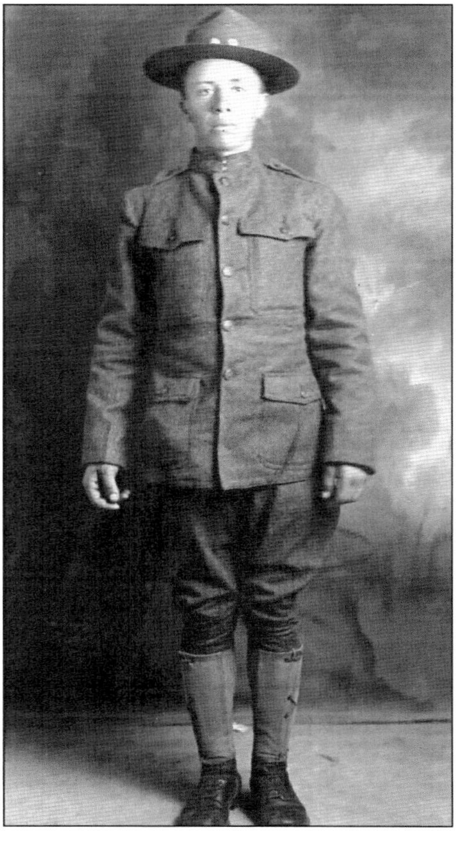

In 1913, the population of Española was about 400. Workers like the men on this crew earned $1.40 for a 10-hour day. From left to right are Fortino Rodriguez, Santiago Fresquez, Santiago Pacheco, Adan Martinez, and Manuel de Atocha Rodriguez. The location is present-day Fairview Lane, on the west side of the Valdez Bridge. Manuel Rodriguez (right) left his job to serve in World War I. He was one of 8,000 soldiers who mustered out on the Chili Line. When he returned to the railroad after the war, he was given a foreman's position, and his wage increased to $4 a day. (Both, Dr. Gerald Rodriguez.)

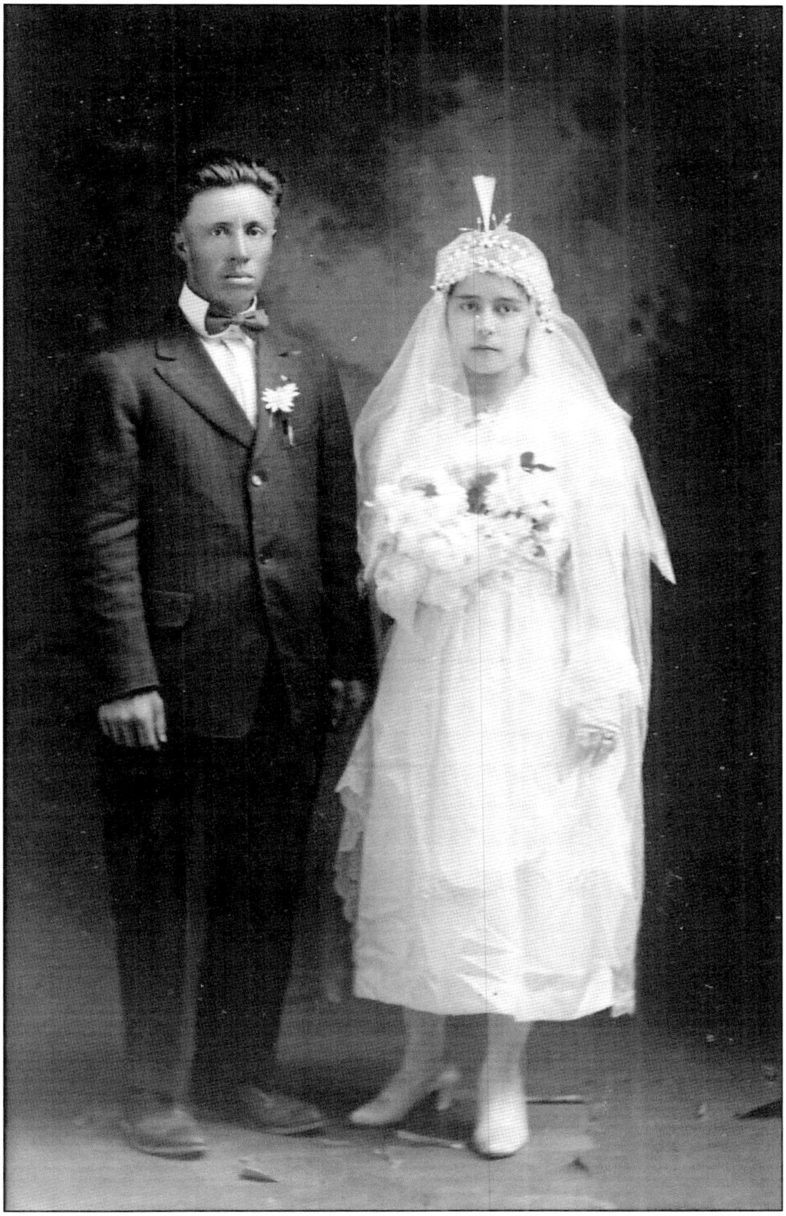

Manuel de Atocha Rodriguez and Lugardita Salazar appear on their wedding day, January 20, 1920. Both are descended, in unbroken lines, from original founding Spanish families of the Española Valley. The families go back at least 14 generations in Corral de Piedra, a village on the north end of Española. Rodriguez retired in 1974 from Cook's Hardware; he had started working there in 1926 when it was Española Mercantile. Manuel and Lugardita had seven children: Guadalupe, 90 years old and a retired university professor; Bertha, owner of Rio Grande Sales with her husband Santiago Martinez; Angelina Valdez, beloved schoolteacher; Manuel, formerly a monsignor in the Catholic church and a graduate of the Harvard Law School; Candido, a retired priest; Flora Russel, a retired attorney with eight children of her own; and Dr. Gerald Rodriguez. (Martha Archuleta.)

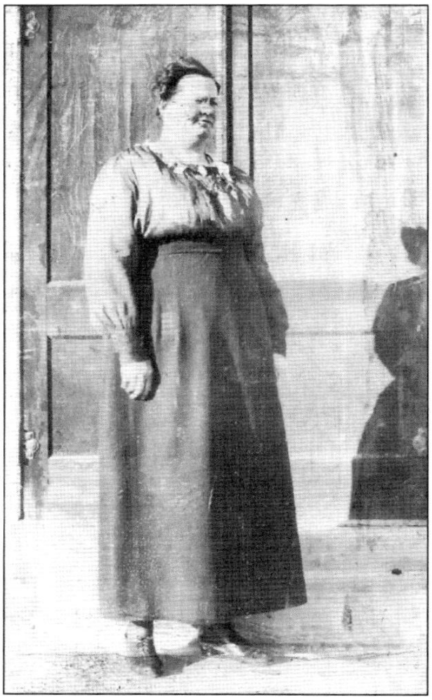

Mellie Perkins arrived in New Mexico in October 1912. She had come to the Española Valley to be teacher, preacher, and caretaker of a budding Methodist congregation in Velarde. This congregation began as a vision of Rev. Clarence Schlotterbeck, a Congregationalist minister from Kansas. With a $1,000 donation from a Texas family named Hauser, Mellie reoccupied an abandoned Baptist church. She was a thoughtful and serious person and had learned Spanish in preparation for her new work. Her little missionary church survived for many years thanks to volunteers like the women below, who saw themselves as improving the lives of the Valley people. In 1915, Miss Perkins negotiated the purchase of two acres of land in Santa Cruz, where she created the McCurdy School, which remains there to this day. (Both, McCurdy School.)

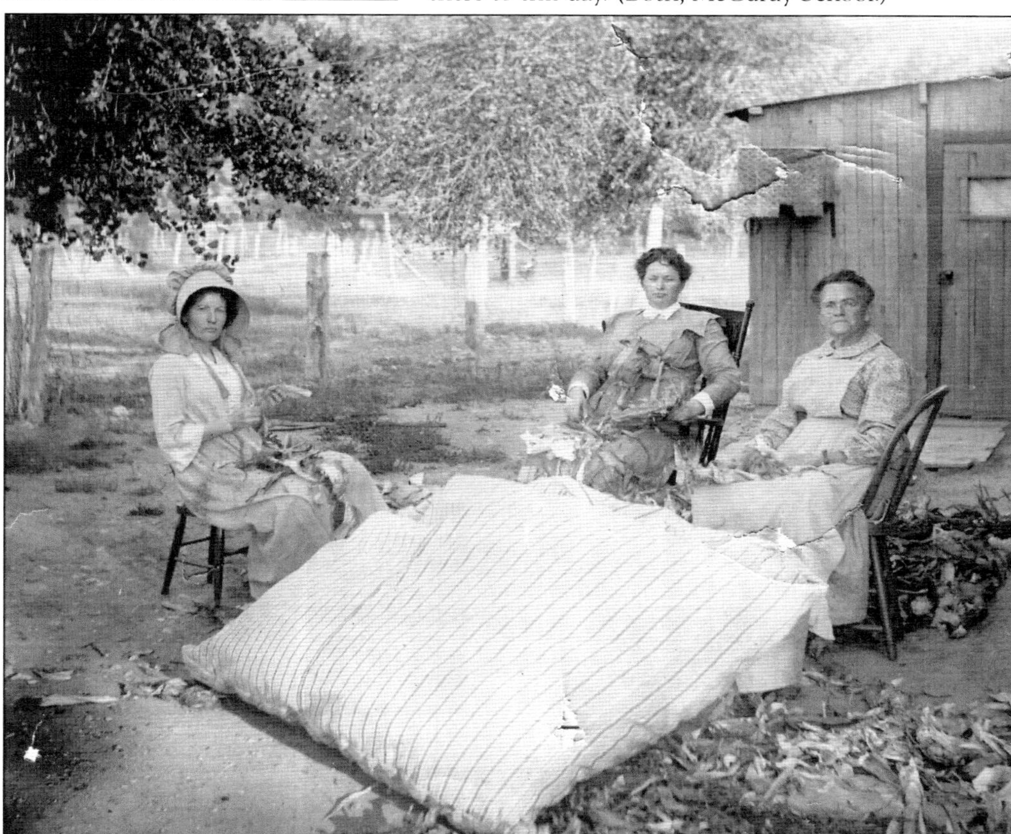

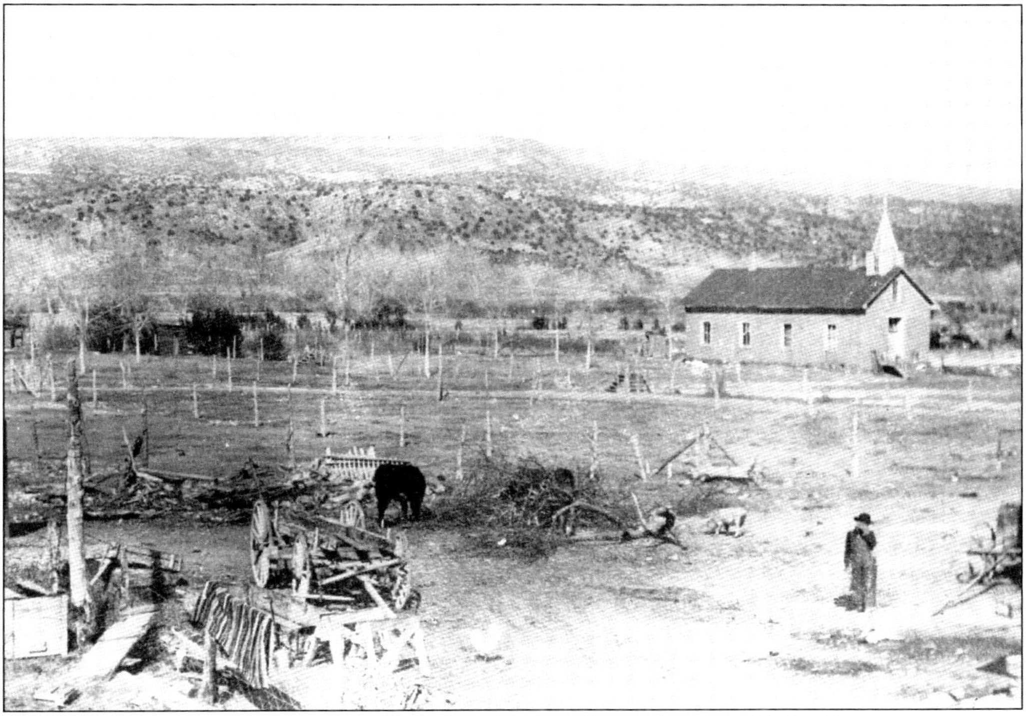

This is the little Baptist church in Velarde, where Mellie Perkins established her congregation. She started her first year with four students. By the following May, she had 43. The sign on the front of the church, which is illegible in this picture, reads, "Hauser Mission Church," in tribute to the family that made it possible. Children of Velarde—and some from Ohkay Owingeh—thrived and learned with the Methodists. A group of parents in Alcalde saw benefit in what Perkins was doing and gave her free land and materials to build a church in their village. The Alcalde school opened in September 1917, under the direction of Ella Shanklin, who had been a missionary in Africa. (Both, McCurdy School.)

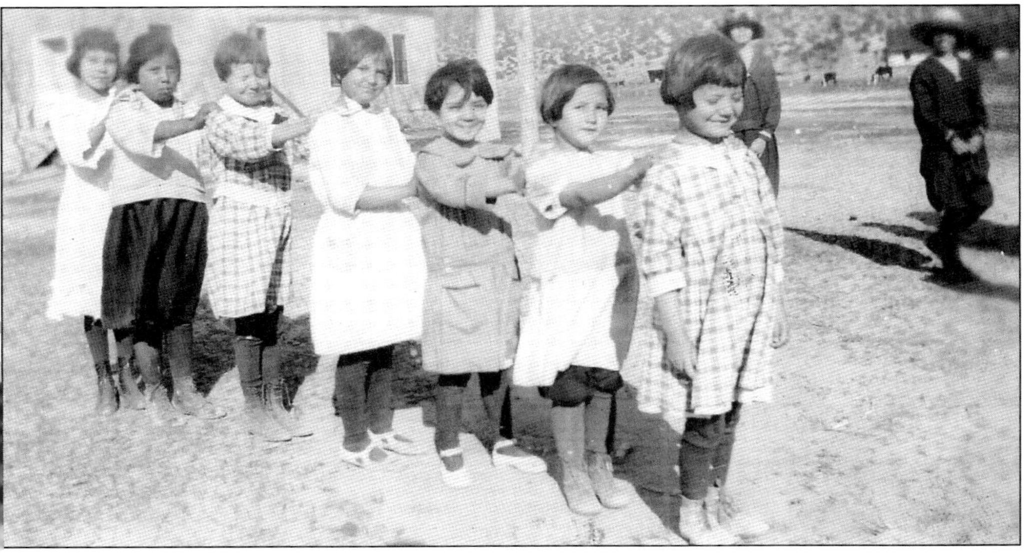

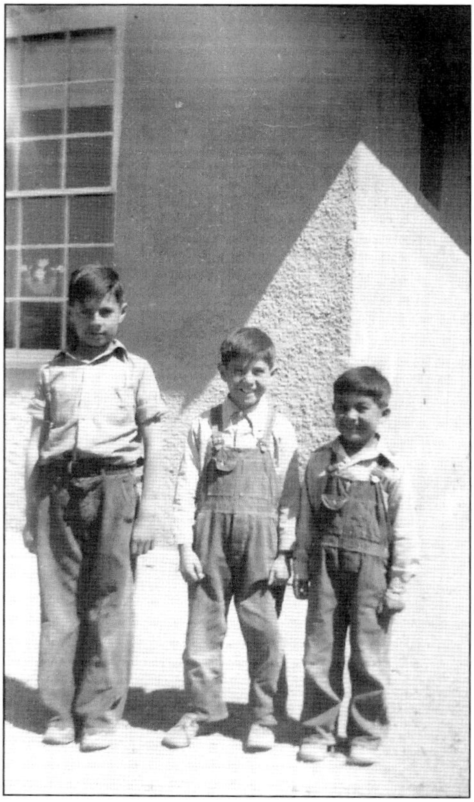

The Gutierrez brothers—three of eleven children in their family—appear in 1939 at the Methodist School in Velarde. Because the school was near their home, they could walk to it. The brother on the left, Fidel, is the husband of Angelina, of Angelina's Restaurant. Ray, in the middle, taught high school in Española for many years. Mellie Perkins's Spanish teacher at Campbell College in Kansas was a beautiful young Wellesley graduate named Edith McCurdy. She was a wonderful teacher and encouraged Miss Mellie in her efforts. But she fell gravely ill and returned to her family in Pennsylvania. After she died, her people gave Mellie Perkins enough money to build the McCurdy School in Santa Cruz. The school is shown here, as it appeared at its very beginning. (Both, McCurdy School.)

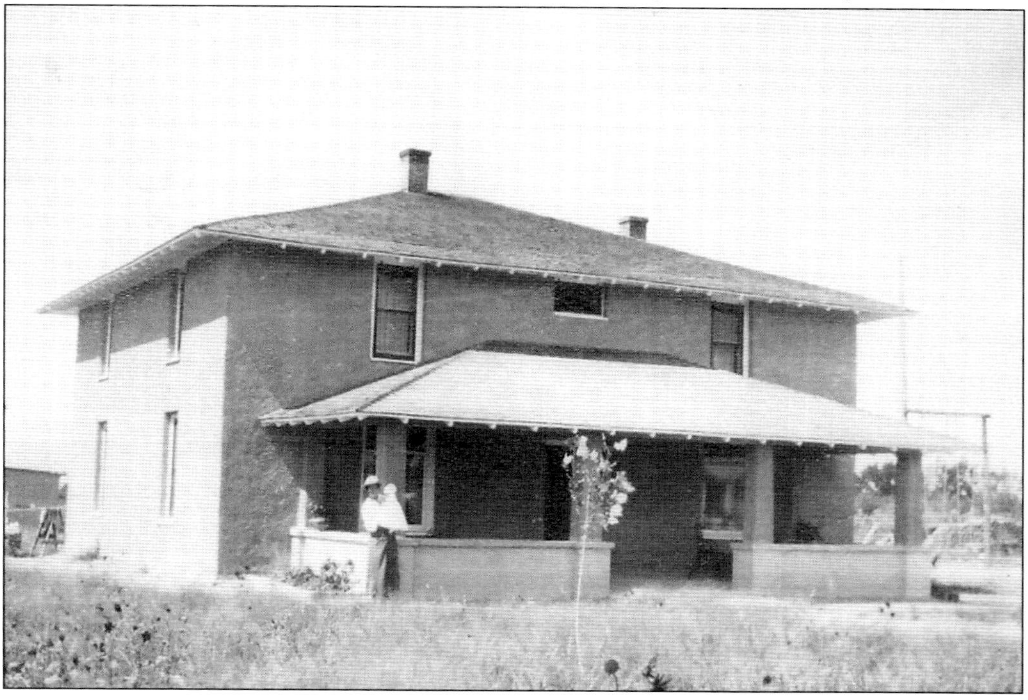

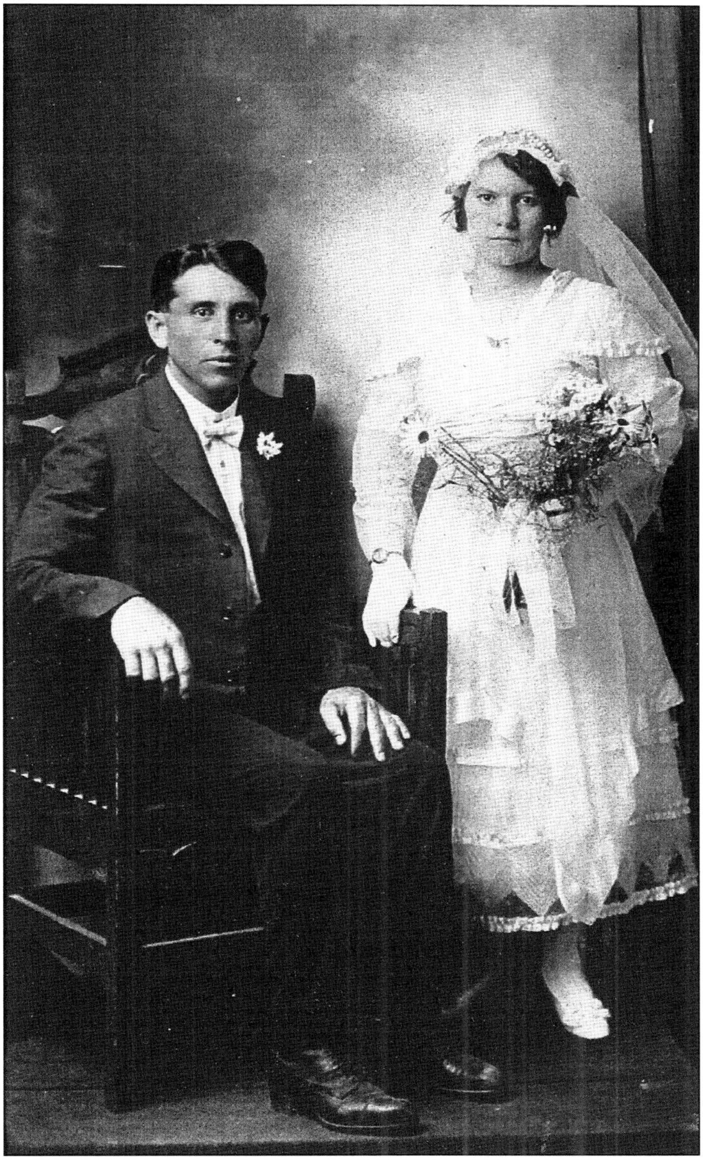

The term "normal school" does not mean *normal* in the everyday sense of the word. It comes from the French *école normale*, which refers to the setting of an educational standard. The first normal school in the United States opened in Vermont in 1823. The Spanish-American Normal School was created by the New Mexico Territorial Legislature, in preparation for statehood, to train teachers for the Spanish-speaking population. The school opened in El Rito in September 1909. Porfirio Vigil, from Guachupangue, shown with his bride, Ramona, was in the first graduating class of the Spanish-American Normal School. At that time, the people of Española Valley were just beginning to transition from a barter economy to a cash economy. George Martin, the principal of the Normal School, had to accommodate his students' needs by adjusting the school schedule to the demands of planting and harvesting. This interesting arrangement produced a situation that was conducive to the education of the unique population of the Española Valley, and in 1915, the Normal School graduated 26 elementary schoolteachers. (Martha Archuleta.)

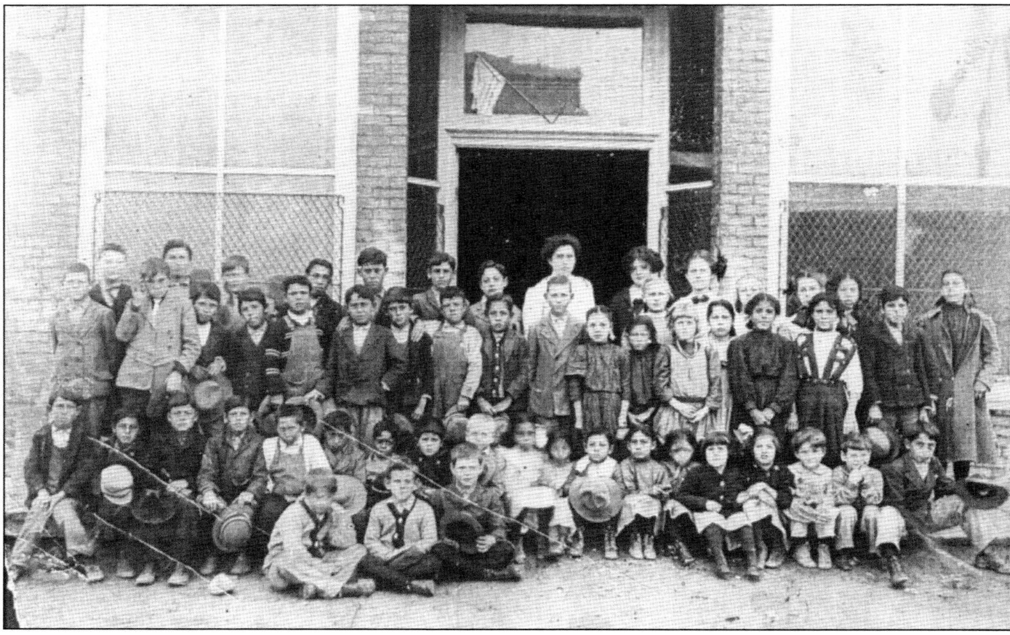

Taken in 1909, the above picture is a class portrait from the one-room Rio Arriba County Public School in the Archuleta Building at the bottom of Hill Street. Max Vigil Sr. is sitting fourth from left in the first row. At that time, only 45 percent of school-age children attended school, and the school year lasted about three months. The picture below, taken in 1935, is of a class in the newly built Española Public School at the top of Hill Street. Pictured are, from left to right, (first row) Maimie Jo Peabody, Blanch Lowe, Eulalia Quintana, Ofilia Valdez, Juanita Garcia, Florence Gonzales, Felicitas Espinosa, Susie Vigil, Virginia Drace, and Martha Jean Lee; (second row) Alex Salazar, Frank Chavez, Harvey Wise, Emilio Rodriguez, Daniel Martinez, unidentified, Jim Henry, Ignacio Martinez, Elias Trujillo, Fidel Archuleta, Manuel Vigil, Gregorio Garcia, Felix Martinez, and teacher J.C. Roybal. The historic buildings on Hill Street still stand, but they are no longer used as classrooms. (Above, Max and Frances Vigil; below, San Gabriel Historical Society.)

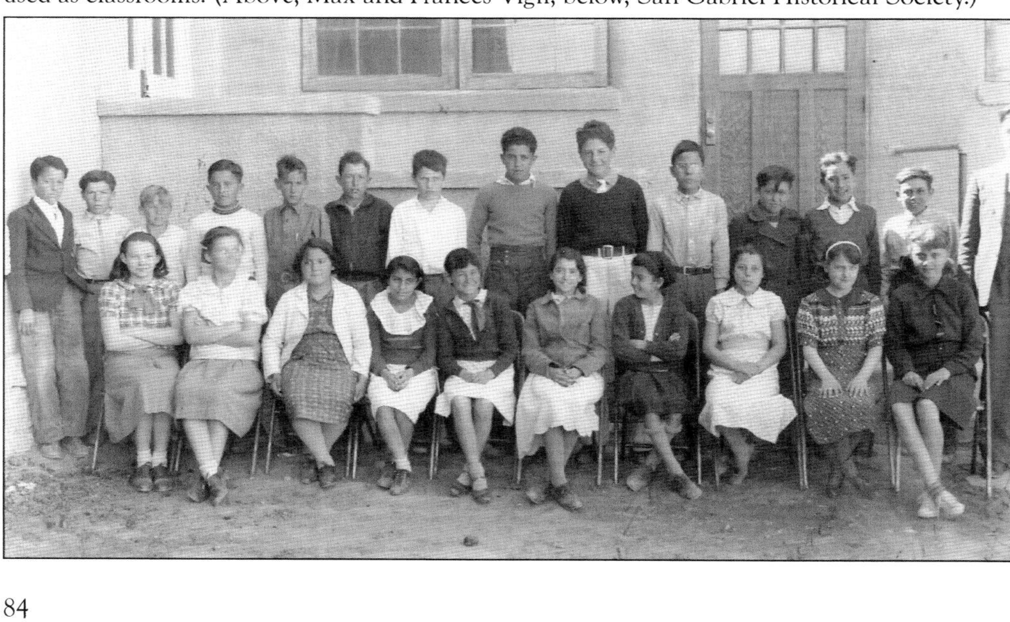

Eliseo Margarito Valdez was born in about 1880 in Tierra Amarilla, 80 miles north of Española. Valdez attended Rio Arriba County School until the age of 12. Of the 36 schools in the county at that time, only 10 taught in English; the rest taught in Spanish. Valdez was married to Josefita Montaño, and they had four children: Herminia, Ofilia, Olivama, and Eliseo Jr. When Josefita died, Eliseo moved his family to Española. Little Ofilia, sitting on her mother's lap, now lives in San Pedro. Ofilia remembers the family home at the south end of Railroad Avenue. She remembers the printing shop across the road that her father owned and managed. She would help him set the type by hand. In the bottom photograph, Eliseo looks every bit the scholar that his community considered him to be. (Both, Ofilia Quintana de Valdez.)

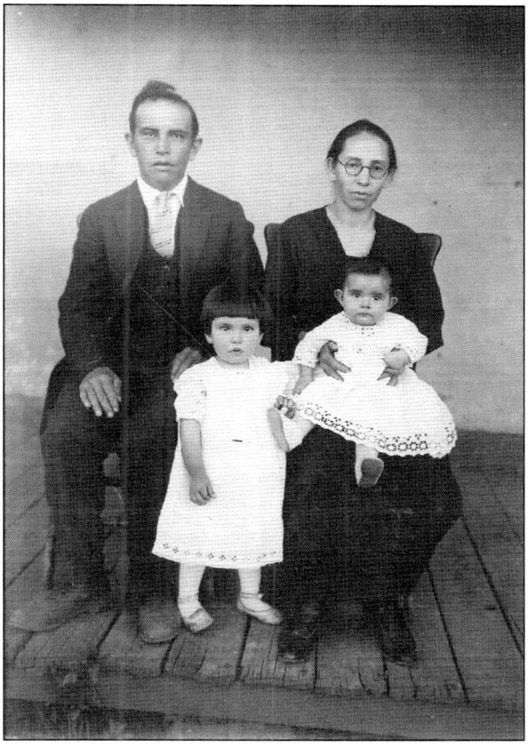

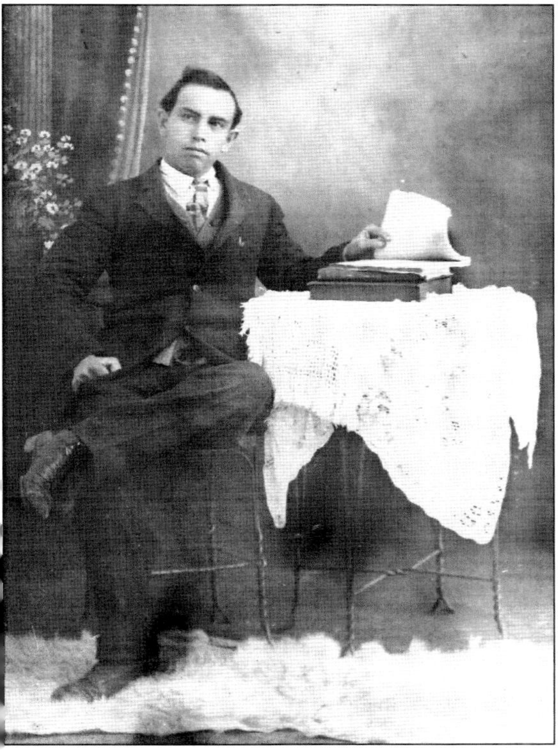

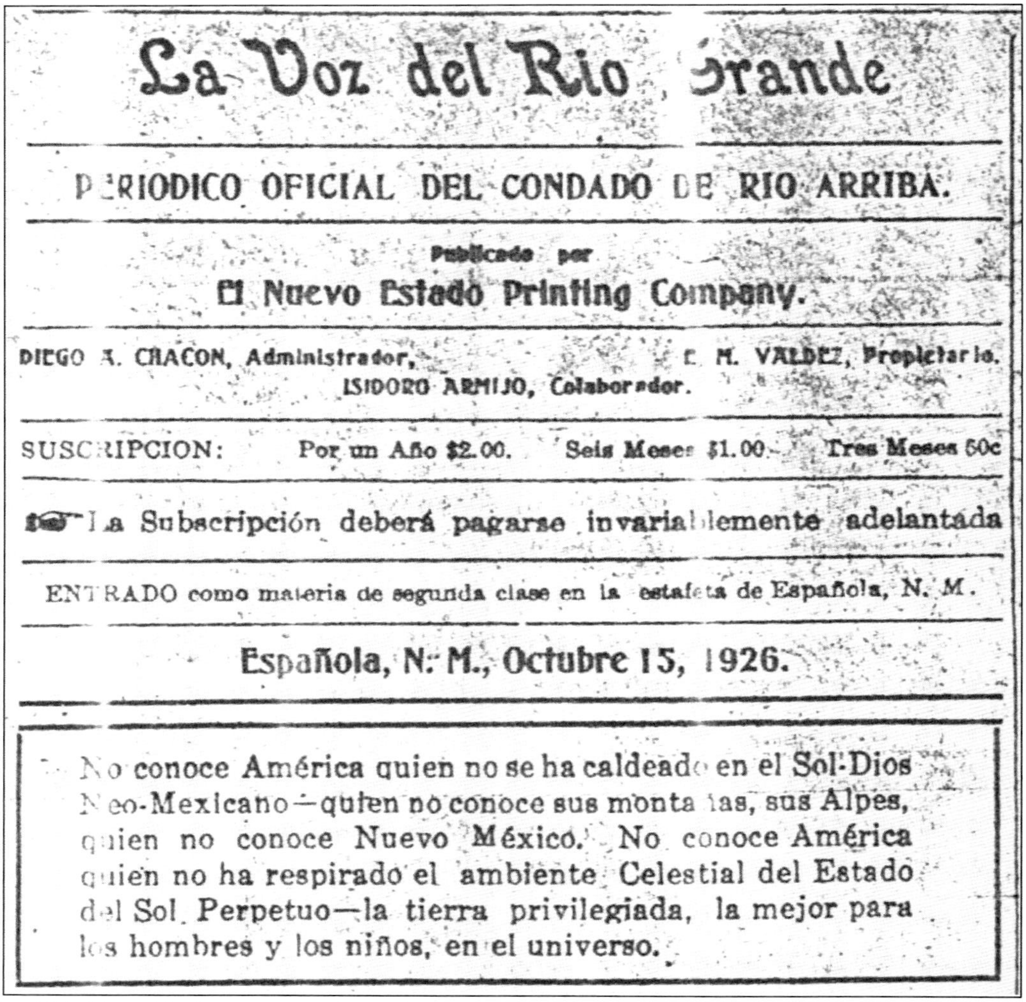
La Voz del Rio Grande

PERIODICO OFICIAL DEL CONDADO DE RIO ARRIBA.

Publicado por

El Nuevo Estado Printing Company.

DIEGO A. CHACON, Administrador, E. M. VALDEZ, Propietario.

ISIDORO ARMIJO, Colaborador.

SUSCRIPCION: Por un Año $2.00. Seis Meses $1.00. Tres Meses 60c

La Subscripción deberá pagarse invariablemente adelantada

ENTRADO como materia de segunda clase en la estafeta de Española, N. M.

Española, N. M., Octubre 15, 1926.

No conoce América quien no se ha caldeado en el Sol-Dios Neo-Mexicano—quien no conoce sus montañas, sus Alpes, quien no conoce Nuevo México. No conoce América quien no ha respirado el ambiente Celestial del Estado del Sol Perpetuo—la tierra privilegiada, la mejor para los hombres y los niños, en el universo.

In 1907, Eliseo Valdez—a printer by trade, a poet by nature, and a Republican by conviction—started the first newspaper in Rio Arriba County, *El Nuevo Estado*. When he brought his family to a new home near the river in Española, he renamed his paper *La Voz del Rio Grande*. In researching *La Voz*, the author discovered, to her surprise, that almost no paper copies exist. Shown here is the masthead of *La Voz del Rio Grande*, with Valdez's lyrical observation of the week: "To know America, one must feel the heat of the New Mexican Sun God, her mountains, her Alps. To breathe the celestial vapor of the Sun State's privileged earth is the best in all the universe for old and young." Valdez was also a musician; he played trombone in the Tierra Amarilla County Band. His home still stands at the south end of Railroad Avenue, near Cook's Hardware, and is occupied by his granddaughter. (Samuel Quintana.)

Margaret Tafoya, of Santa Clara Pueblo, was born into an ancient line of potters. She lived almost 100 years—from 1904 to 2001—and is considered one of the greatest of traditional Pueblo potters. In this old postcard, she is standing with her husband, Alcario Tafoya, and some of her remarkable wares. Pueblo pottery and design became extremely popular in America, and familiar to many thousands of travelers in such places as the La Fonda Hotel in Santa Fe and the El Rancho Hotel in Gallup. This is because an entrepreneurial English immigrant named Fred Harvey used the Pueblo artistic sensibility to create a vast hospitality empire of hotels, restaurants, and dining cars throughout the Southwest. Fred Harvey invented the concept of the chain restaurant and left an enduring mark on the cultural landscape of America. He also ran tours through Española. (Right, Leopoldo Trujillo; below, Palace of the Governors Photo Archives, photograph by T. Harmon Parkhurst.)

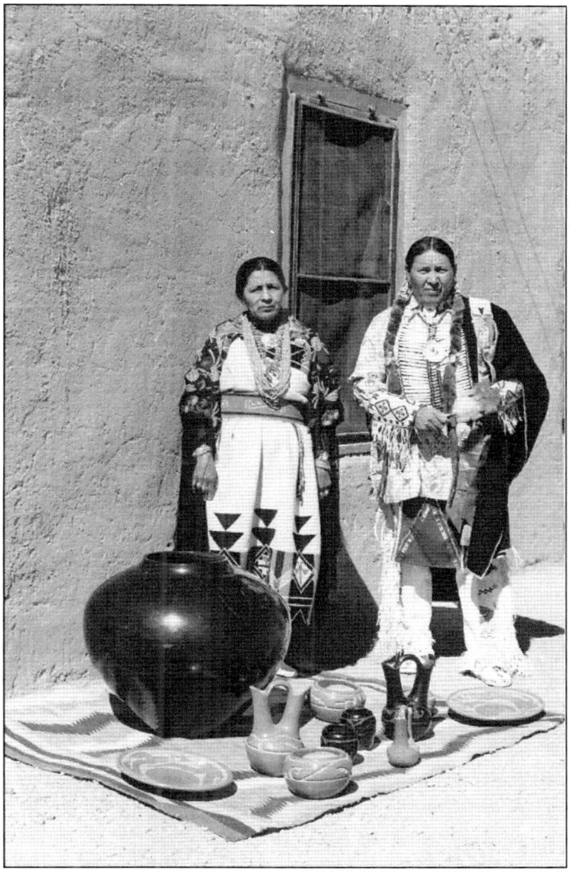

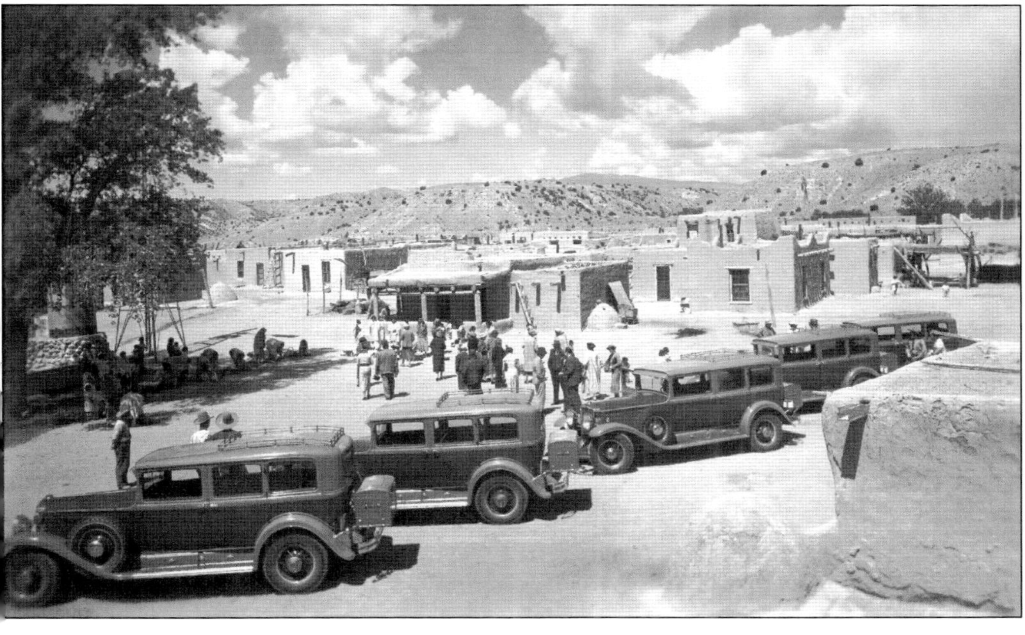

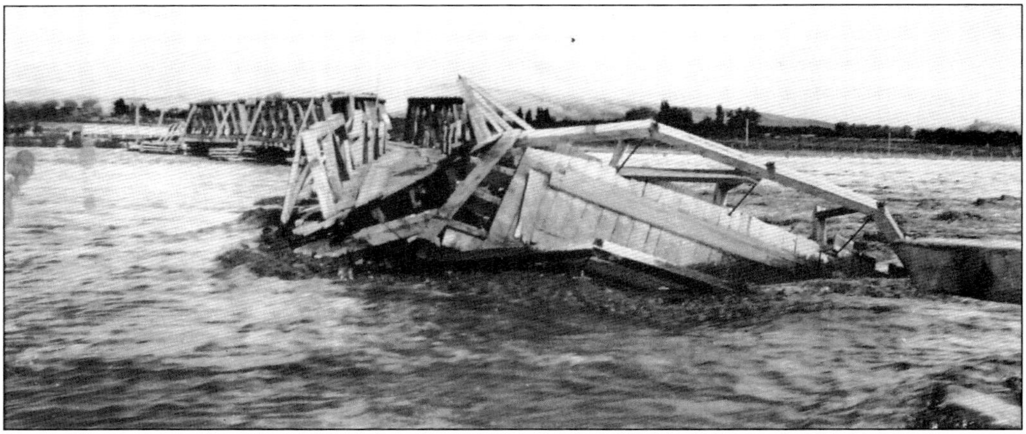

This bridge was an early attempt to span the Rio Grande. In 1920, the river flooded and swept the bridge downstream, as frequently happened with trestle bridges in those days. Española's Middle Bridge was built on this spot in 1940. Far more than a bridge was being overwhelmed. Indeed, an entire way of life was about to change in the face of a huge constellation of forces. A strangely gifted man, Policarpio Valencia, was coming to the end of a life that had been lived entirely in the old patterns. He was born in 1856, but beyond that, almost nothing is known about him except what he left behind: a few astonishing patchwork-embroideries on sheets, bedspreads, and clothing—magical, incantatory, and visionary things. Unique and unclassifiable, they incorporated both imagery and the written word, a vanishing universe encoded in art. (Above, San Gabriel Historical Society; below, Museum of International Folk Art.)

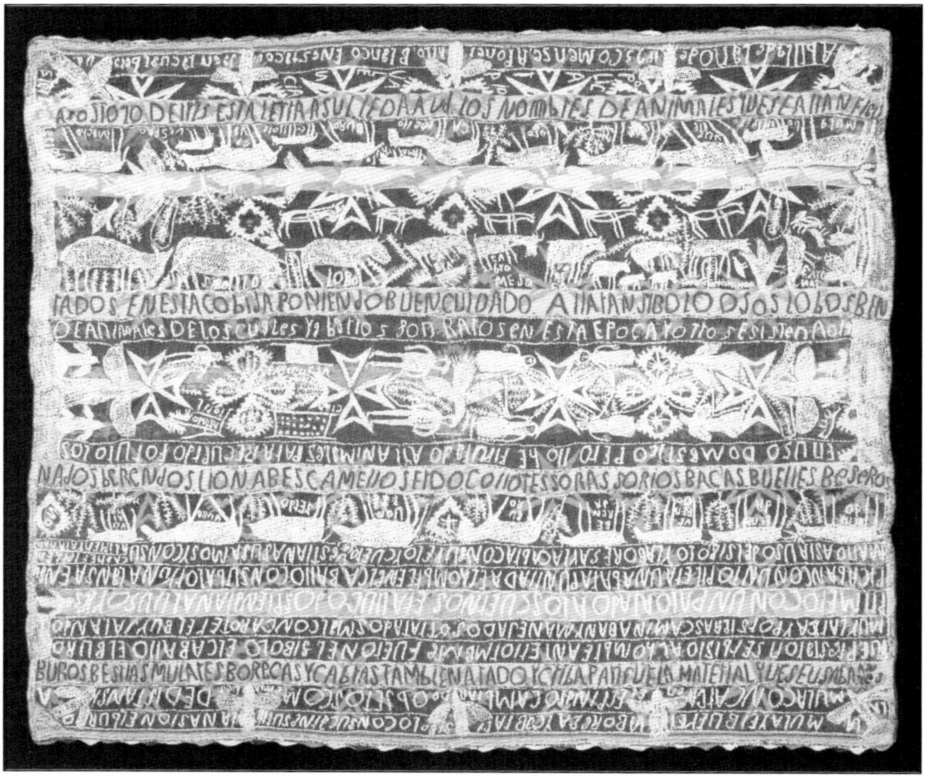

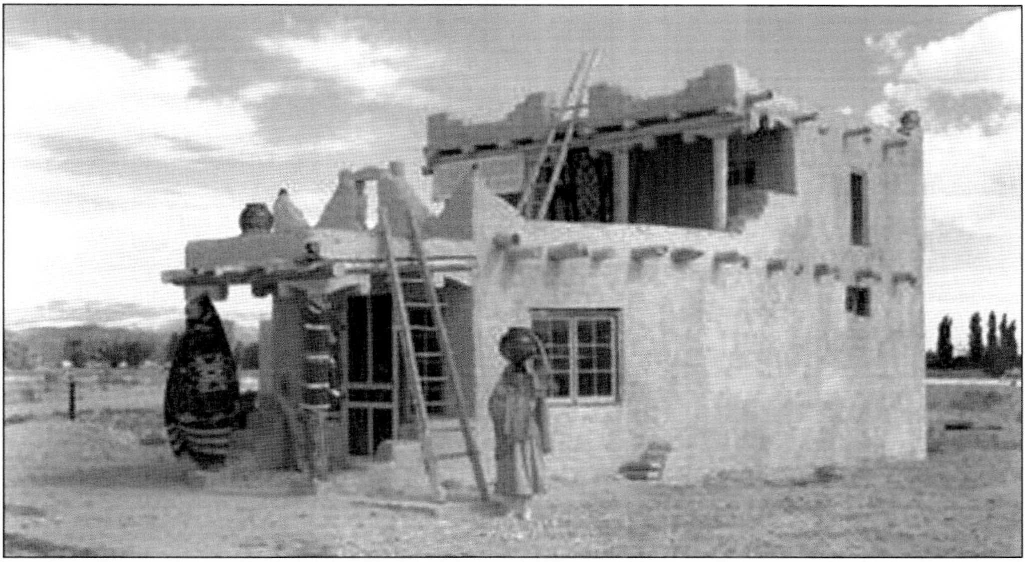

In 1929, Esquipula De Aguero "E.D." Trujillo built the Chimayo Trading Post at the Y in Española. Born and raised in Chimayo, and possessing a fine artistic sense, he filled his store with Indian pottery, clothing, weavings, and jewelry. In those days in Chimayo, many families made a living by weaving. Trujillo contracted his neighbors to produce rugs, vests, and jackets, which he sold. His store was unique in the region, and attracted many visitors, including tourists from far-off places. In 1939, a devastating fire destroyed the Chimayo Trading Post. At that time, Española did not have its own fire department, so fire fighters and equipment had to be called in from Santa Fe. During the blaze, two firemen were trapped in the basement of the burning building, but survived. (Both, Leopoldo Trujillo.)

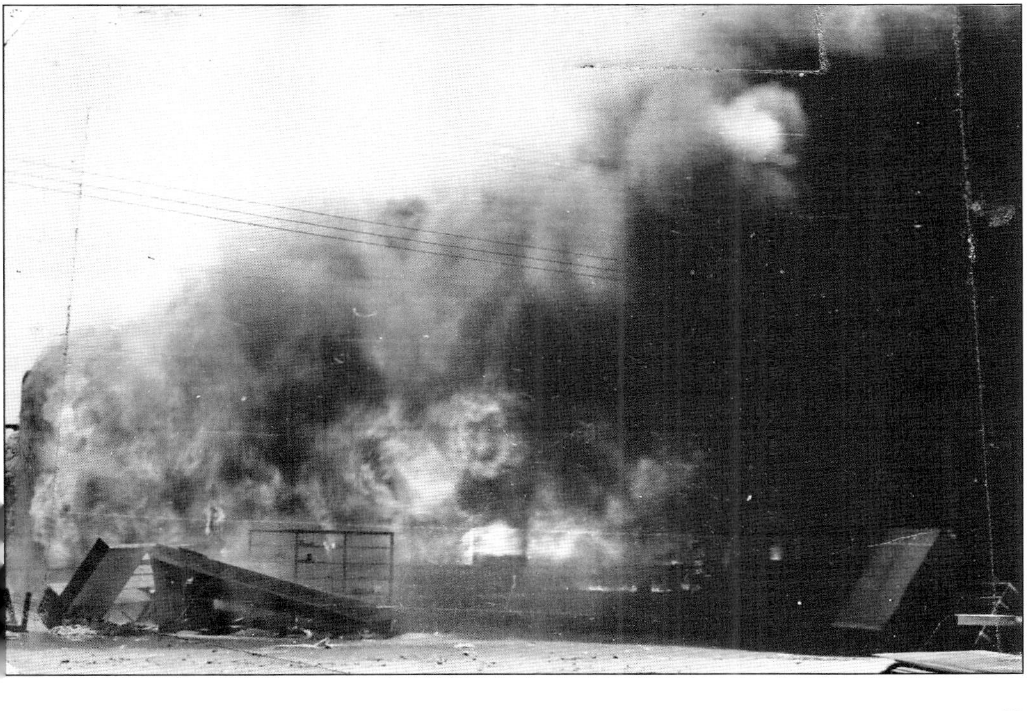

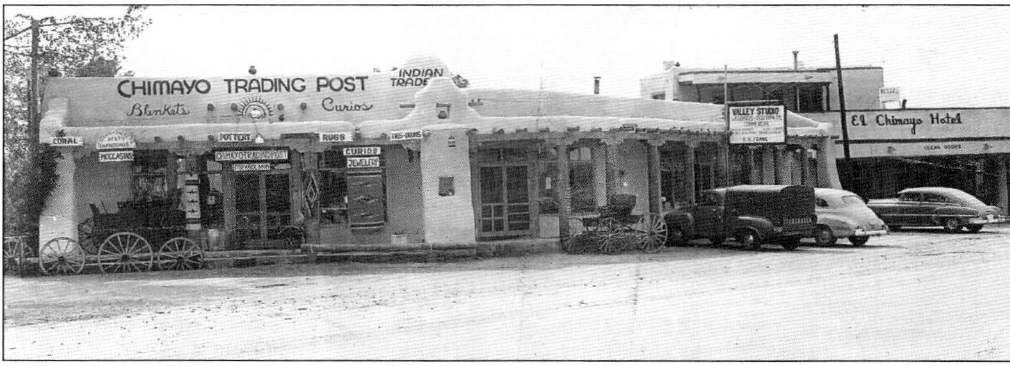

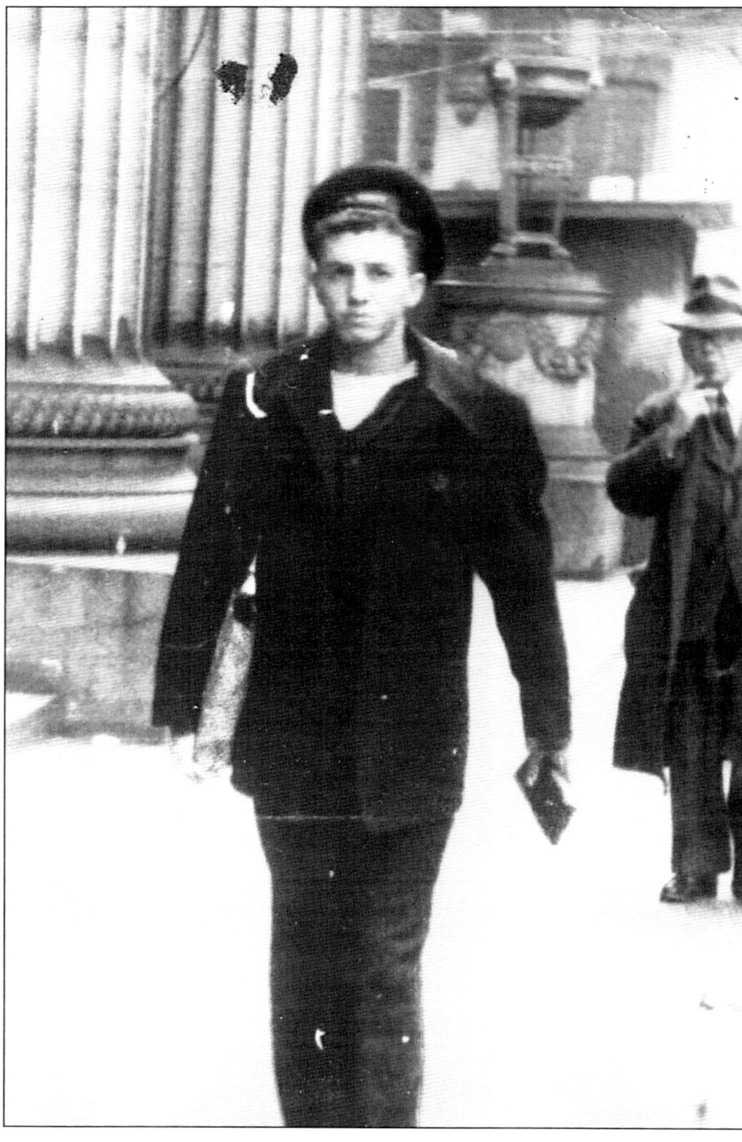

The Trujillo family rebuilt the Trading Post, and by the late 1940s, it was a thriving business again. In addition to the store, the Hotel Chimayo had been added to the property, along with living space for the family. E.D. Trujillo also ran a bar in the back. The Trujillos' youngest son, Leopoldo, left the Española Valley to attend the Naval Academy School in Bainbridge Maryland. He appears in uniform at left, a country mouse loving the big city. He also enrolled in culinary classes at Maxim's of Paris in New York. After that, he worked for Pan Am Airways for many years. (Both, Leopoldo Trujillo.)

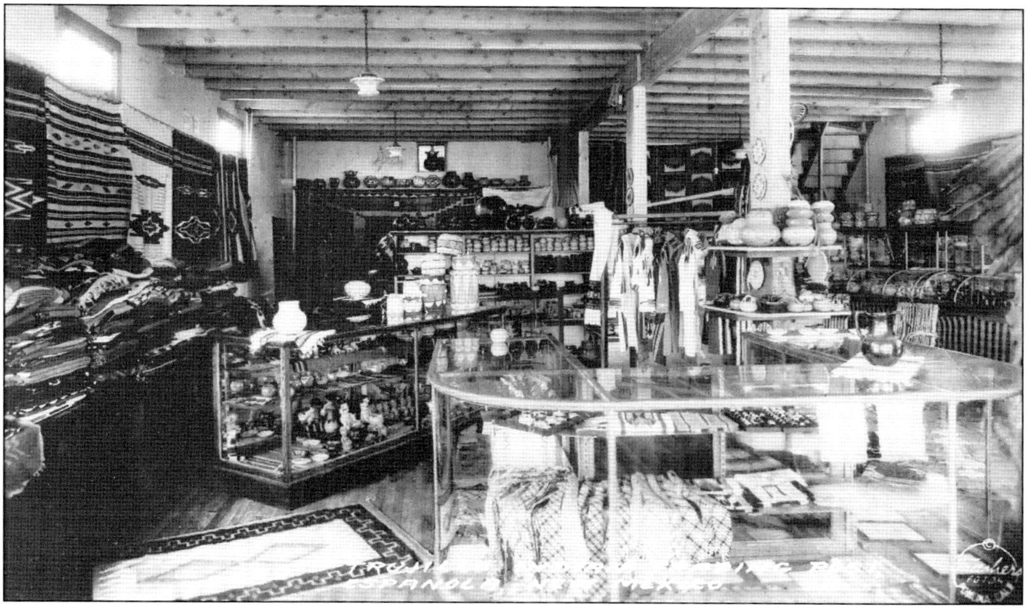

E.D. Trujillo set a high standard with the Chimayo Trading Post. Another store that the family ran in Pojoaque did well, but had to close when the Pojoaque Valley Schools leased the property from Pojoaque Pueblo for a new elementary school in the late 1960s. Today, that property is the site of the Pueblo's City of Gold Casino. (Leopoldo Trujillo.)

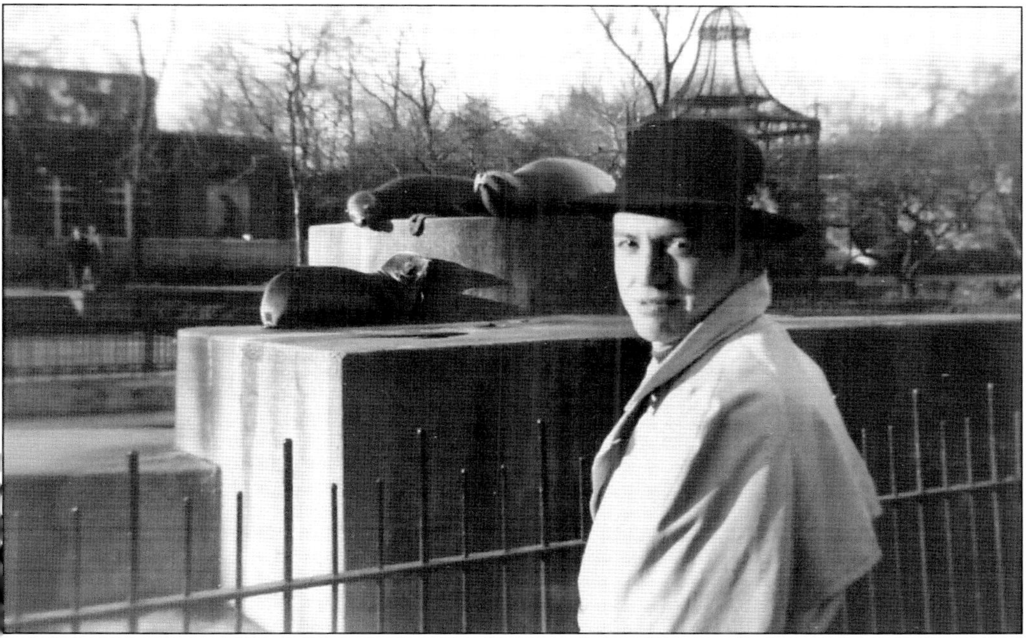

Leopoldo Trujillo lived in New York City for 30 years. He traveled widely and led a very exciting and interesting life, witnessing things many people of that time could only read about, like these seals at the Central Park Zoo. In the 1990s, he retired from Pan Am and came back to Española. Today, he takes care of his father's Trading Post, and can be found there most any day of the week. (Leopoldo Trujillo.)

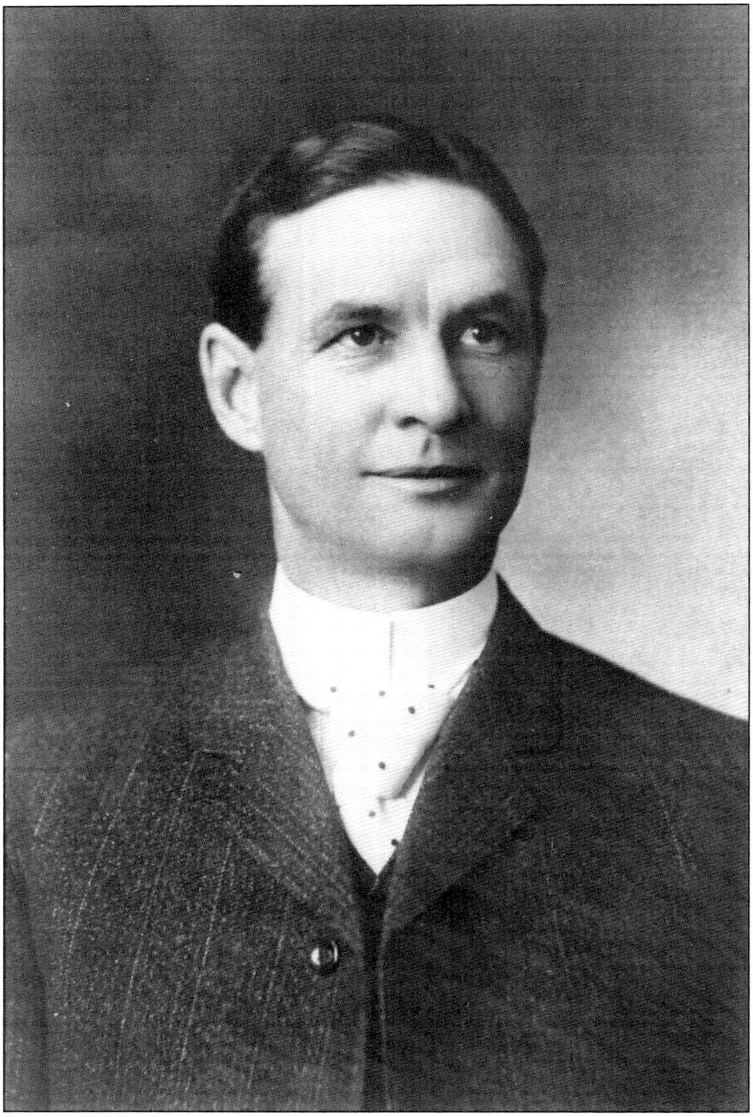

The Bond Company was established in 1883, when G.W. and Frank Bond, brothers from Canada, bought out the inventory of Scott & Whitehead, the commissary for the Chili Line's Española Depot. They built corrals and chutes near the depot for shipping livestock. They bought large tracts of land, including the Ramon Vigil Grant and the Baca Location in the Valle Caldera. The Bonds built an empire based on sheep. Their herds numbered in the thousands. The Bond & Nohl store, which carried everything for the home, including groceries, extended easy credit to their *partidarios*, who sharecropped herds of Bond-owned sheep. The store was located at the site of the present-day Convento. (Both, San Gabriel Historical Society.)

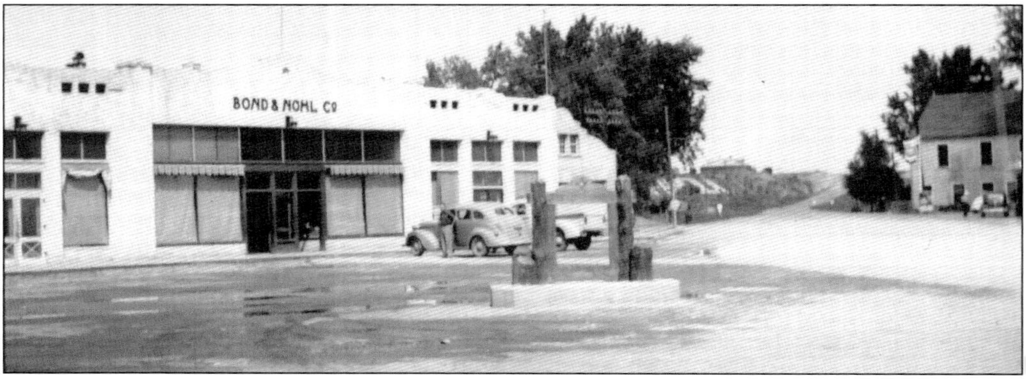

From 1909 to 1926, the Santa Barbara Tie & Pole Company harvested 16 million railroad ties from the Mora Grant, above Embudo, to feed the appetite of the Atchison, Topeka & Santa Fe Railroad. Ties were milled year round and held at the mouth of the Embudo River, until released in spring to sail downriver, past Española, to a place called Boom. From there, they were hauled out of the canyon and taken to Albuquerque. The Hallack & Howard Lumber Company set up a camp near La Madera, where they cut lumber that helped build Denver. For 11 years, 300 men were employed by the company. Shown below with their tools is a tough crew of tree-cutters, who worked for Hallack & Howard in the early 1900s. The man on the left is Desiderio Vigil, the father of Wilfredo Vigil. (Right, Palace of the Governors Photo Archives, photograph by T. Harmon Parkhurst; below, Wilfredo Vigil.)

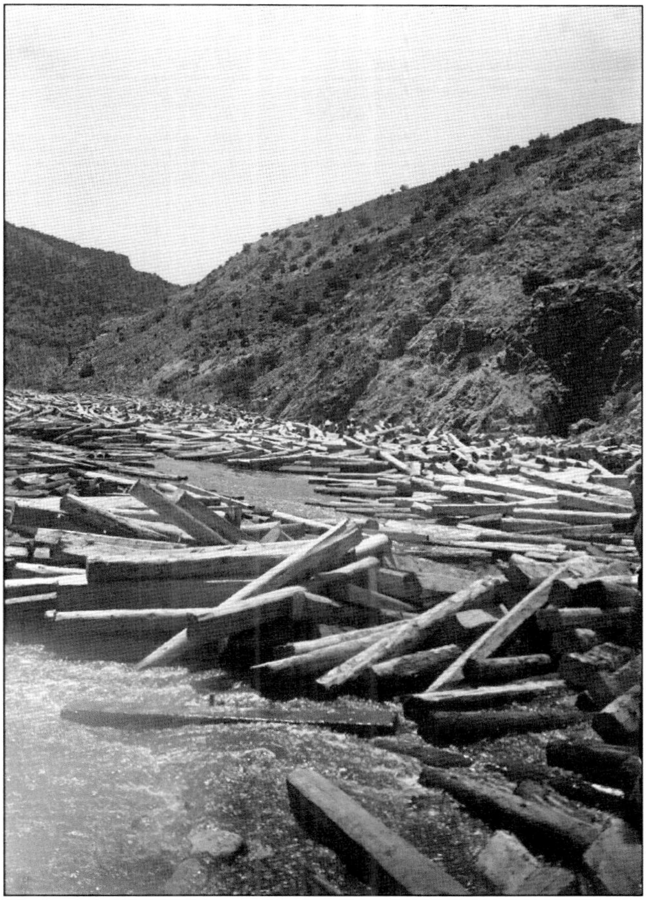

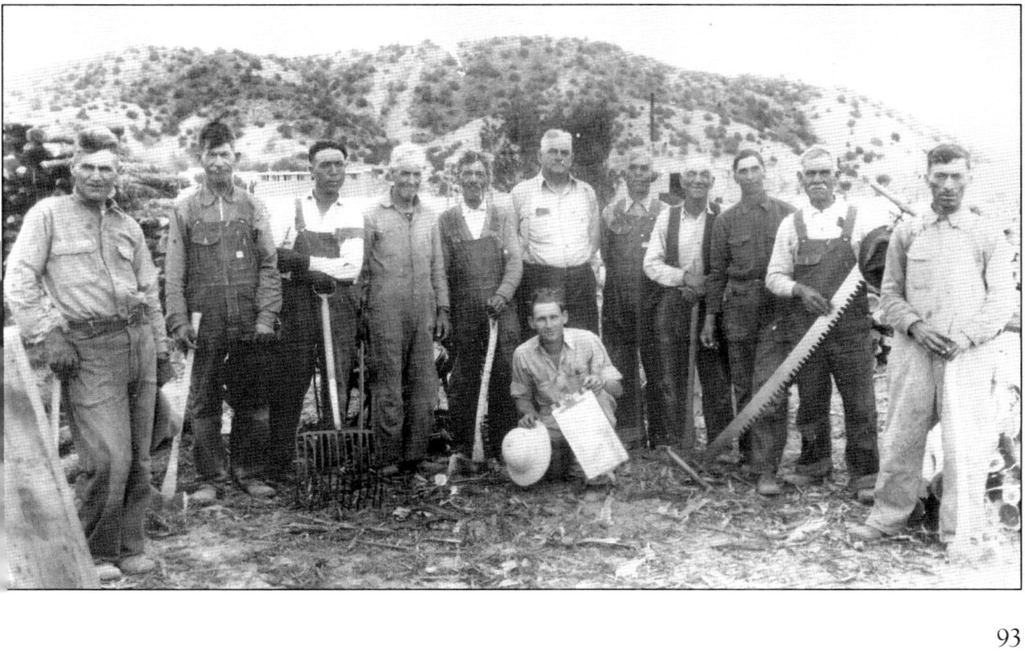

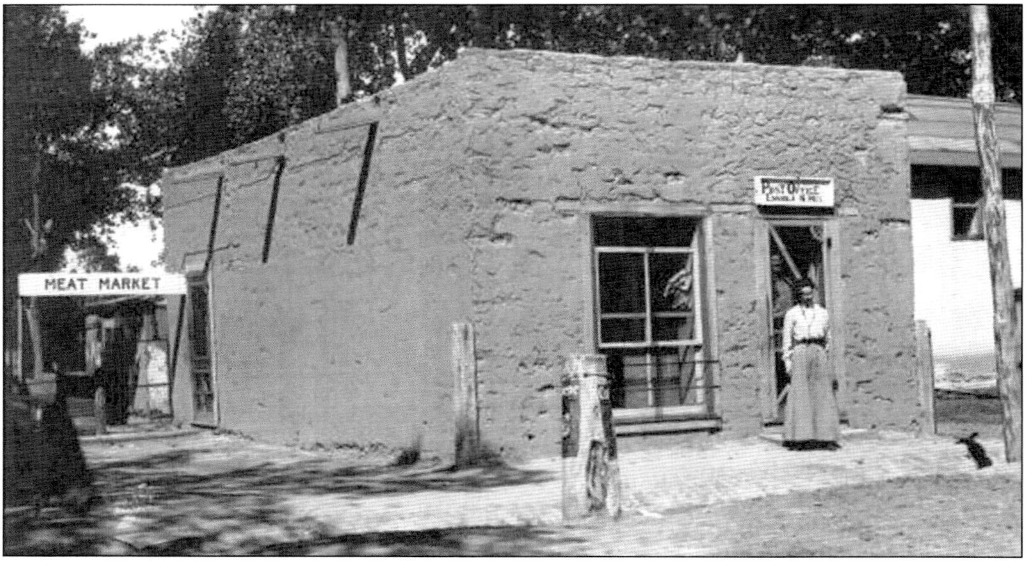

As Española grew into a town, the scenery changed. Española's first adobe post office was on tree-lined Oñate Street, across from present-day Cook's Hardware. William P. Cook bought his store from the postmaster, who was also Española's first mayor, Frank Frankenburger. Originally from Kansas, Frankenburger settled in Española in 1903. He worked for Pollard & Company General Store before he bought it and changed the name to Española Mercantile. In 1916, Frankenburger started the Española State Bank, remembered by many as Brashar Bank. During his tenure as mayor, from 1925 to 1928, Frankenburger approved electricity and telephone franchises for the village and helped establish the Santa Cruz Irrigation District. (Both, San Gabriel Historical Society.)

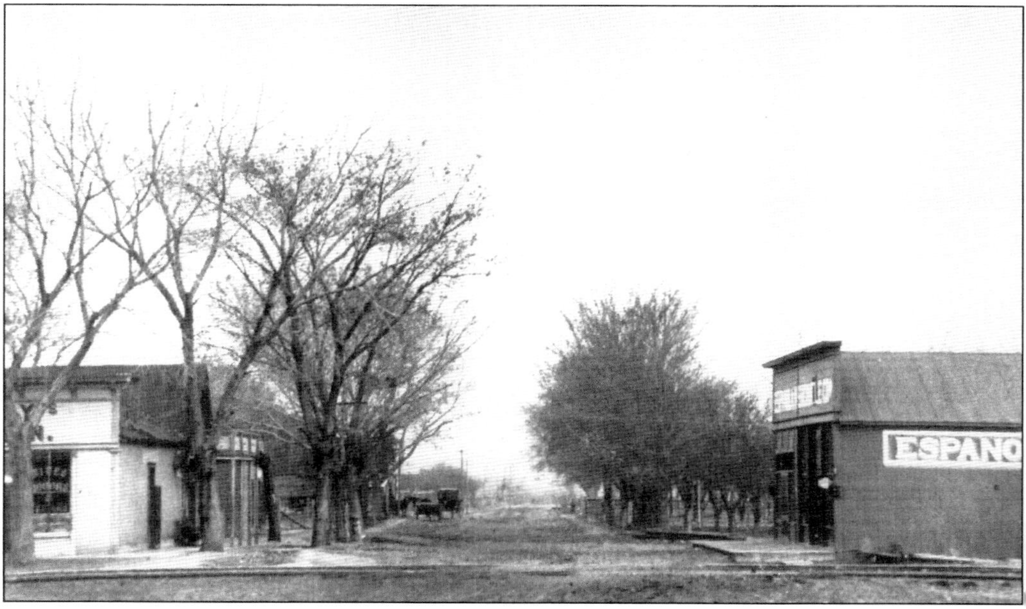

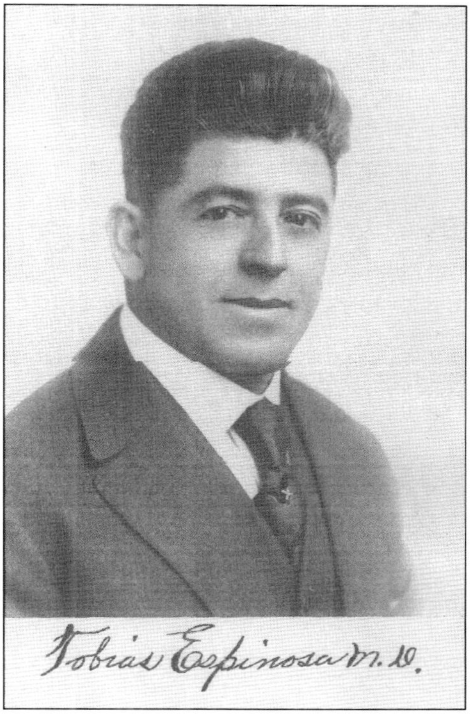

Española's second mayor was Dr. Tobias Espinosa (right), a beloved man who served three terms from 1927 to 1933. Dr. Espinosa was born in Colorado and spent his first year practicing medicine as the Chili Line surgeon in Chama. He took his practice to Albuquerque, San Francisco, the Navy submarine service, and Belen, before settling in Española. Dr. Espinosa continued to practice medicine in the Valley, and he delivered 6,000 babies. Dr. Espinosa was chosen to play Oñate in the 1934 Fiesta. Española's third mayor was Diego Salazar, shown below with his bride, Sarafina, in 1909. He was from Corral de Piedra and served as mayor for 16 years. A self-taught scholar, Salazar could type and was able to write letters and prepare documents for fellow villagers. With Peres Quintana, he operated a grocery store that was eventually sold to J.W. Owens. (Right, San Gabriel Historical Society; below, Martha Archuleta.)

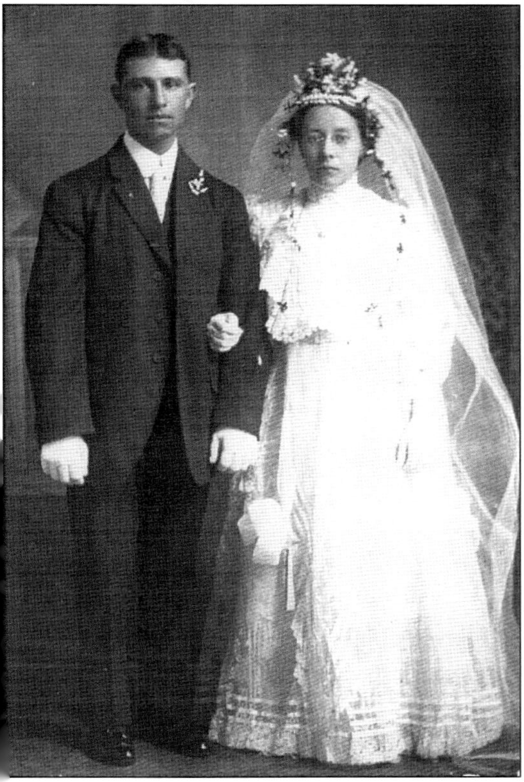

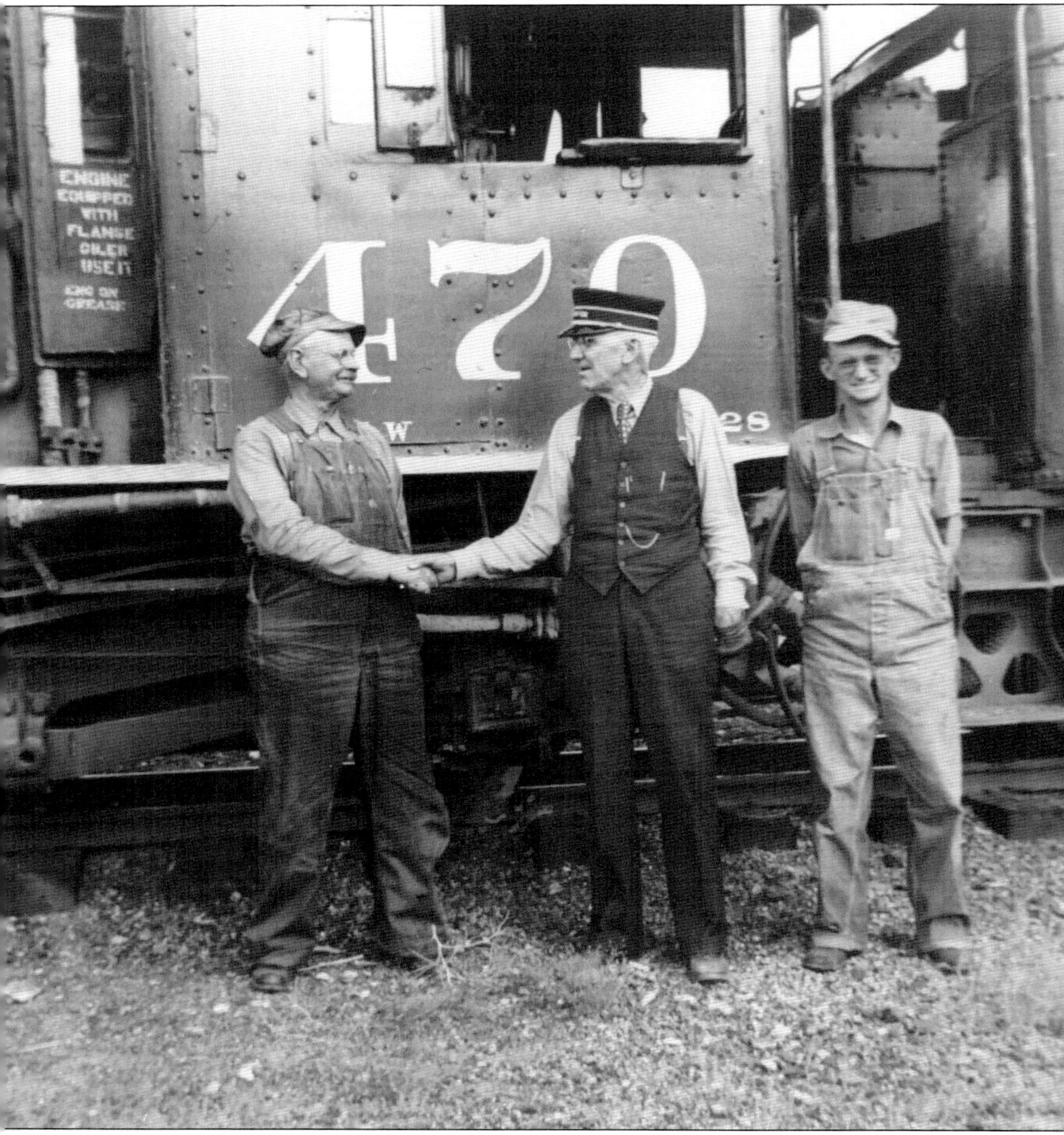

Conductor Willis shakes hands with engineer C.R. Arnell and fireman Roy J. Brown on September 1, 1941. The Chili Line is over. Trucking, faster and cheaper than the train, had cut into the rail's dominance and reassigned much of rail travel to the tourist industry. During the previous summer, news had spread through the Valley that the end of the Chili Line was coming. Engine No. 470 chugged into Antonito for the last time. Cleanup crews began removing track. Train engines were sold to the Army or scrapped. An era had ended. In three months, the United States would be at war. The Manhattan Project would soon call upon the Valley for support and discretion. (Palace of the Governors Photo Archives.)

Five

PROJECT Y

When the author's mother, Lydia Trujillo de Roybal, was a child, her father, Procopio, would make a little house in the bed of his Chevy pickup truck. He would lay down rugs to make a floor, like the one in their home in Pojoaque; he would secure some benches for sitting and make a roof with a canvas tarp tied to the *barandales*. Lydia and her siblings were packed safely into the back, Grandma and Grandpa rode up front, and the Roybal clan would head up La Culebrilla, the snaking road that wound up past Los Alamos to El Valle Grande.

The family would spend a week at the San Antonio Hot Springs, where Grandma Toñita and the girls washed blankets in the stream, and Grandpa stayed busy with the boys, fishing and making camp for the family. At week's end, they all headed back down to the Valley, refreshed and ready for another summer of hard work.

The land the Roybal family camped on has an interesting history. It was part of a 34,000-acre parcel that in 1742 had been granted by the viceroy of Spain to Pedro Sanchez, a loyal soldier. Some generations afterwards, in 1851, a Sanchez heir sold the land to Jose Ramon Vigil for a few cows and some cash. Sold again, to a priest, in the 1880s, the Vigil grant changed hands often. At one time, it was owned by Española businessman Frank Bond, and later by Ashley Pond, the man who would build a boys' school in Los Alamos.

By the time Lydia Trujillo de Roybal was a teenager, the land would be in the hands of Project Y, otherwise known as the Manhattan Project. In one short year, in the secret labs of Los Alamos, the mysteries of the universe would unfold, spectacularly and terribly—and World War II would end.

The author's grandfather, if he could see how things turned out, would remove his hat, scratch his head respectfully, and say, as he often did, "*Dios es muy grande*." God is quite large.

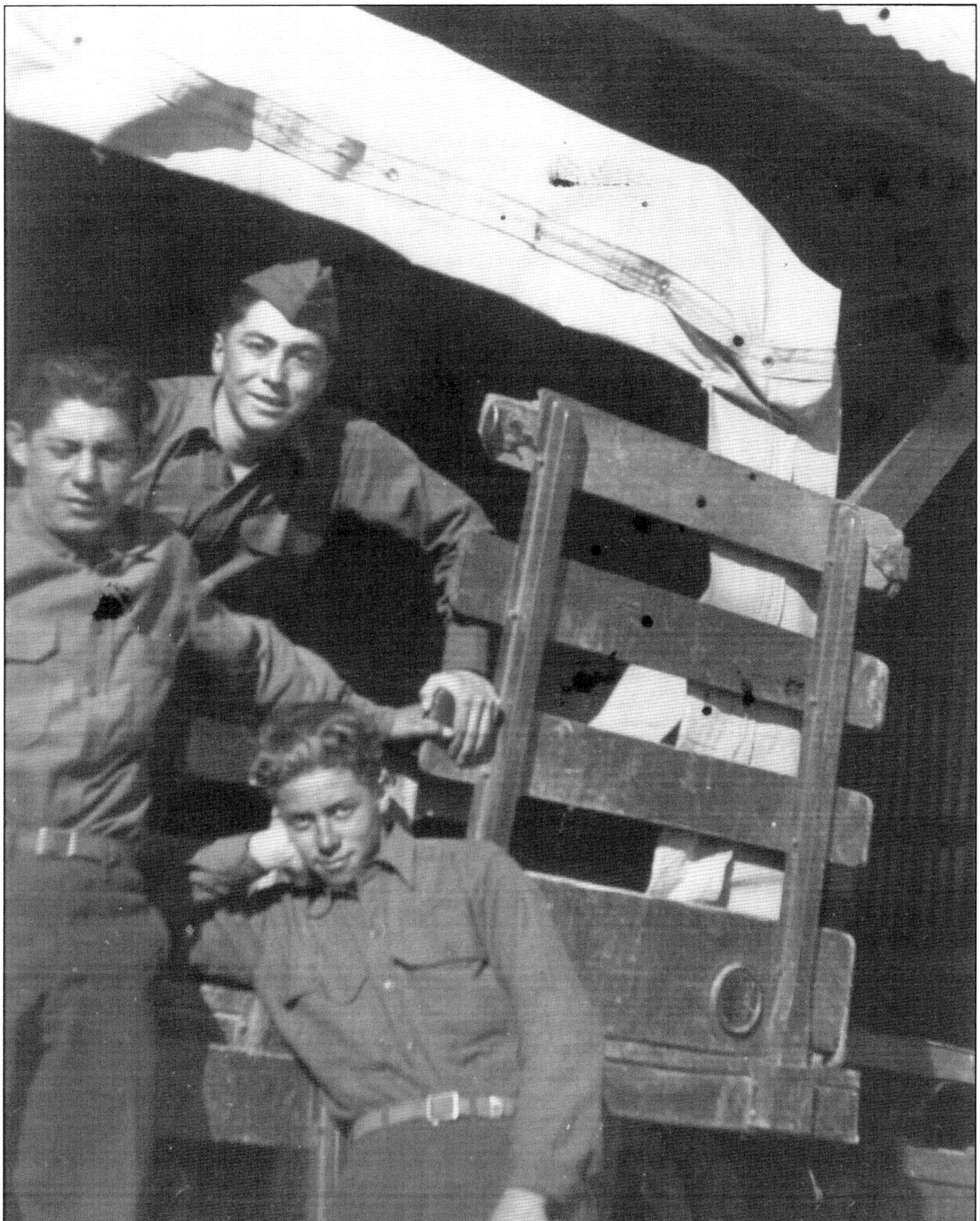

The Civilian Conservation Corps (CCC) was a New Deal program that stimulated local economies and provided jobs during the Great Depression. Seen here at a CCC camp in Bandelier National Monument in 1939 is Amadeo Quintana, from San Pedro, then 21 years old. He earned $30 a month. By the time the CCC ended in 1942, at the start of World War II, 32,000 men had worked on New Mexico's state parks. (Jonathan Quintana.)

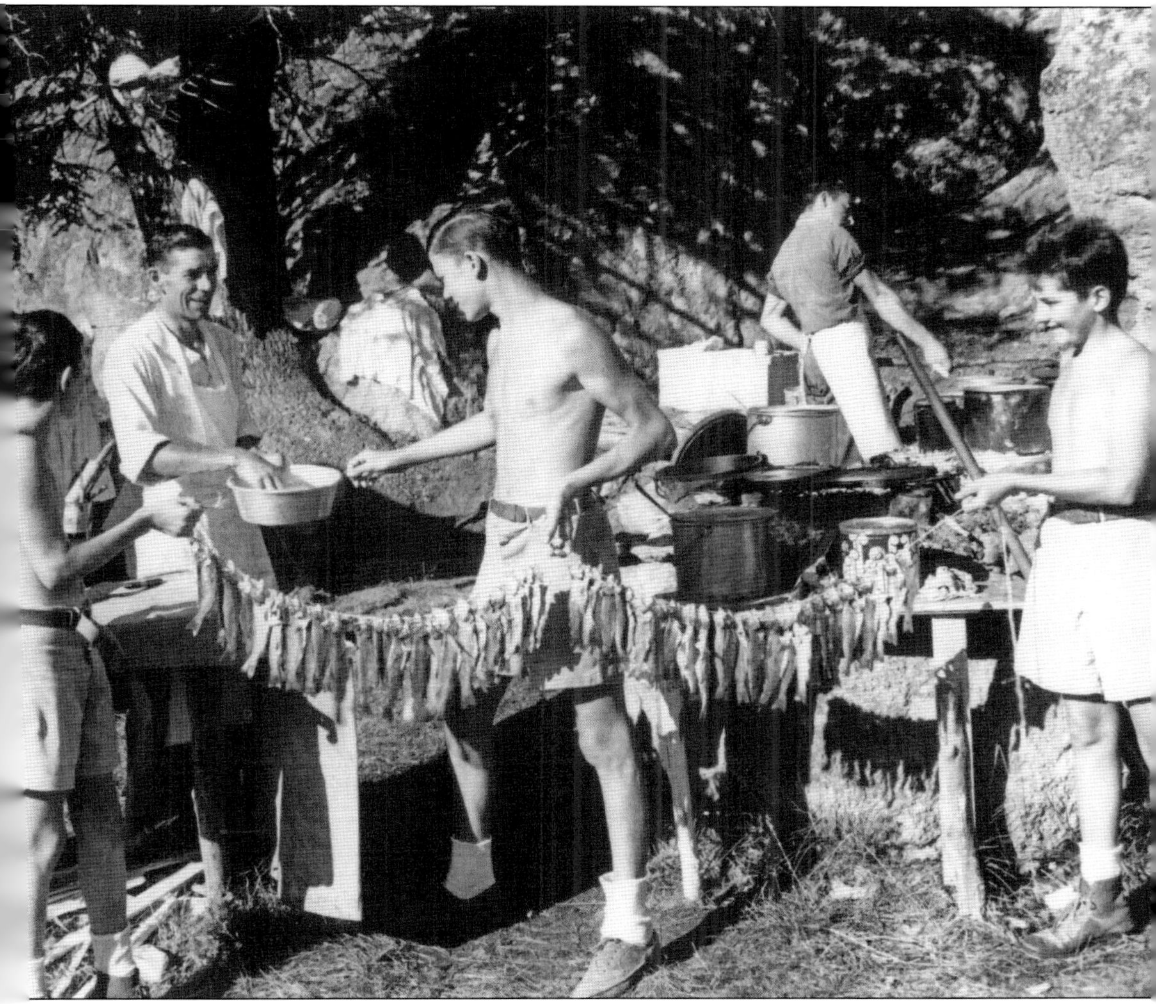

If something needed doing at the Los Alamos Ranch School, the man most often called upon was Bences Gonzales, who lived in a cabin on the Pajarito Plateau with his wife, Ernestine, a descendent of generations of Los Alamos homesteaders. The Gonzales home had hot water, indoor plumbing, and a bathtub—luxuries almost unheard of in those times. They even had a car and, therefore, were considered wealthy by their Valley relatives. Gonzales ran the Los Alamos Trading Post for the school, where he traded Stetson hats to local men for lambs. Once, Gonzales went clear across the Valley to Ojo Sarco to find a hunting guide. He brought the man and his helper back to the school. That night, after everyone had gone to bed, Gonzales heard talking from one of the rooms. Peeking through the window, he saw one of the men from Ojo Sarco standing on a chair, trying to blow out the light bulb, a thing neither of them had ever seen before. "*Jale el mecate*," Gonzales told them. "Pull the string." (Los Alamos Historical Museum Photo Archives, photograph by T. Harmon Parkhurst.)

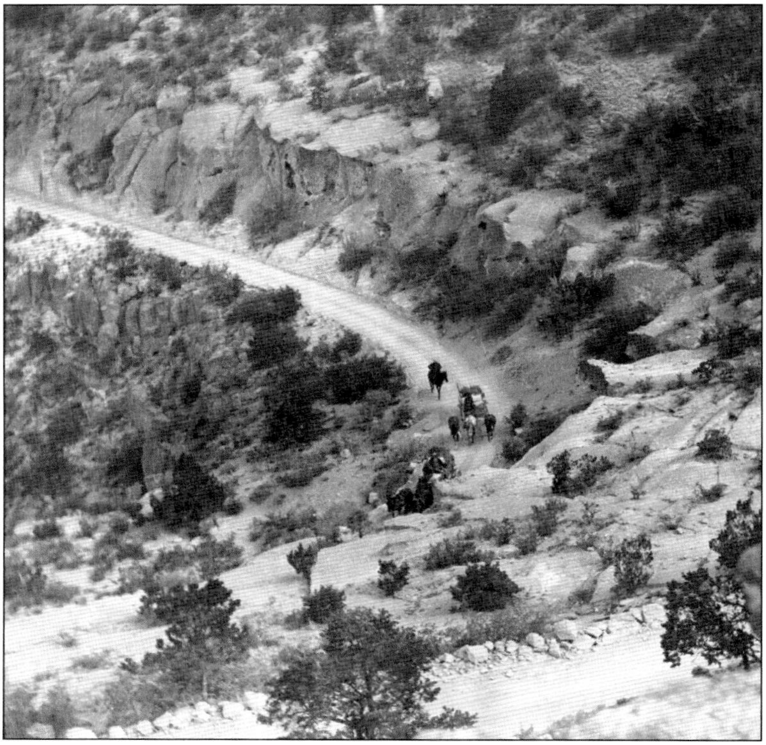

The Pajarito Plateau was opened for homesteading in 1906, and some Valley people took advantage of the Homestead Act to acquire land up on the Rio Frijoles, as cash-crop farming was replacing subsistence farming. Each spring, Bences Gonzales's father in law, Victor Romero, rode to Los Alamos with his family in a horse-drawn wagon, laden with supplies. In 1915, the Romeros harvested 2,100 pounds of beans and 1,800 pounds of corn. (Los Alamos Historical Museum Photo Archives.)

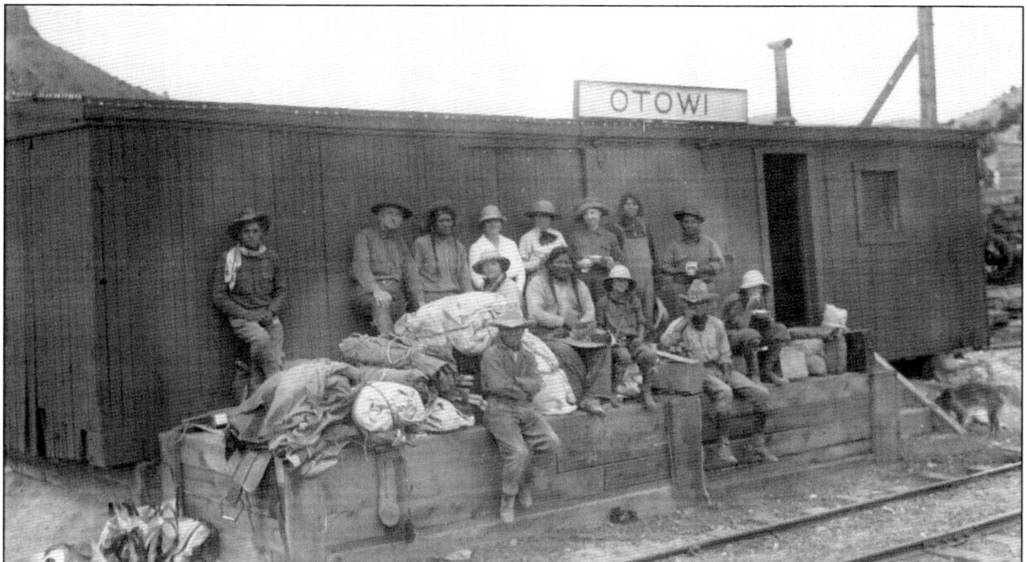

Archeologist Edgar L. Hewett is seen here with Santiago Naranjo, governor of Santa Clara Pueblo. Hewett opposed the Forest Service's plan to increase the habitation of the Pajarito by granting more grazing rights. Hewett knew that important remains of pre-Columbian settlements would be destroyed if the Forest Service continued its policy of private expansion into public lands. Dr. Hewett was the first director of the Museum of New Mexico in Santa Fe. (Palace of the Governors Photo Archives.)

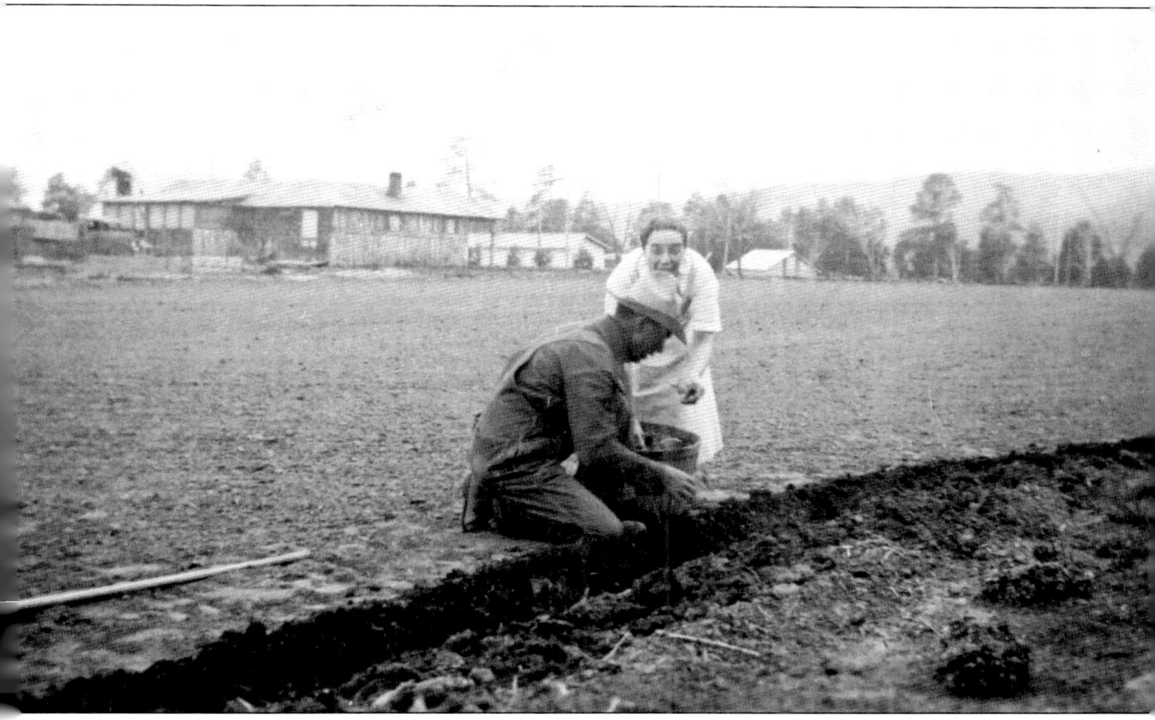

Bences Gonzales and Adolfo Montoya were as close as brothers. Montoya and his wife, Elaisa, established a homestead on the Pajarito Plateau around 1918. Adolfo Montoya was a meticulous man who grew magnificent gardens. He and Elaisa are shown working their land, which adjoined the Los Alamos Ranch School. Adolfo was the school gardener; his main job was to provide fruit, vegetables, and cut flowers. Whatever was left, he would give to his neighbors. His daughter Margaret Caperton remembered her father making big barrels of sauerkraut in their cellar and bringing home deer that he had hunted. A man of incredible energy, Montoya also maintained a small herd of cows and had even wanted to open a meat processing plant on the plateau. After the school was condemned for the Manhattan Project and closed by the federal government, the Montoyas and the other Pajarito Plateau families relocated to the Valley. A.J. Connell would often visit with the Montoyas at their eight-acre farm in San Pedro. Adolfo Montoya was a pallbearer at A.J.'s funeral. (Los Alamos Historical Museum Photo Archives.)

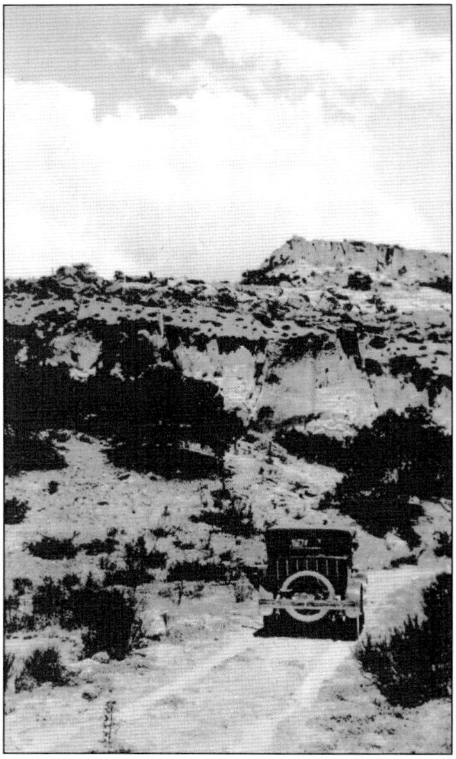

In 1942, the federal government created a small, highly secretive organization of scientists with a mission to develop the atomic bomb. The project chief was a man who had spent boyhood summers in the thin dry air and sunshine of New Mexico, J. Robert Oppenheimer, a physics professor at the University of California, Berkeley. He chose the Pajarito Plateau for the urgent undertaking that would change the world completely, known as Project Y. The new residents of Los Alamos rode the train to Lamy and then checked in at 109 East Palace Avenue in Santa Fe, where all the details were worked out for their entry into the "Secret City." Next was a 35-mile car trip that could take up to four hours, depending on the conditions of the dusty or muddy arroyos and the steep, winding mountain road. (Both, Los Alamos National Lab Archives.)

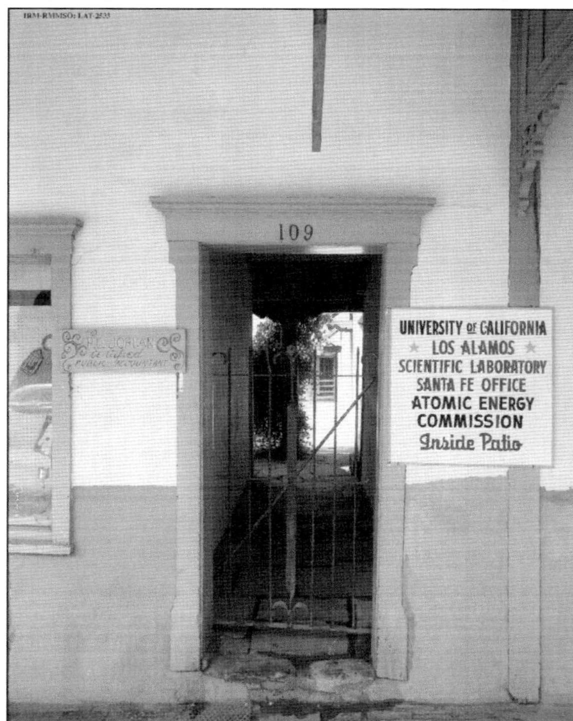

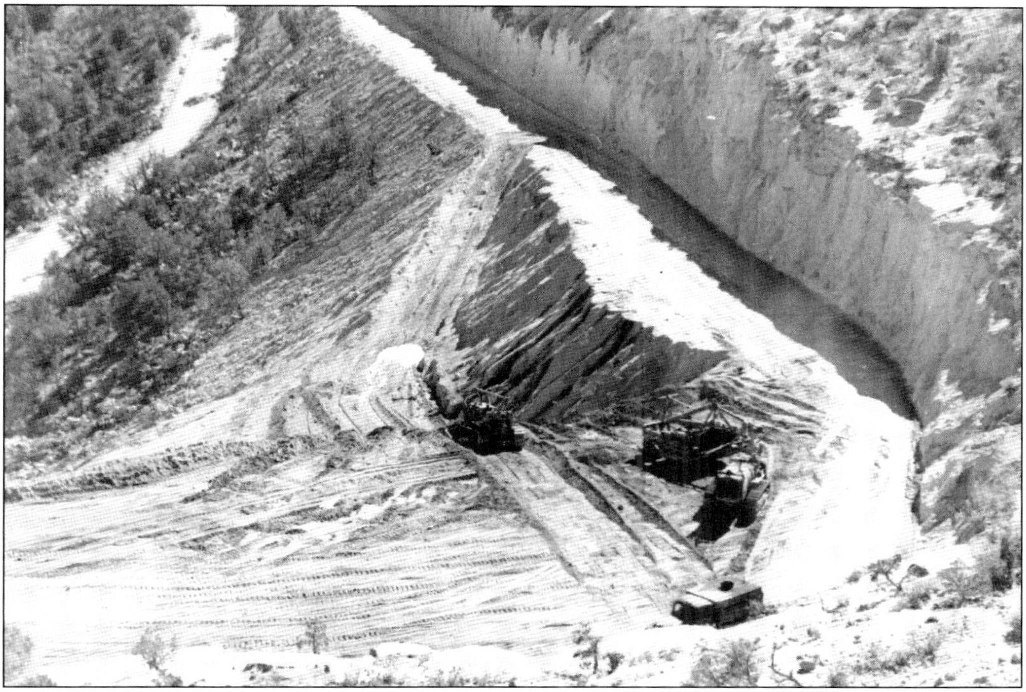

On March 22, 1943, Secretary of War Henry L. Stimson requested 49,000 acres on the Pajarito Plateau to create a "demolition range." Of the 49,000 acres, 8,900 were privately owned and would be purchased or condemned so they could be acquired for Project Y. Homesteaders were offered \$7–\$15 an acre for their lands and \$20–\$30 per head of livestock. The Los Alamos Ranch School was purchased for \$343,000. The Sundt Company was hired to build housing. A.O. Peabody, of Santa Fe, surfaced roads, and Lowdermilk Brothers of Denver supplied the gravel for the site. The Lowdermilks eventually settled in Española, where they ran a sand and gravel business that was located behind today's Lowe's. After the war, when the Atomic Energy Commission took control of the area in 1946, Project Y became Los Alamos National Lab. (Both, Los Alamos Historical Museum Archives.)

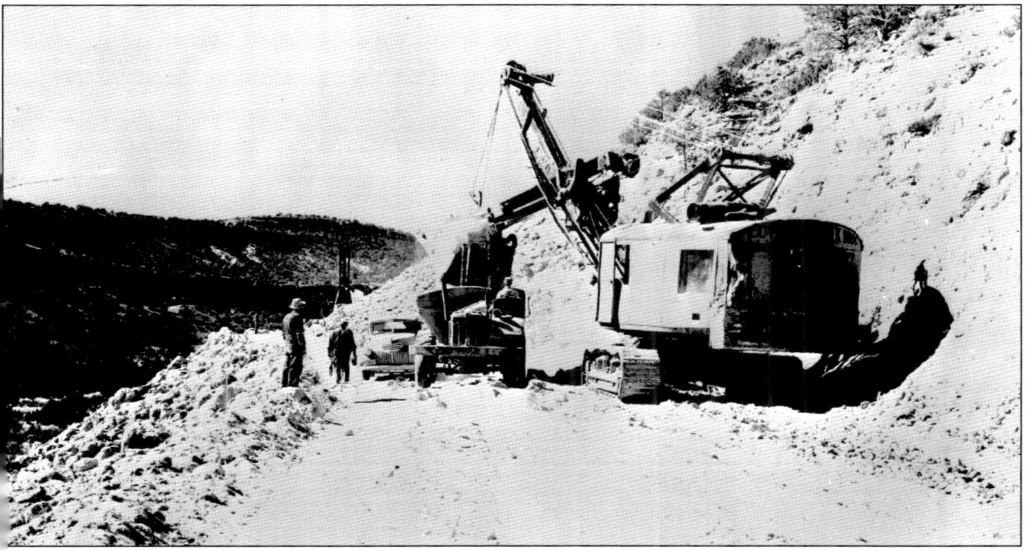

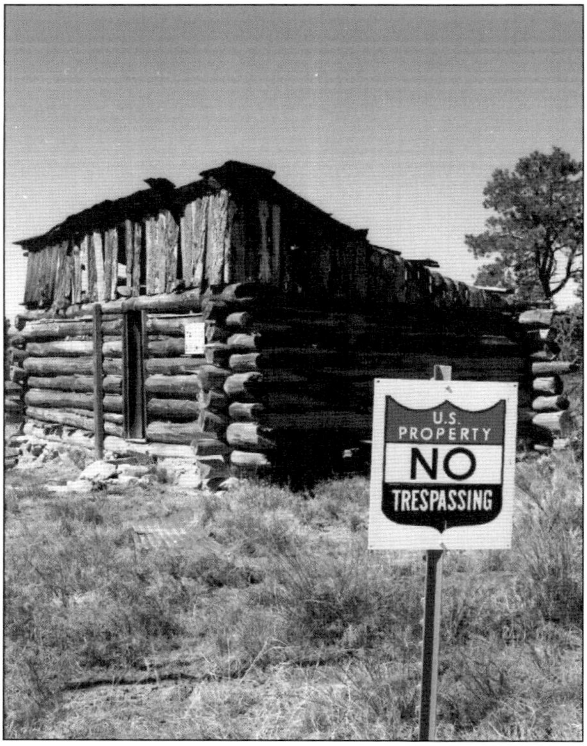

After the Ranch School closed, Bences Gonzales stayed on at Los Alamos during the Manhattan Project, and operated the Post Exchange (PX) from the former Trading Post site. A well-liked, friendly man, he took the sons of lab personnel camping with his own sons. All of Gonzales's six children finished school in Los Alamos. His sons Severo and Ray worked various jobs in Los Alamos, including caring for Kitty Oppenheimer's horses. Gonzales was appointed to the Los Alamos school board. He retired to his home-place in San Pedro, where his son Severo now lives. Few homesteaders remained on the plateau after the confiscation of their houses and land. Most relocated to their homes in the Valley. Here, Mrs. Marcos Gomez wipes a tear as she and her husband visit their former cabin on the Pajarito Plateau, for which they received $1,000. (Both, Los Alamos Historical Museum Archives.)

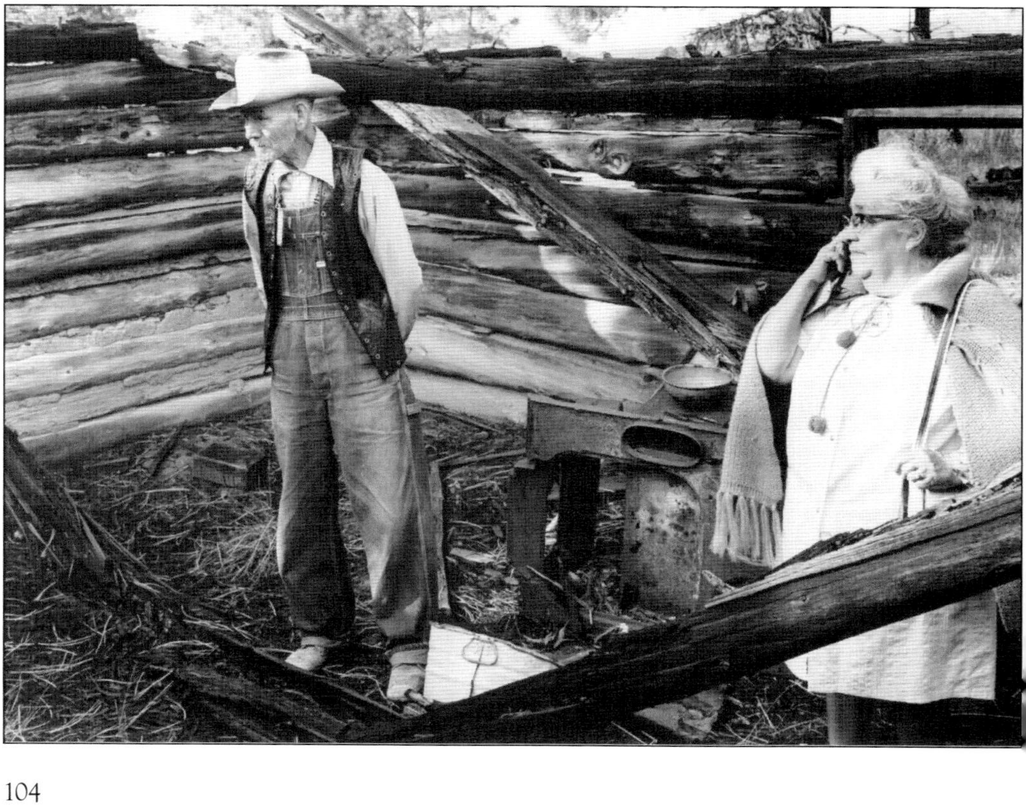

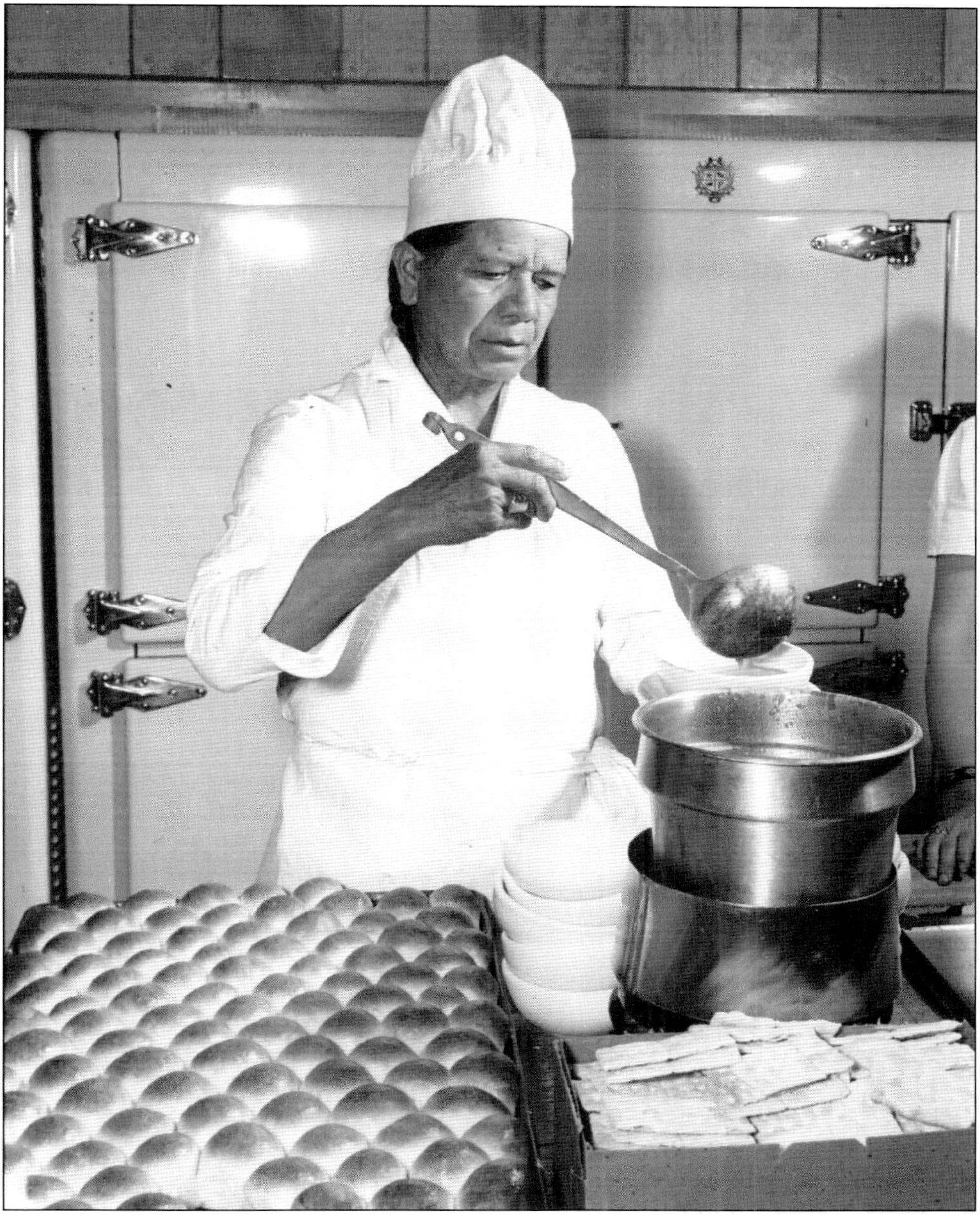

Sundt, an enormous construction company, was contracted to build an entire town on the plateau. In just 14 months, Sundt built homes, research buildings, and infrastructure to support the Los Alamos community of scientific, military, and technical personnel. Project secrecy was amazingly effective—not until 1945 did the company learn the facility's true purpose. Some of the housing Sundt built for Project Y was replaced with conventional housing after the war, and original Sundt units were transported to Española, where a few people still live in them. When Project Y became Los Alamos National Lab, the need for dependable civilian personnel increased. Zia Company was created to bring in qualified, security-cleared workers from the Valley, such as chef Cleto Tafoya, governor of Santa Clara Pueblo, seen here preparing lunch at the East Cafeteria in 1947. (Los Alamos National Lab Archives.)

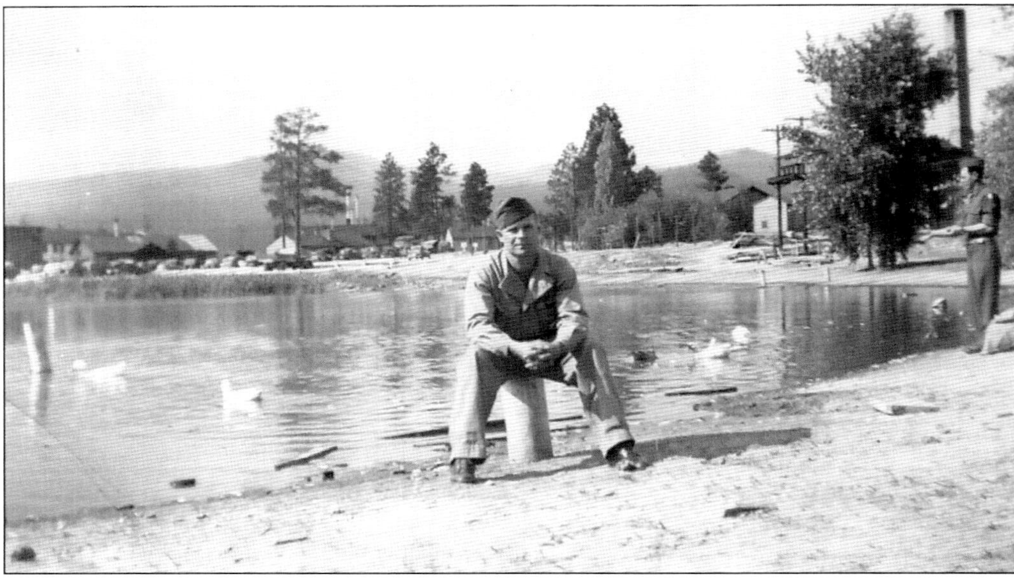

The labs of Project Y were centered around Ashley Pond when Felix DePaula arrived at Los Alamos from New York City early in 1945. He was a driver for the Trinity Site operation. On July 16, 1945, DePaula beheld, with his own eyes, the birth of the Atomic Age at a remote spot in the desert southeast of Socorro—the test blast of the bombs that would be dropped on Japan and bring an end to World War II. Later, DePaula was one of the first employees of Zia Company, which managed warehouses—built from the old military barracks—that supplied the still growing community. Finally, Los Alamos National Lab became his employer for 41 years, until he retired. DePaula was one of those who came to the Pajarito Plateau as military personnel and transitioned to civilian employee life. (Both, Felix and Sadie DePaula.)

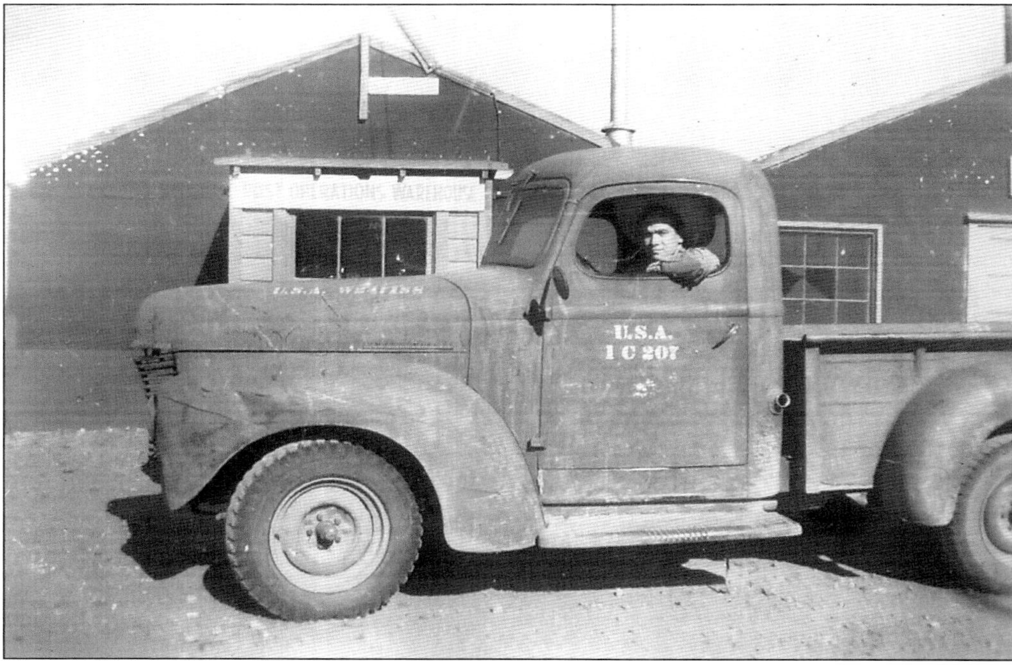

Albert Wilson came from North Carolina to Los Alamos in 1944 and worked there until 1976. He and his wife, Blanche, lived for a time on Trinity Road, next to Dr. Hans Bethe, head of the Theoretical Division of the labs. Once, Bethe asked Wilson to help him with a lamp that would not turn on. Wilson changed the bulb, and it worked fine. Wilson celebrated his 97th birthday in 2010. (Albert Wilson.)

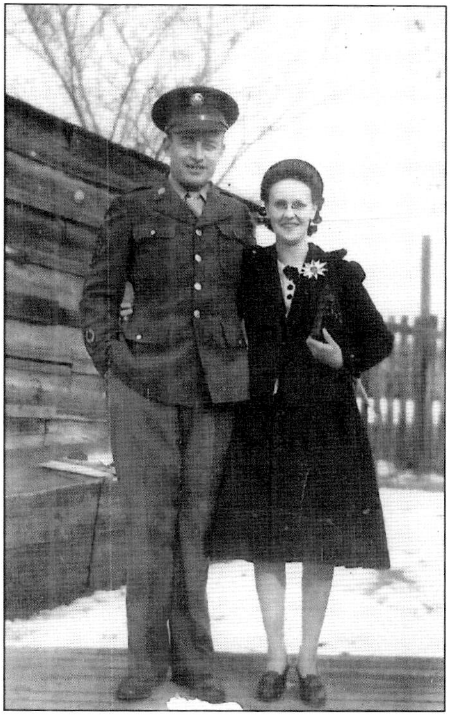

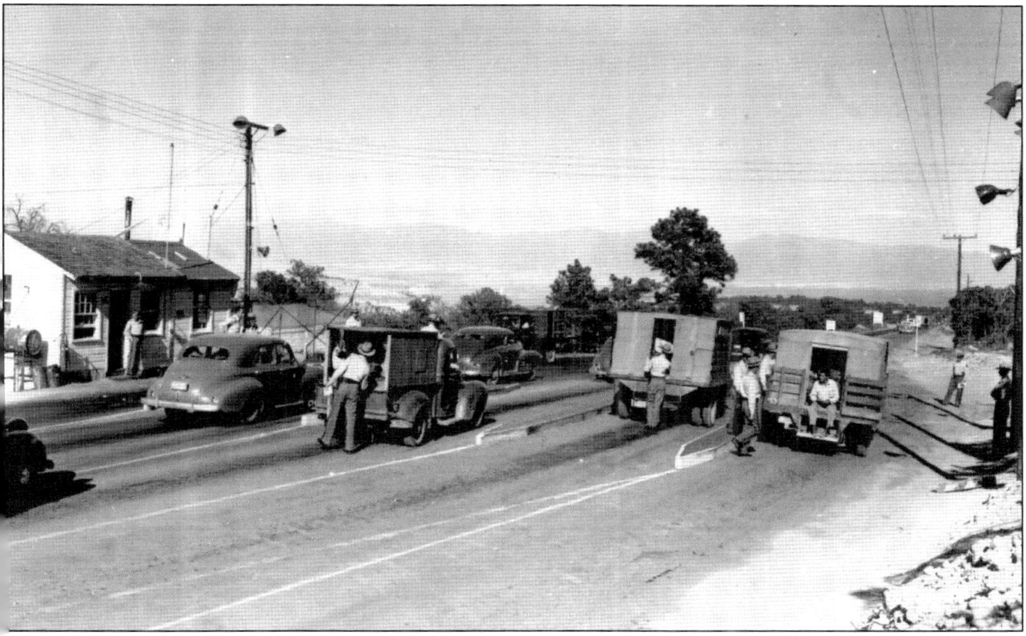

Many lab workers from the Española Valley did not own cars. Valley people in those days still plowed with horses, and some from the villages even traveled in horse-drawn wagons. A shuttle service was provided to transport Los Alamos workers from as far away as Truchas. Shown here at the end of a typical workday is a checkpoint vehicles had to pass through. (Los Alamos National Lab Archives.)

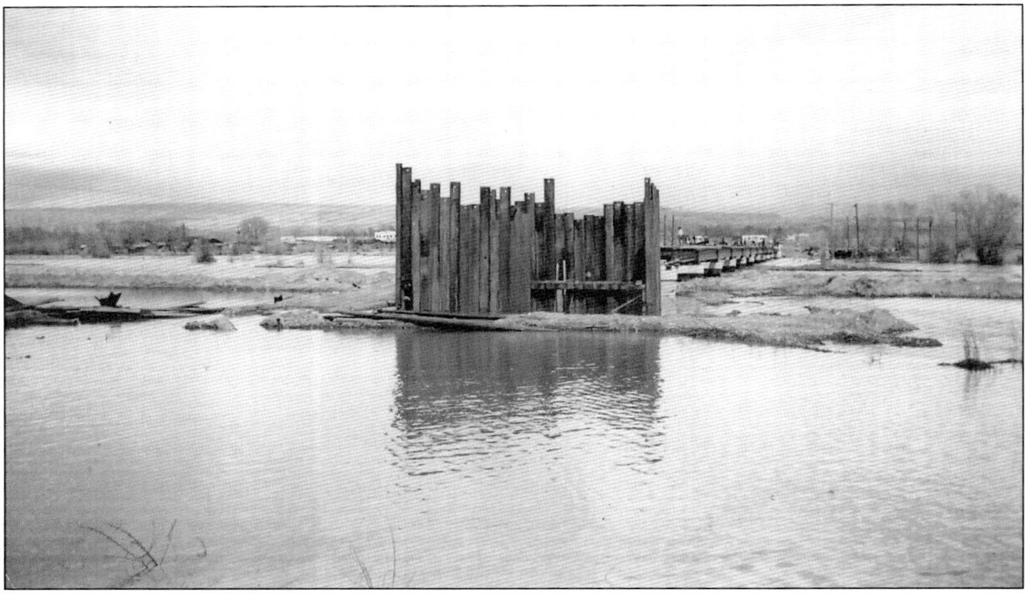

Work on the Oñate Bridge in Española began December 11, 1940, and was completed December 21, 1941. Pilings were anchored 23 feet into the riverbed, and beams from the old wooden bridge were used as reinforcements during construction. The bridge construction required 29,000 sacks of cement and 255,000 tons of steel. In the spring of 1941, construction was delayed because the Rio Grande reached its highest flood level in history and damaged some of the unfinished work. The bridge is 844 feet long and 36 feet wide, including sidewalks. When new, it was the largest and finest bridge in the state, and 300 people turned out for the ribbon cutting ceremony. The Española High School band led the first trip across. The bridge created a permanent link between Riverside and Española. (Both, San Gabriel Historical Society.)

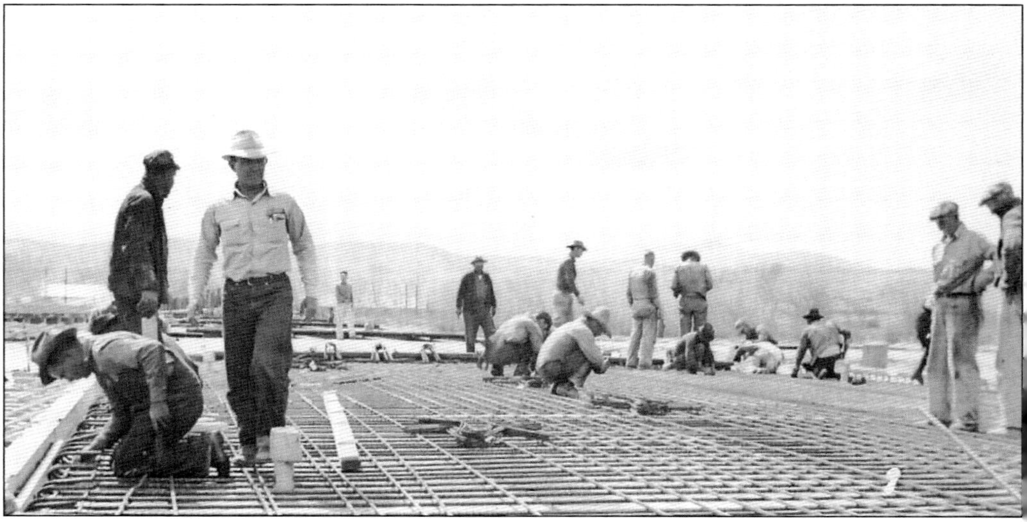

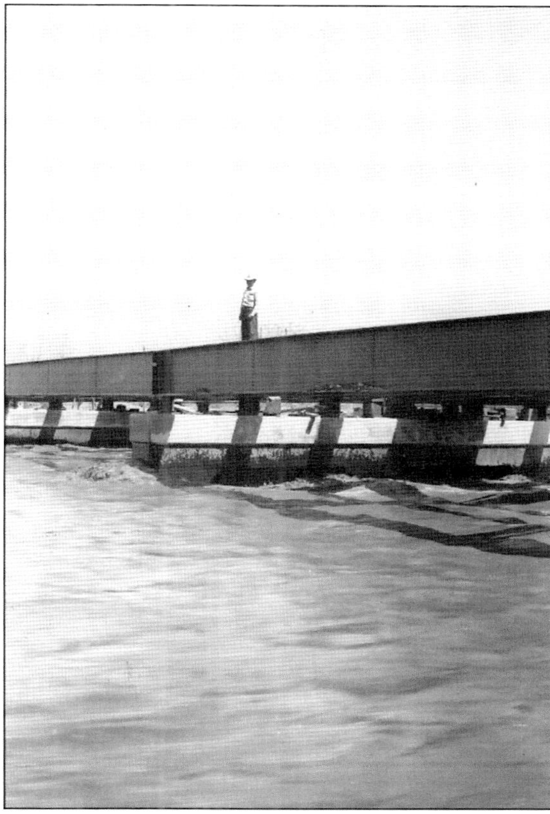

The bridge also served the war effort because it could support the weight of large trucks bringing supplies to the labs. Every night at 10:00, a curfew whistle blew; the streets would clear, and the trucks came through. The new bridge stimulated business in Española. Old-timers will remember some of the businesses in the flourishing Española of the 1940s and 1950s: Becker's, Ponca Pontiac, Bond & Willard, Española State Bank, Hunter Motor Company, El Rio Movie Theatre, Lucero's Five & Dime, Million Electric, J.W. Owens, Evans' Pharmacy, Matilda's Restaurant, Farmers' Supply Feed Store, Farmway Feed, Morton Brothers filling station, Pueblo Drugs, Bridges Radiator Service, Bud's Cleaners, Fairview Foods, Richard's Department Store, Wayne's Auto Parts, Chuckwagon Café, Pike's Jewelry, A&W Drive-In, and Valley Spudnut. (Both, San Gabriel Historical Society.)

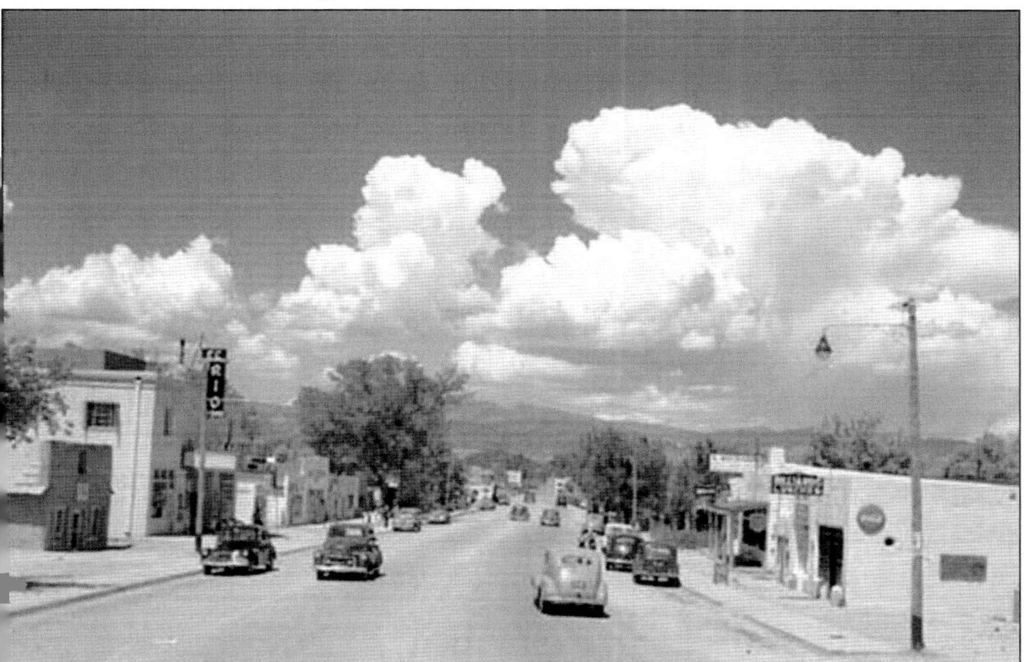

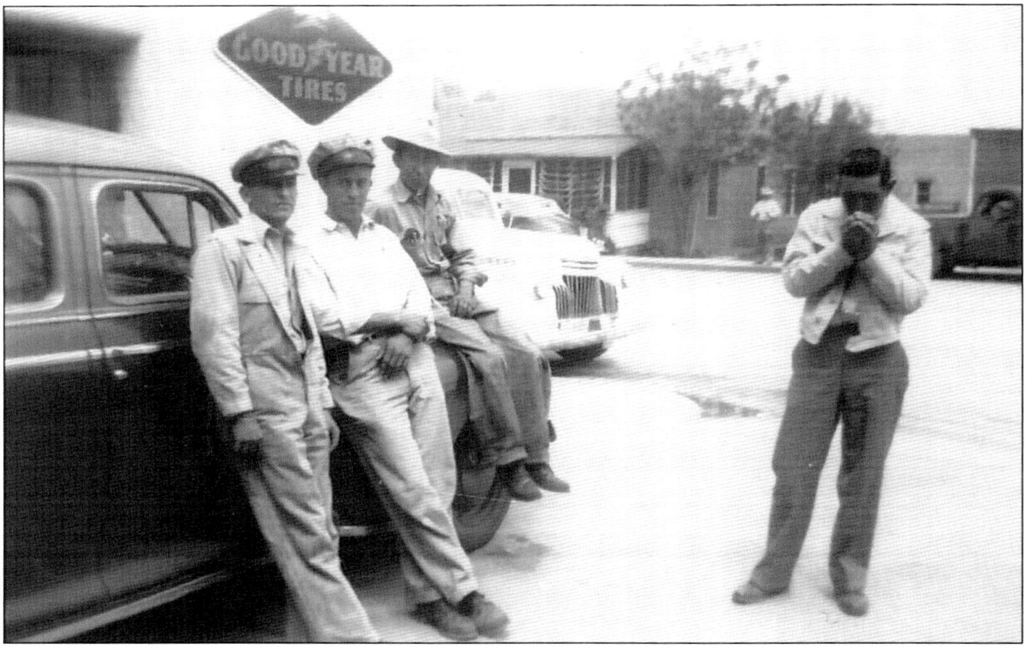

Ofilia Valdez moved to Española from Tierra Amarilla with her father, Eiliseo Valdez, when she was a little girl. Eliseo was a printer by trade, and with his press, he published one of the first newspapers in New Mexico. Ofilia's family lived near the Española depot of the Chili Line, and she remembers a big flourmill on the west bank of the Rio Grande. She was working at Bond & Willard when she met Amadeo Quintana. Amadeo was working at the M&S Garage, where the New Mexico Gas Company is today. They married and raised a family in San Pedro. Amadeo was a gifted farmer; he kept livestock, and his dinner-plate dahlias were truly stunning. Ofilia and Amadeo once grew sugarcane from which they made *miel Mexicana*, a delicious syrup from bygone days. (Both, Ofilia Quintana de Valdez.)

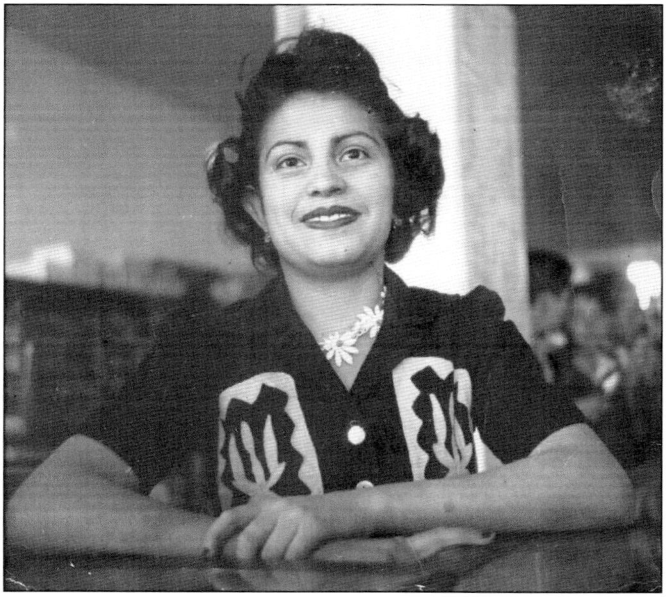

Lydia Roybal came from the Pojoaque Valley to work at Farmers' Supply, her brother's feed store, one of the first businesses on Riverside Drive. In those days, Riverside Drive was a dirt road. Cows would become stuck in the mud near the river. Lydia's grandfather Benigno Roybal had lived in the village of Pajarito near San Ildefonso Pueblo, but moved to Española when the tribe reclaimed the land. (Lydia R. Trujillo.)

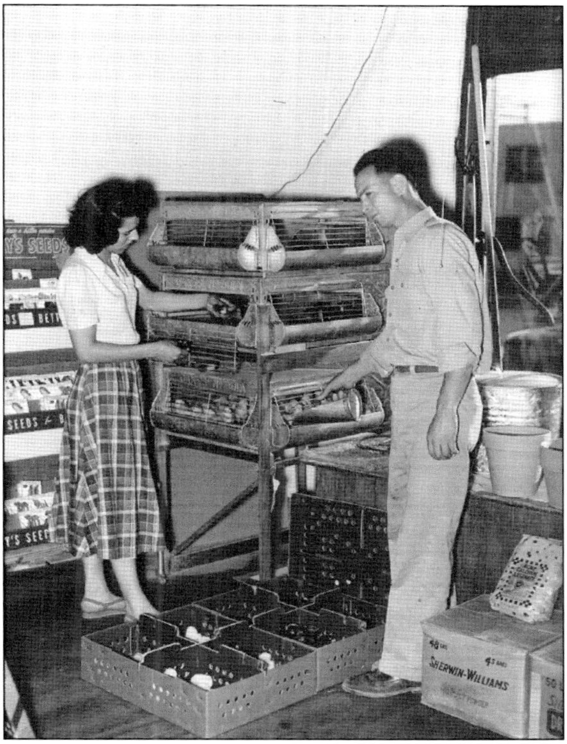

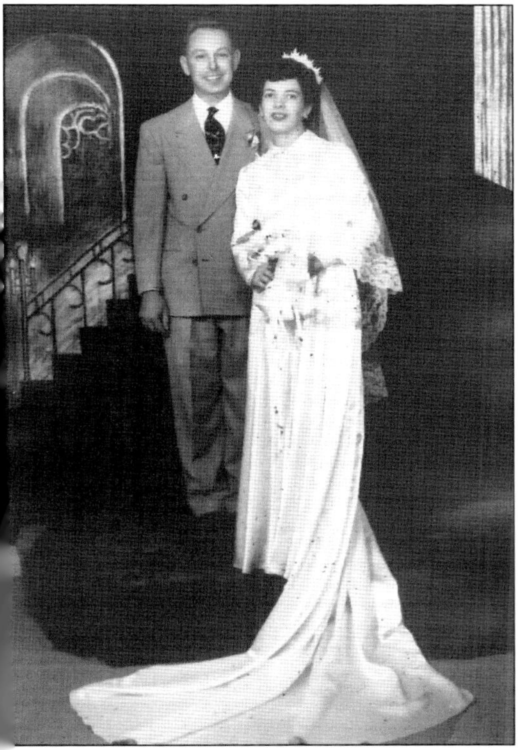

Belle Archuleta married Joe Becker in 1950. They raised their family in Santa Cruz. For 30 years, Belle and Joe ran Becker's, the store that sold the finest clothing and Stetson hats in Española. The first Becker's was by the river on the east side of the Oñate Bridge. When Santa Clara Pueblo reclaimed their land, the Beckers moved their store to Yates' shopping center, next to Hacienda Home Center. (Joe and Belle Becker.)

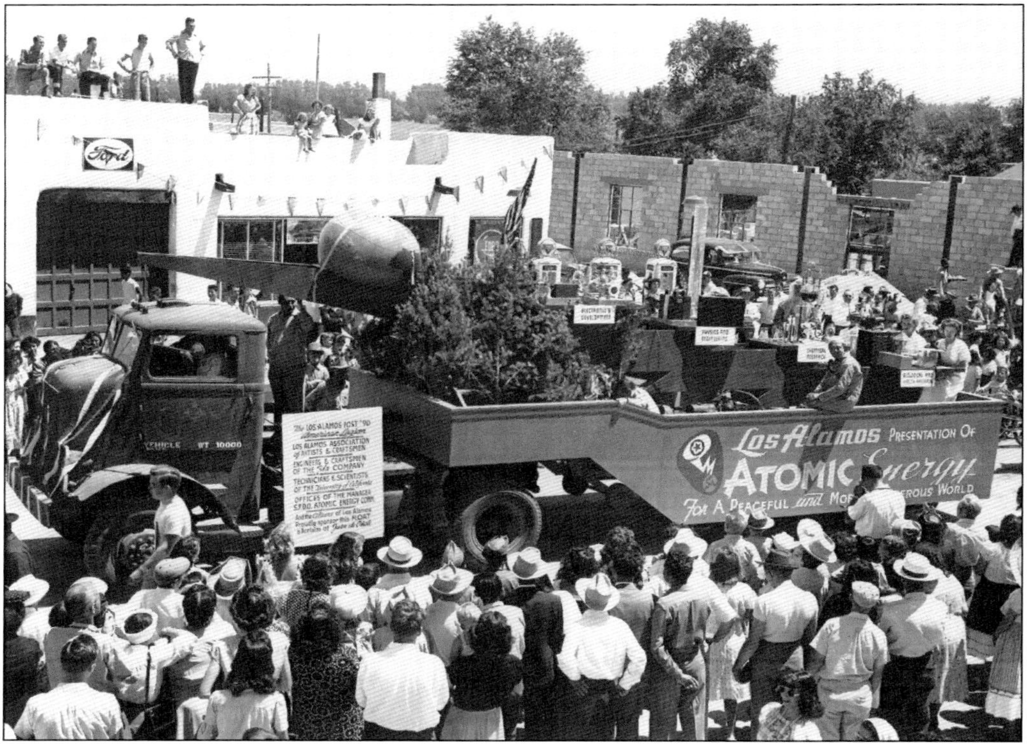

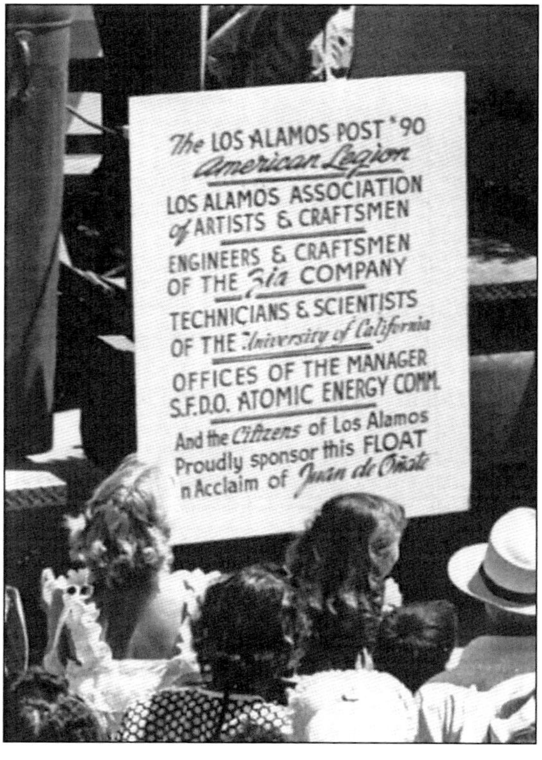

The postwar mood in the Española Valley was buoyant and confident. In the 1948 Española Fiestas, a Zia Company truck pulls a trailer for Los Alamos National Lab. The float depicts a laboratory with people working at various stations. Written on the side of the float is "Atomic Energy for a peaceful and more prosperous world." The dedication sign accompanying the float is enlarged at left. (Both, Ross Olivas.)

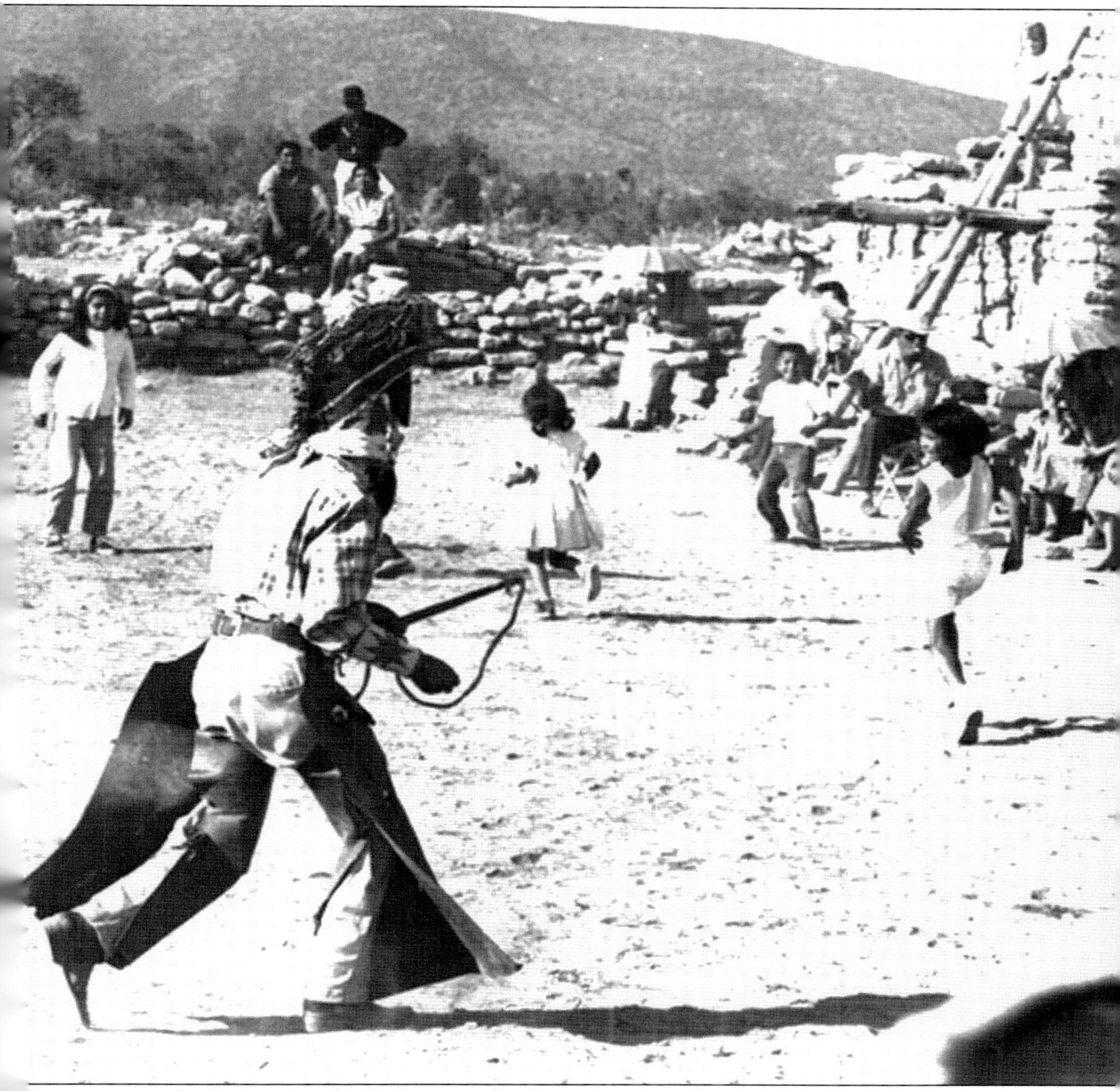

Beginning in the late 1100s, the high mesas flanking the east side of the Jemez Mountains were settled by Anasazi people. At first, there were hundreds of individual, family-size dwellings. By 1300, the people were living in villages, such as Puye, the ruins of which stand on a cliff to the south of Española. Another ancient Anasazi village was Tsirege, which means "little bird" in the Tewa language. Archaeologist Edgar L. Hewett liked the word, translated it into Spanish—*pajarito*—and applied it to a very large area of prehistoric settlement, which is how Pajarito Plateau got its name. The Santa Clara people still conduct ceremonies in Puye, the pueblo of their ancestors. The Matachines' dance, shown here, is a mysterious ceremony associated with old Spanish and Arab culture and the Emperor Montezuma. It is performed throughout the villages of Northern New Mexico. The character portrayed by the Santa Clara dancer in this 1962 picture is called *abuelo*, or grandfather. Puye Cliff Dwellings is a national landmark, owned and operated by the Pueblo of Santa Clara. (Palace of the Governors Photo Archives.)

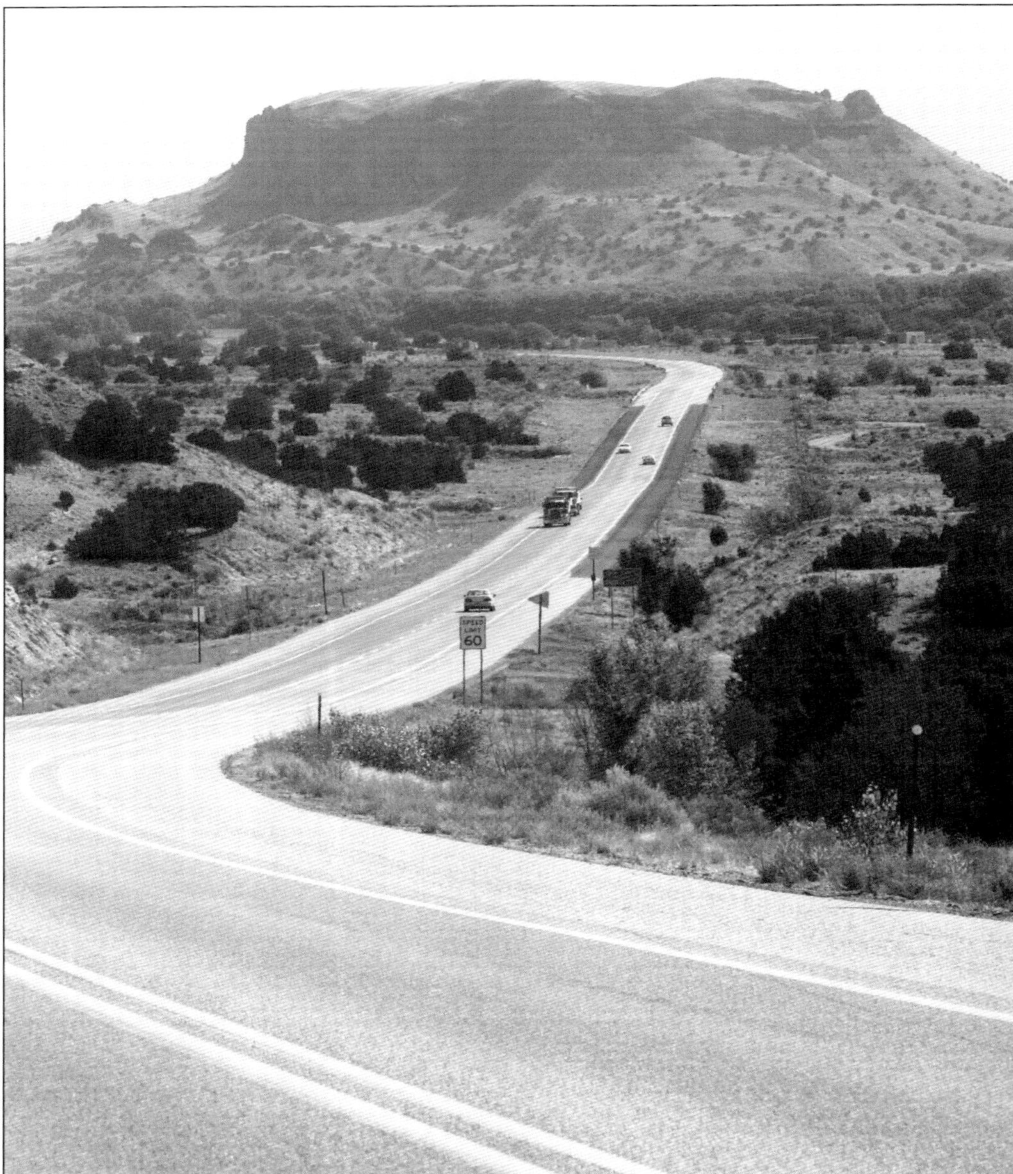

New Mexico State Highway 30 is the road that most Española residents travel on their way back home from work in Los Alamos. The descent from the Pajarito Plateau is a progression through millions of years of natural history. Layer upon layer of silent, seemingly unchanging sedimentary and metamorphic rock belie the violence of the volcanic activity that helped form the Española Valley. The whispers of ancient occupants of the plateau can be heard in the rustle of the raven's wing and the wind in the trees. To the north is Black Mesa, and to the east is the Rio Grande. Each tells its story of timeless endurance and passing seasons. (Los Alamos National Lab Archives.)

Six

La Cosecha

Everyone in Española has a favorite food story. My little sister Pinky told me this one: when she was quite small, she and my older sister DiAna went with our father to visit Uncle Bernardo in Taos. Uncle Bernardo raised sheep, and had butchered one just for this occasion. He gave my sisters some little crunchy things to eat. Pinky had munched through her third one when she noticed DiAna looking at her with a mixture of disgust and glee. "Do you know what you're eating?" DiAna asked Pinky. "Mmm," said Pinky. "It's delicious." "You are eating sheep guts!" DiAna laughed. Pinky stopped munching, wrapped the thing in a napkin, and inconspicuously (she hoped) stuffed it into her pocket. Of course she was later to learn that it was a burrañate—indeed, a stuffed and deep-fried sheep intestine.

One of the references used for this book is the 1935 *Tewa Basin Study*, Volume 2, a federally funded survey of everyday life in Northern New Mexico villages during the Great Depression. The survey was done after a three-year drought, from 1931 to 1934. Though hardly anyone had money, and many families in the Valley were receiving federal relief, the wealth of harvest during those tough times is impressive. Village for village, food production was extraordinary. The study found that in 1935, in El Guache, a village typical of the Española Valley at that time, one acre of land yielded 800 pounds of wheat, 750 pounds of corn, 625 pounds of oats, 750 pounds of barley, 600 pounds of beans, 450 pounds of peas, and 500 *ristras* of chilies.

There is a certain way of preparing red chili in the Valley that earns it the name, *Chile de Casorio*, or wedding chili. The sweetest red chili pods are selected. The dry pods are cleaned, washed, and roasted lightly. Soaked for a quarter hour in warm water, the pods are pureed in the blender with fresh garlic. The thin sauce is simmered until it thickens. Cooked meat can be added, and it is served with fresh *horno* bread.

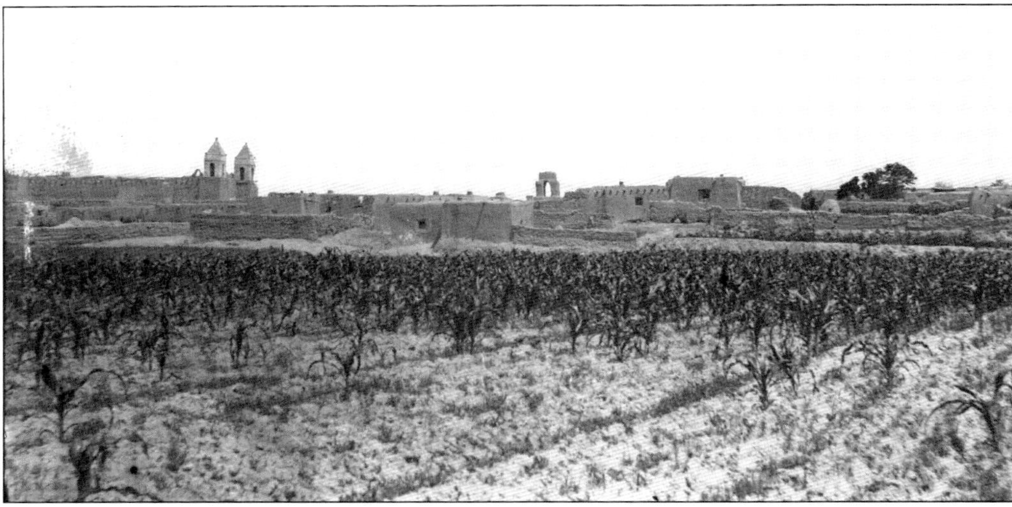

Ocho meses de invierno y quatro de infierno (Eight months of winter, four months of hell) is a *dicho* describing the harsh conditions encountered by early Spanish farmers in the Española Valley. They survived by planting native crops -- corn, beans and squash -- using Spanish knowledge of irrigation, and an ancient Spanish method of weather forecasting, still used today, called cabañuelas. The corn field shown above in this 1872 photograph lay between the Santa Cruz de la Cañada Church and the Santa Cruz River. Today, this field is a large mobile home park. (Palace of the Governors Photo Archives, photograph by H.T. Heister.)

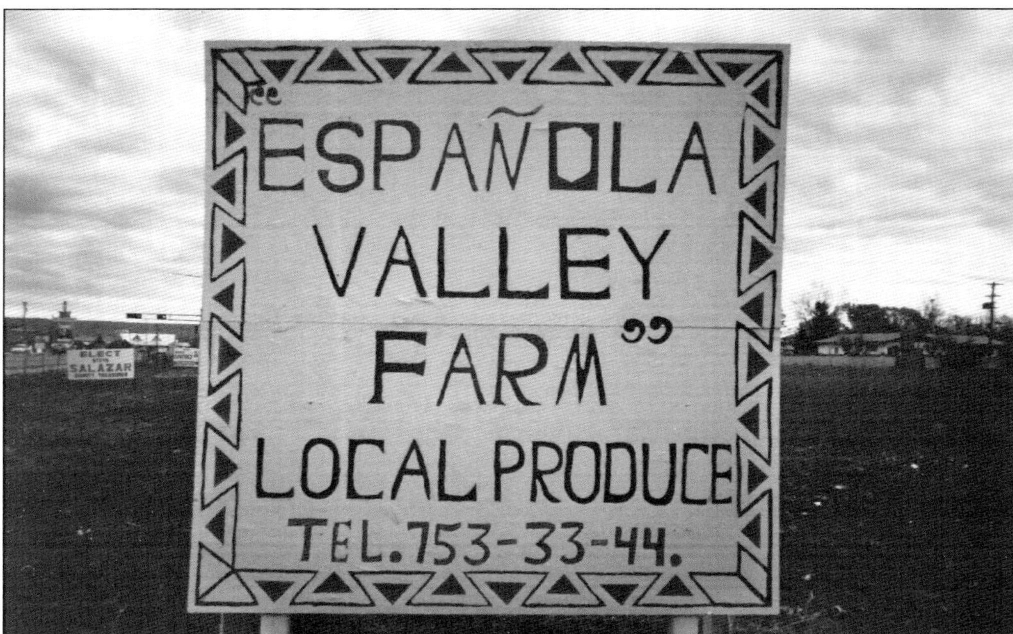

Joseph Merhege's parents ran sheep on Mesa Prieta, north of Española, in the early 20th century. Today, his 30-acre farm is managed by Salvador Corona Chavez, who takes a truckload of produce every week to the Española Farmers' Market. A convenient stop on North Riverside Drive, Española Valley Farm specializes in sweet peas, onions, corn, and squash, as well as traditional dried foods. (Salvador Corona Chavez.)

Come March of every year, a familiar sight throughout Northern New Mexico is the cleaning of the acequias. Each parciante is responsible for cleaning his portion of the ditch. Under the old water laws -- which are based on Iberian law -- individuals own the land, but the community owns the acequias. Here, Samuel Quintana and his daughter Maclovia clean the ditch in San Pedro, 1991. (Camilla Trujillo.)

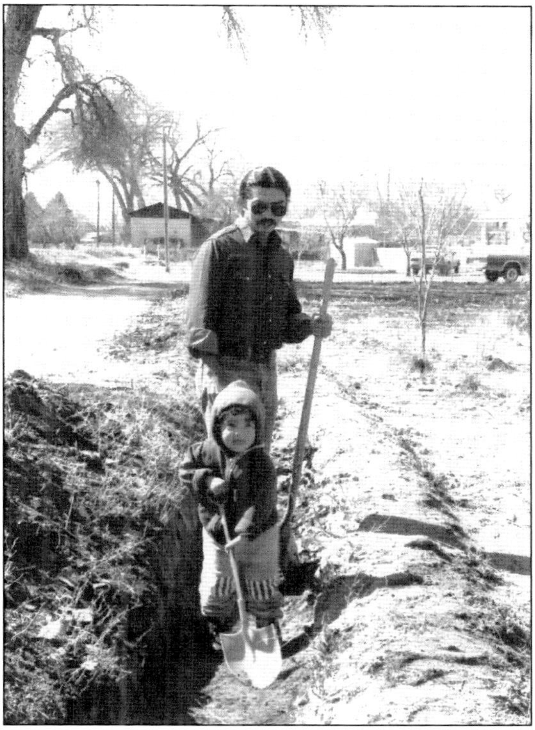

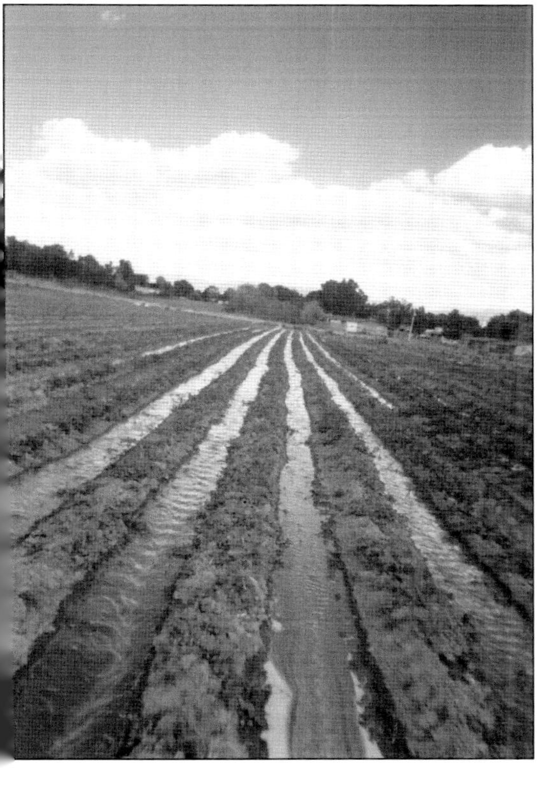

The first irrigation ditches in the United States were dug in the Española Valley, and were already in use at Ohkay Owingeh when the Spanish arrived. The first apples and pears produced in the Rocky Mountain region were grown in the Valley. Fruit trees commonly bore fruit for hundreds of years. "We were always poor, but never hungry," is how elders of the Valley remember the Depression. (Salvador Corona Chavez.)

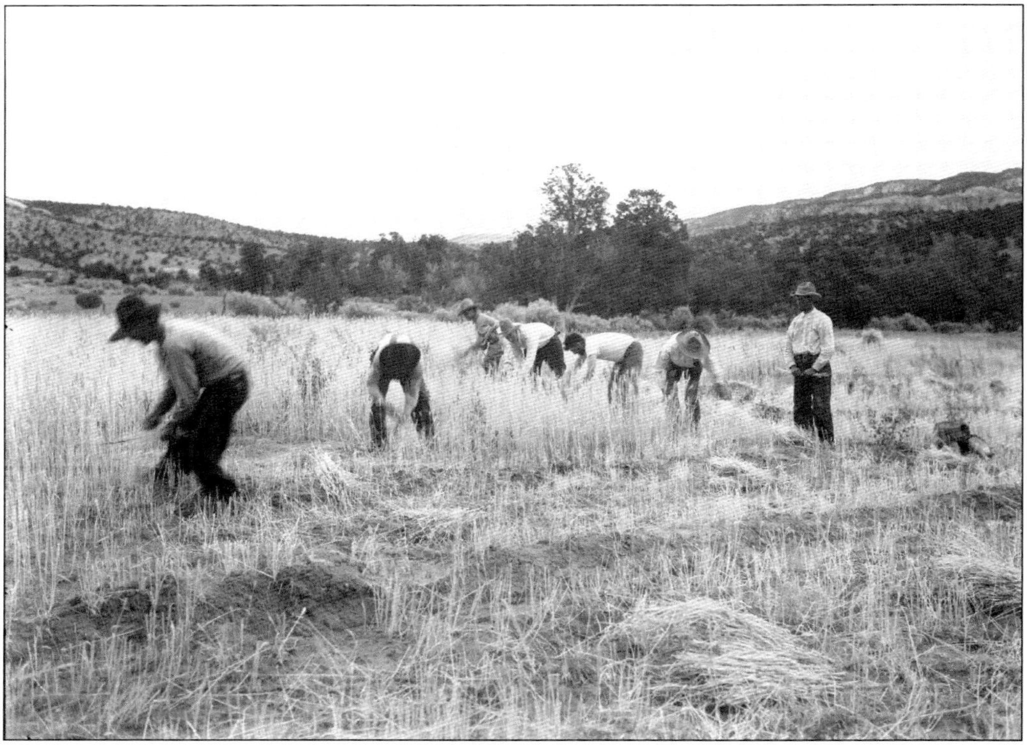

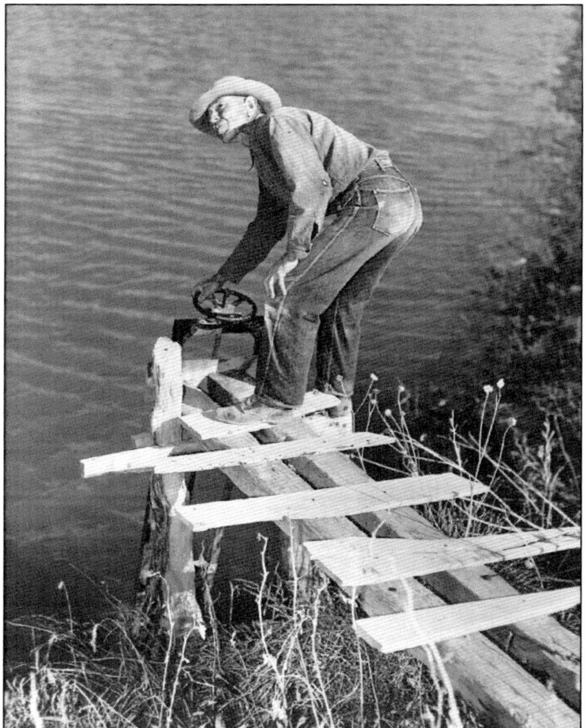

The Spanish brought wheat to the Valley. These men are using the sickle, or *hóz,* to harvest the grain. In the 1920s, the wheat was taken to an *era*, or a place of hardened dirt, where goats or horses were made to trample it. The berries, now separated from the stalks, were winnowed in the wind and washed, then dried in preparation for grinding into flour. (Palace of the Governors Photo Archives, photograph by T. Harmon Parkhurst.)

The *mayordomo* of an acequia is chosen for his familiarity with the community, his understanding of the waterways, his physical strength, and his ability to communicate, sometimes in three languages, with the *parciantes*. Procopio Roybal, mayordomo of Acequia Ancón in neighboring Nambé, releases the water from a holding pond into the acequia in 1948. (Lydia R. Trujillo.)

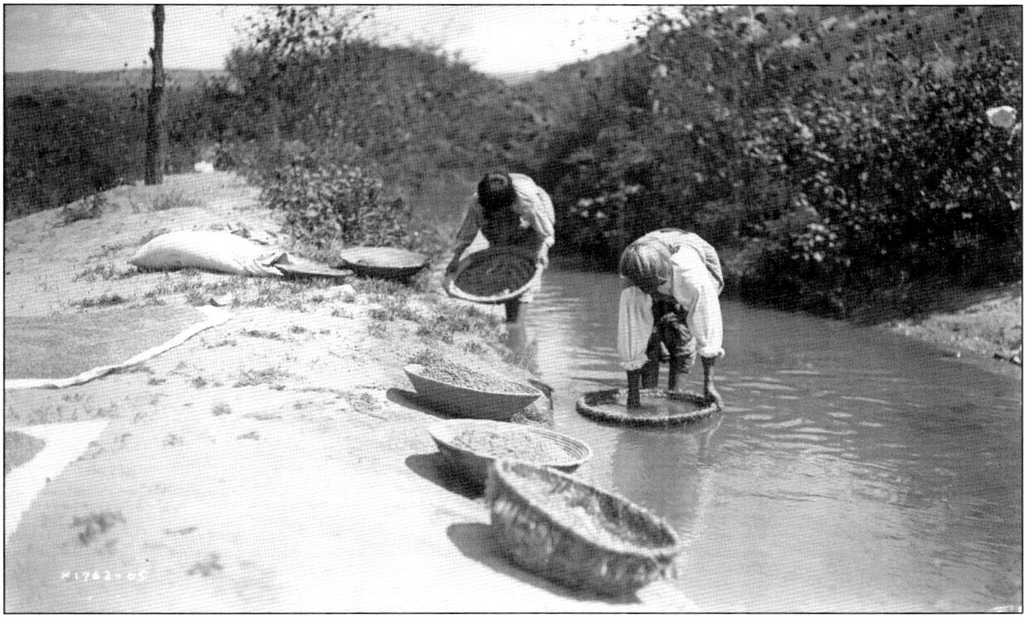

Women from Ohkay Owingeh wash and rinse wheat berries in the acequia. Rio Arriba County commissioners are taking steps to protect irrigated lands in the Valley from careless building practices. Commissioner Alfredo Montoya says, "Restrictions on construction will protect water rights and farmland for future generations, as well as honor and maintain our cultural traditions. These are the things that really enhance the value of our property." (Palace of the Governors Photo Archives, photograph by Edward S. Curtis.)

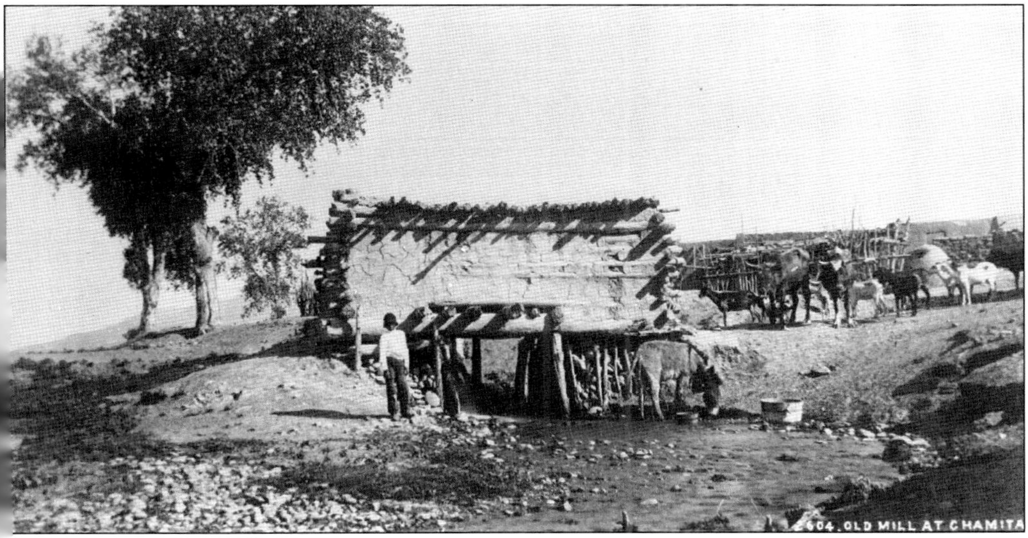

n the early 20th century, there were a number of small flourmills, or *molinos*, throughout the spañola Valley, such as this one in Chamita, photographed in 1881. They were powered by water nd were always situated on or alongside acequias or creeks. The miller understood not only the vorkings of his mill, but the economy and culture of his region. Villagers would bring him their rain to be to ground, often paying him with flour. (Palace of the Governors Photo Archives, hotograph by William Henry Jackson.)

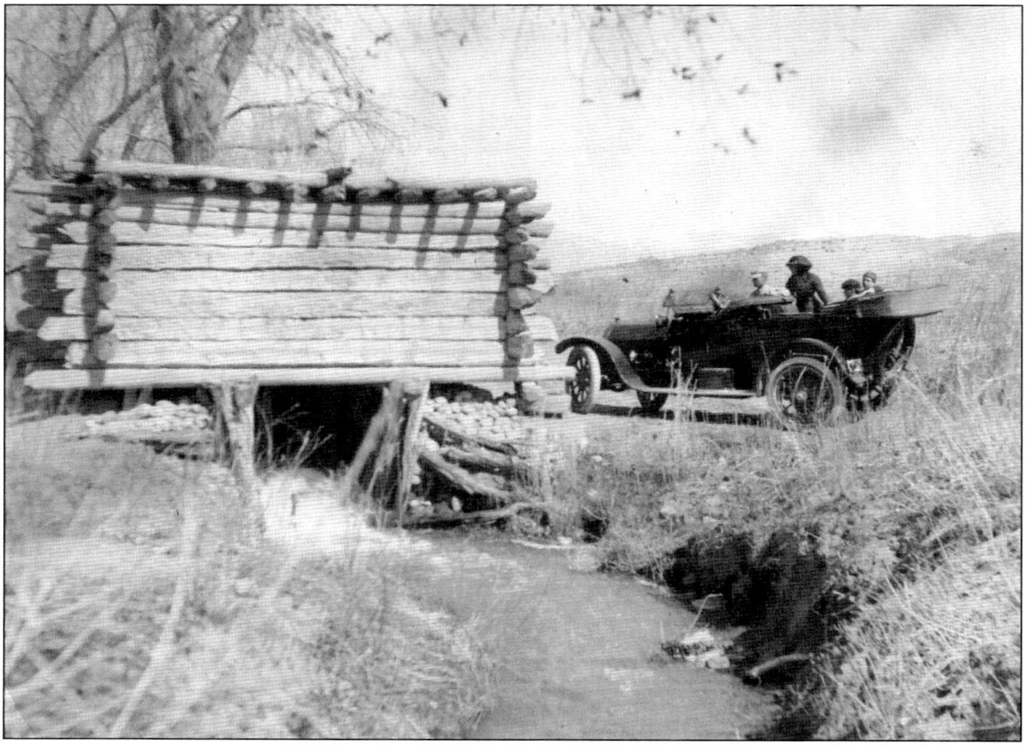

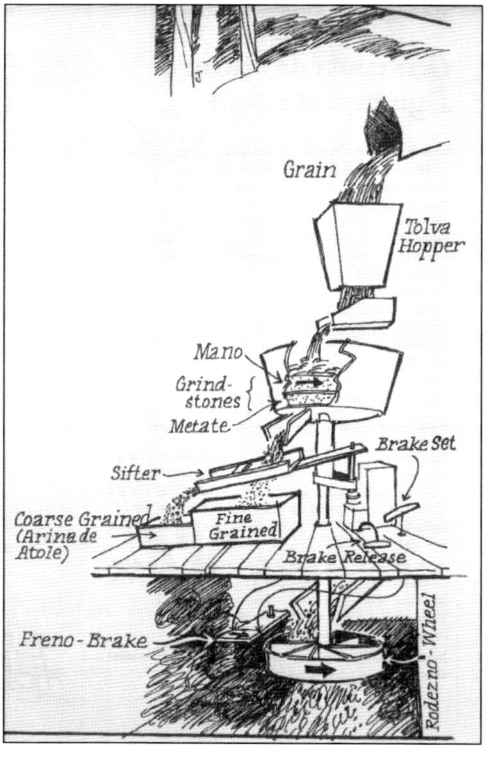

A carload of tourists admires the Truchas Molino, built of notched, hand-hewn timbers and still working in 1934. The brilliantly simple engineering of the Barela Mill is illustrated in this diagram. The technology of the water-powered grain mill was already many centuries old when the Spanish brought it to the New World, where grain was still being ground by hand on *metates*. The mill benefited everyone and had a unifying cultural and economic value for the people of the Valley. (Above, Palace of the Governors Photo Archives, Asplund Collection; left, Palace of the Governors Photo Archives, photograph by Louann Jordon.)

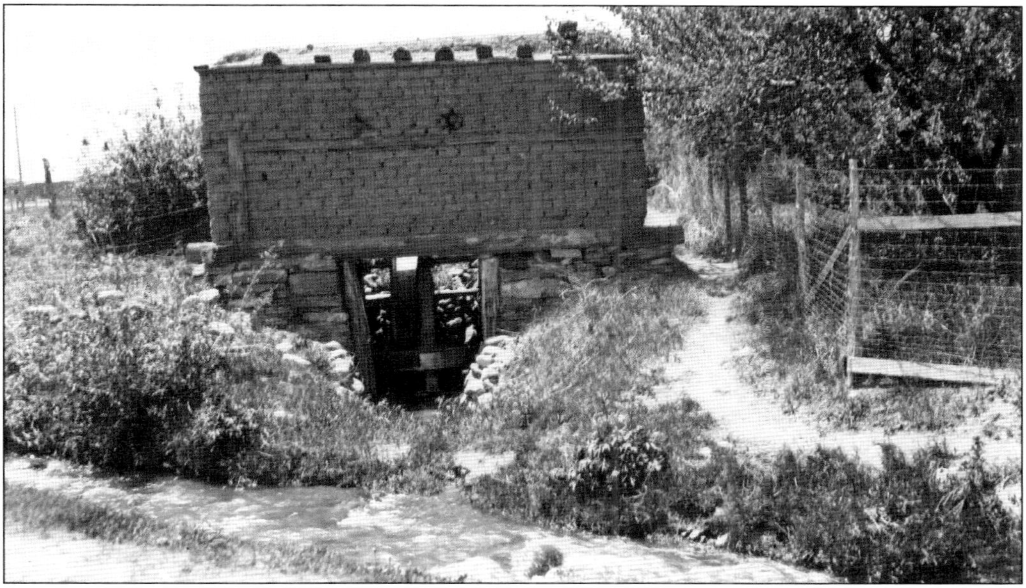

Marta Martinez remembers a *molino* in Potrero, possibly built in the less commonly seen adobe brick style above. Note the horizontal waterwheel. According to the 1935 *Tewa Basin Study*, virtually 100 percent of the populace of Chimayo engaged in agriculture at that time. Trade was on a barter basis, and ancient measurements were still in use: one *almud* (16 pounds) of beans was worth two *ristras* (strings) of chili; a sack of potatoes was worth one-and-half *ristras* of chili; a *fanega* (140 pounds) of wheat was worth two *ristras* of chili. The chilies drying on the roof of this house in Santa Cruz (below) show that it is September. The heap of blue corn in the foreground will be ground into *atole* and the white corn, perhaps, into *chaquegue*. (Both, Palace of the Governors Photo Archives; above, photograph by William H. Roberts.)

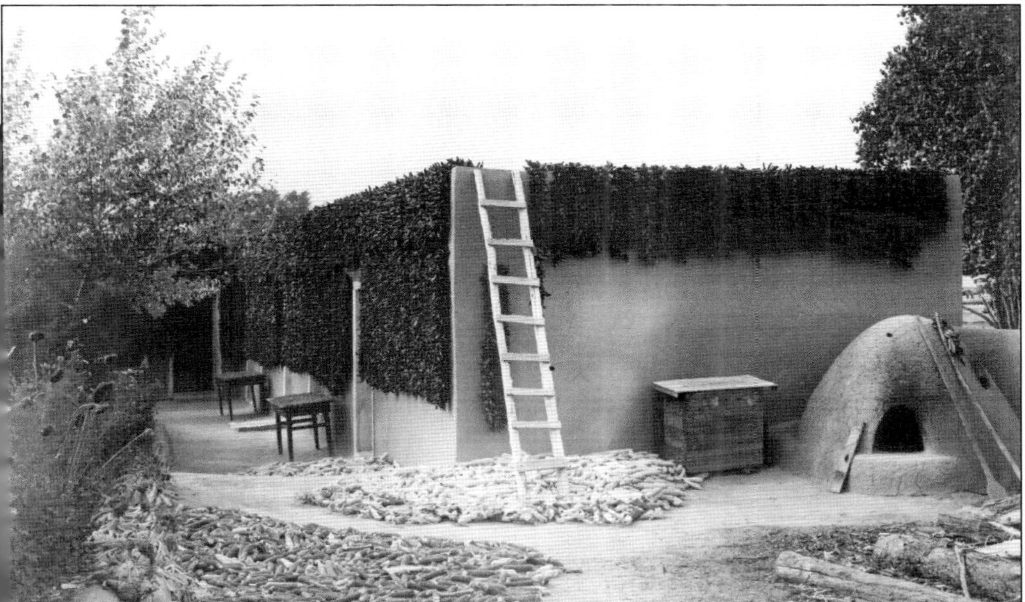

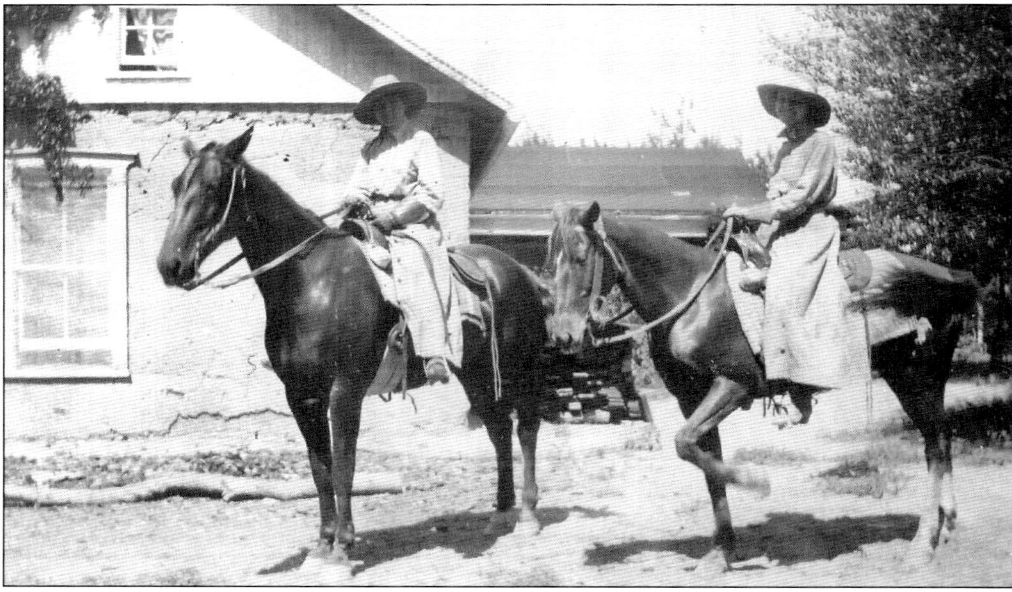

The Becker home was built in 1886 by Father Frankalon while he was serving at Santa Cruz Parish. He brought apple trees from France and planted a 50-acre orchard. In the 1930s, when this photograph was taken, Stark Brothers Nursery was using seeds from Frankalon's apple orchard to create rootstock to sell in their catalog. Where the orchard used to be is now Yates subdivision. A few of Father Frankalon's wonderful trees remain. (Joe and Belle Becker.)

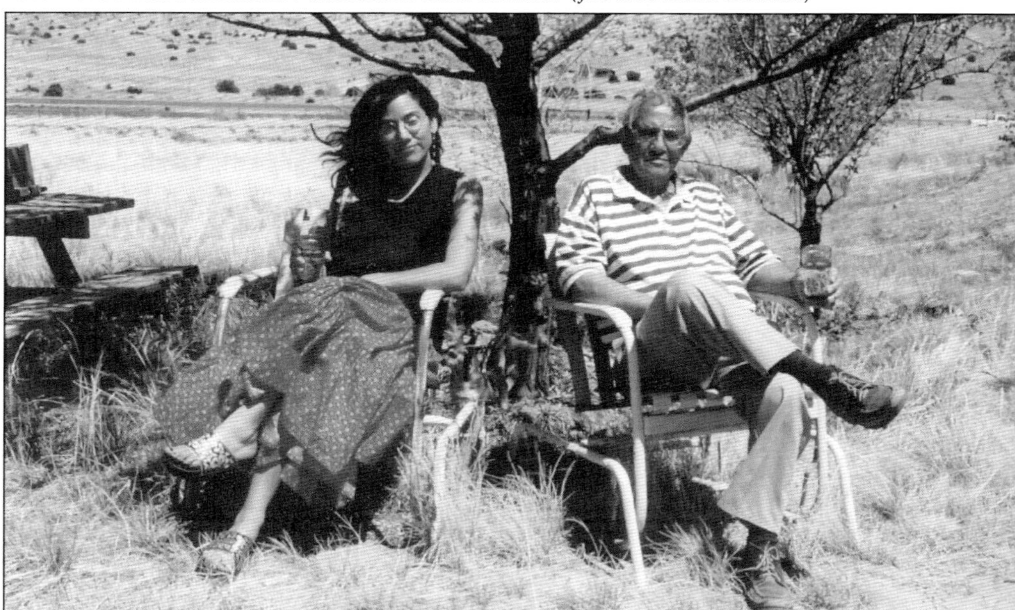

Paul Trujillo, shown in 1998 with his daughter Camilla, was the County Extension agent for Rio Arriba County from 1948 to 1980. He survived the Bataan Death March and recalled eating the *verdolaga* that he discovered growing around the prison camp. Originally from Taos, Trujillo was instrumental in bringing to Velarde the Bloom-Delay Through Sprinkling Program, an effort to save the apple crop from the yearly freeze. (Camilla Trujillo.)

Lucia Roybal and Margaret Caperton, daughters of Adolfo and Elaisa Montoya, are shown at their Pajarito Plateau cabin in 1943. Adolfo's years on the plateau ended with Project Y. He moved his family to San Pedro, where he continued to farm. For many years, Lucia and her husband, Stan, ran Farmers' Supply Feed Store on Riverside Drive. Margaret, a beloved educator, died unexpectedly in a car accident in Amarillo, Texas, in December 2000. (Los Alamos Historical Museum Photo Archives.)

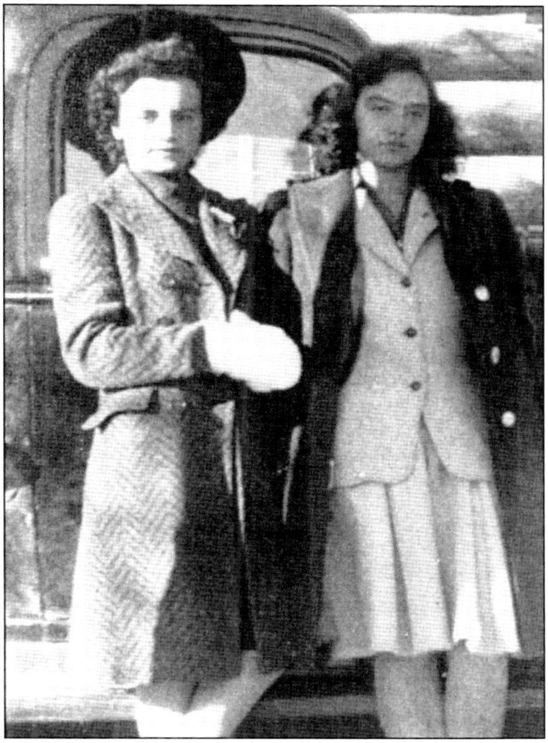

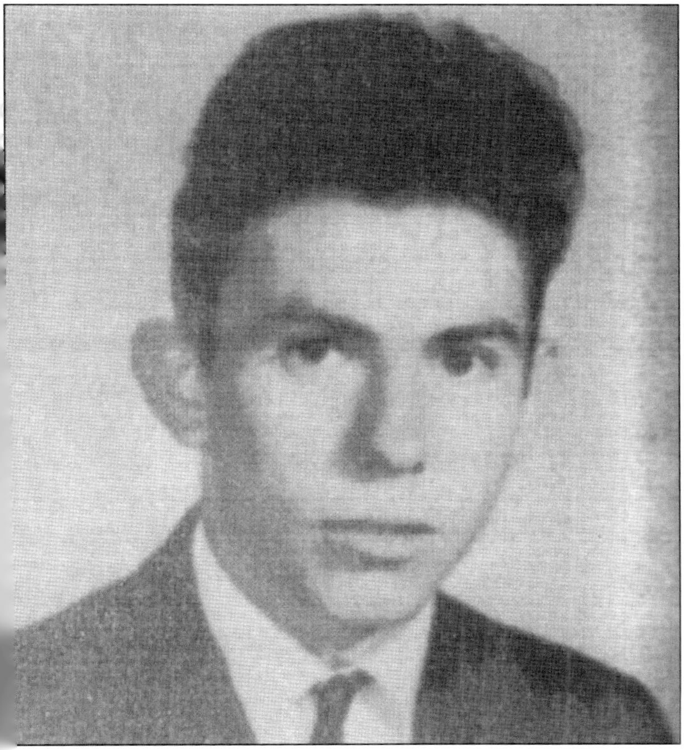

Phil I. Valdez, a 1965 graduate of Española High School and a US Navy hospital corpsman, was killed in Vietnam while saving the lives of two Marines under heavy enemy fire. Phil was posthumously awarded the Navy Cross for "conspicuous gallantry and intrepidity in action." Española named the North Bridge after him, and the US Navy honored him by naming a ship after him—the USS *Destroyer Escort Valdez*. (San Gabriel Historical Society.)

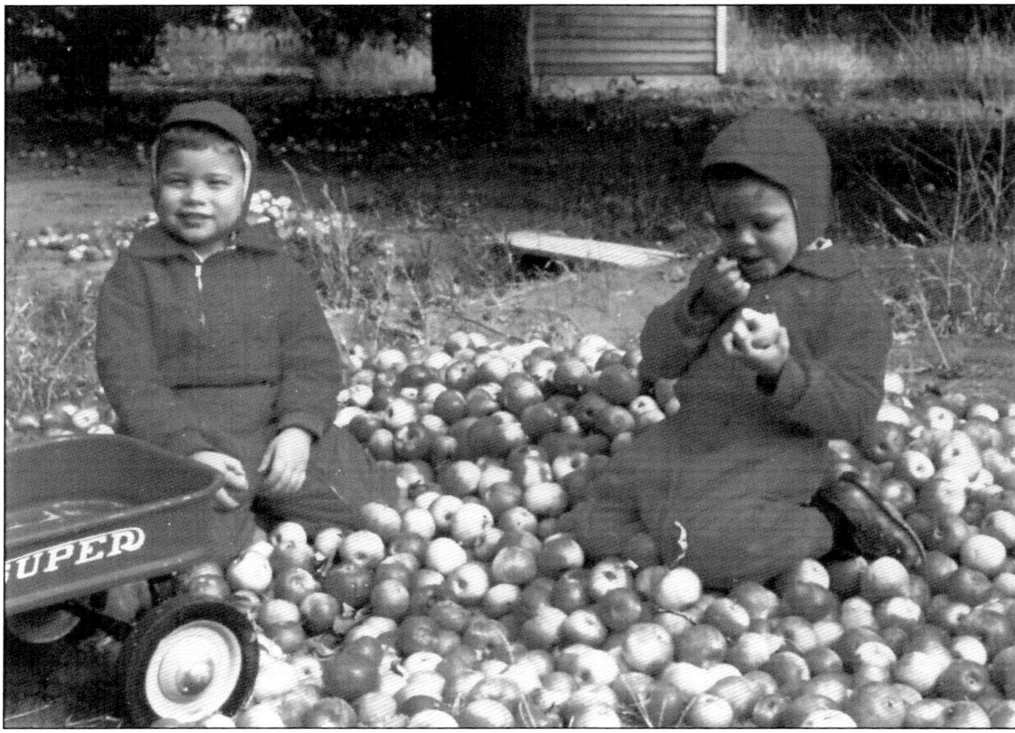

Steve and John DePaula are enjoying the fall apple harvest in 1955. The 1935 *Tewa Basin Study* found that one-fourth of Santa Cruz, or 500 acres, was planted in fruit trees, especially apples, the most frost-resistant of the fruits. In the days of the Chile Line, 200 bushels of apples a week were exported out of the Valley. Former New Mexico governor L. Bradford Prince bought a 200-acre farm in Española to grow apples. (Felix and Sadie DePaula.)

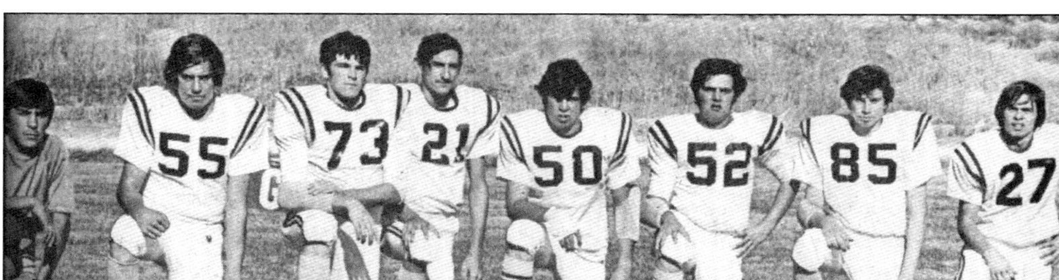

Before there were Sun Devils, there were Hornets (Española High School) and Crusaders (Santa Cruz High School). Española High School used to be on Hunter Street, and Santa Cruz High School was on Old Church Road. Pictured in this 1973 Hornets lineup are, from left to right, Ronnie Martinez, Johnny Montoya, Bruce Law, Ruben Borrego, James Farmer, Española city manager James Lujan, Raymond DePaula, and Bobbie Martinez. (Santa Fe New Mexican.)

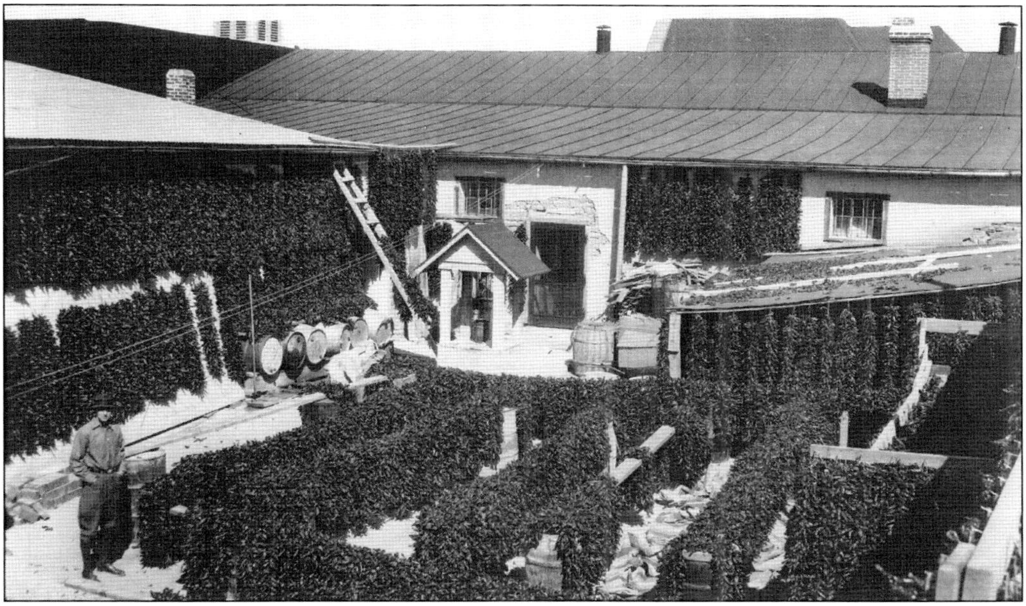

In 1937, chili production in the Santa Cruz, Pojoaque, and Lower Chama Valleys amounted to 60,000 *ristras*. Of these, 8,000 were marketed through Murrhege Brothers; 15,000 through Bond & Nohl; and 15,000 through Reuth & Kramer of San Juan, shown here. None of these stores paid cash to the growers. Instead, credit was extended, which was often applied to existing debt. Seldom did cash pass hands. Nowadays, chili growers in the Valley get up to $20 per pound of heirloom variety chilies, and a five-foot *ristra* can sell for $45. Españcla's famous Stop & Eat is still run by the Gus Martinez family. One morning, the author was having breakfast at a cafe in New Haven, Connecticut. On the wall was a photograph exhibit by the Yale Architecture School. To her amazement, she saw a photograph of Stop & Eat! (Above, Palace of the Governors Photo Archives, photograph by Irving Galloway; below, Kent Bowser.)

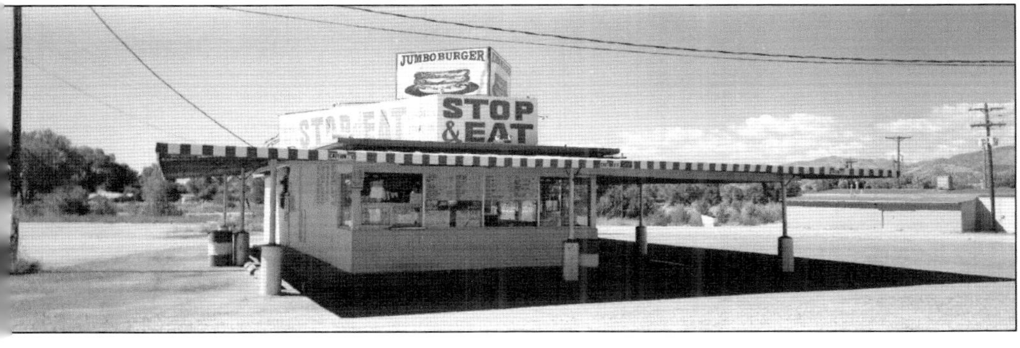

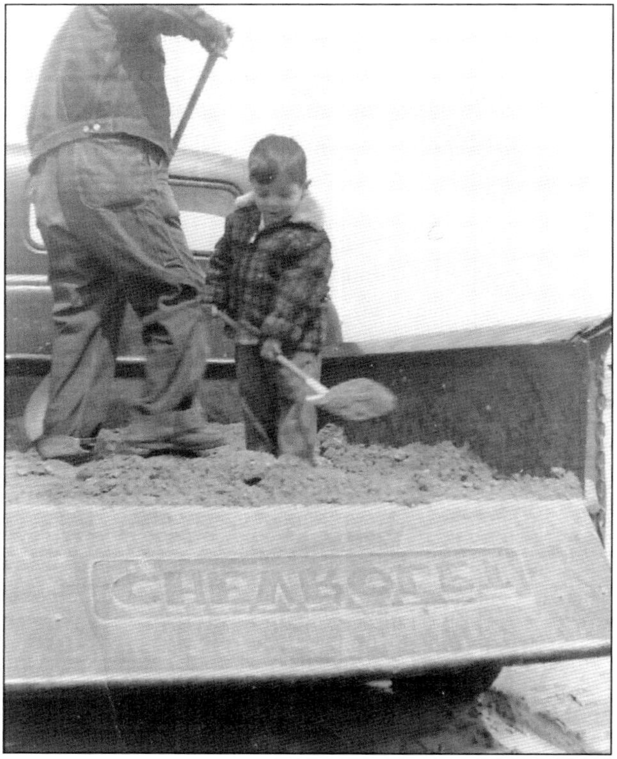

In this 1959 picture, which could easily be titled, "The Making of an Española Valley Man," little Rosenaldo "Ross" Olivas helps his grandfather Toribio Olivas at their El Llano farm. Raised by his grandparents, Ross learned the necessity and joy of working the land. He also learned the particular ways of doing things characteristic of the region and culture. Today, Ross still works his seven acres, taking care of them immaculately and lovingly with his grandpa's 1950 Ford tractor. He is experimenting with composting and water-saving methods. One of his greatest wishes is to find a way to keep his apricot trees from freezing in the spring. Ross's way of life is in tune with commissioner Alfredo Montoya's call to preserve traditions, water, and land—the source of the values held by the people of Española Valley. (Both, Ross Olivas.)

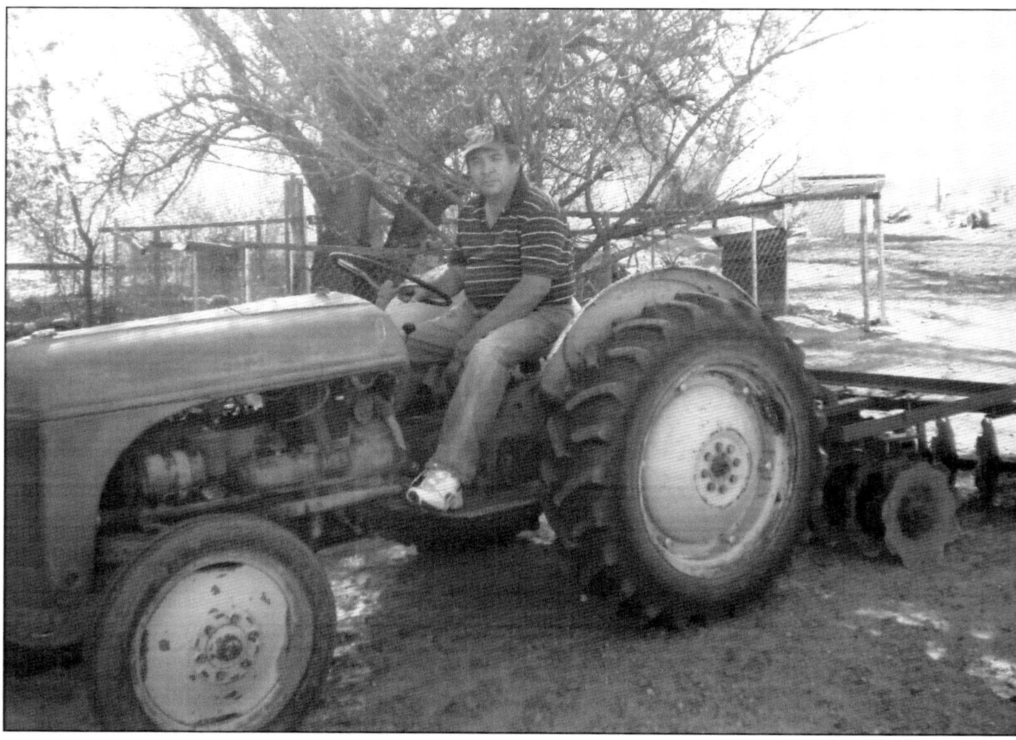

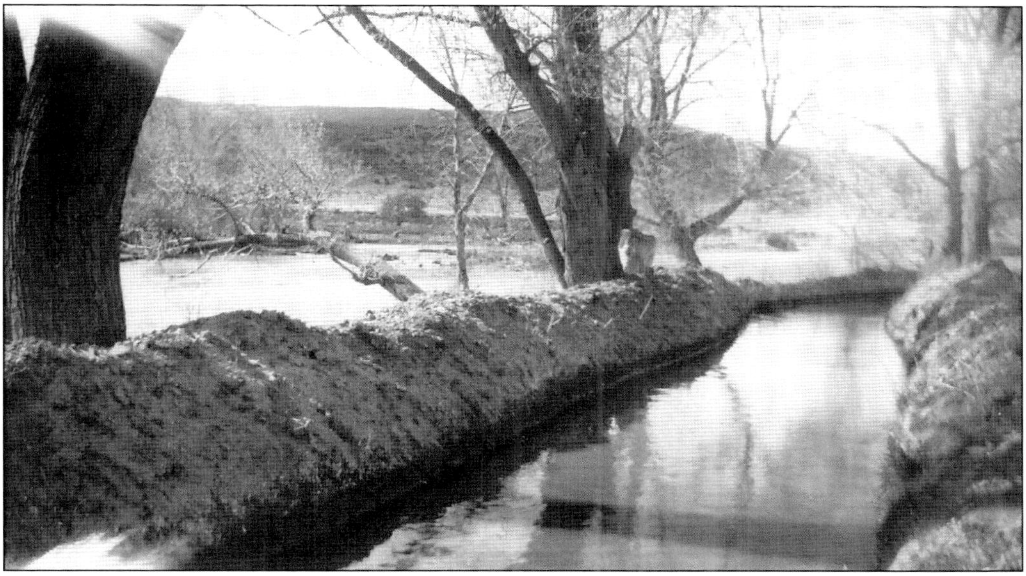

In the valleys of Northern New Mexico, *la acequia madre*—the mother ditch—is the artery that takes water from the river and delivers it to the gardens, fields, and orchards of the community. An endearing tradition in the Española Valley is called *Paseando el Santo*—an archaic expression that suggests a Saint "dropping by," as a neighbor would. Katherine Teba, shown carrying a statue of Santa Clara, leads a group of women from her pueblo to the *capilla* at Pajarito in celebration of the feast day of San Isidro in mid-May. They are taking the Saints out of their sanctuary and walking them across the fields for a visit with the village. A meal is shared, and the saints are returned. The fields of the Valley's people are blessed for another year. (Above, McCurdy School; right, Bob Wilson.)

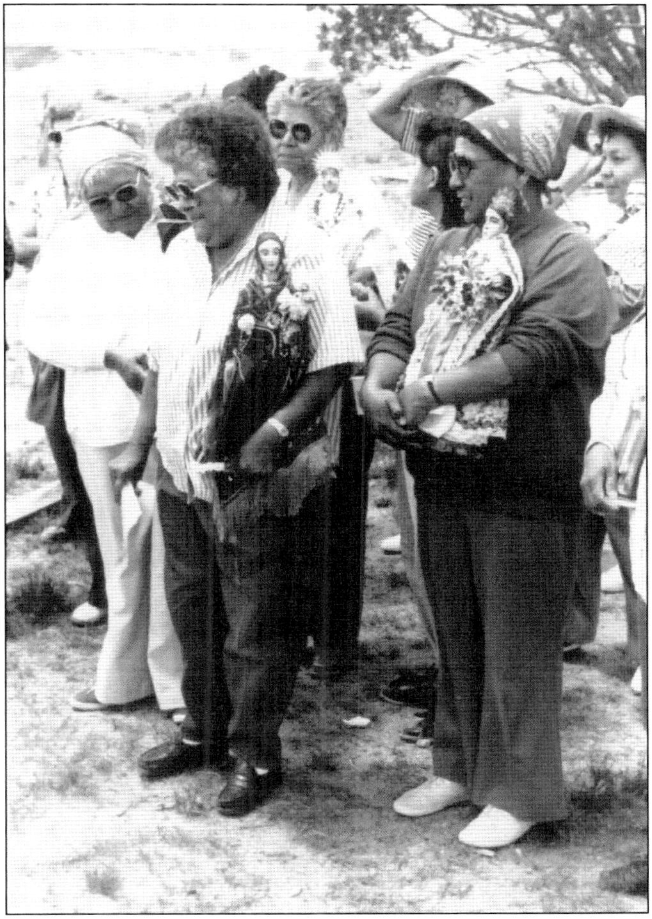